Labor Market Institutions and Public Regulation

CESifo Seminar Series
edited by Hans-Werner Sinn

Labor Market Institutions and Public Regulation

Jonas Agell, Michael Keen,
and Alfons J. Weichenrieder,
editors

 Seminar Series

The MIT Press
Cambridge, Massachusetts
London, England

Set in Palatino on 3B2 by Asco Typesetters, Hong Kong. Printed and bound in the United States of America.

Library of Congress Cataloging-in-Publication Data

Labor market institutions and public regulation / Jonas Agell, Michael Keen, and Alfons J. Weichenrieder, editors.
  p.   cm. — (CESifo seminar series)
Includes bibliographical references and index.
ISBN 0-262-01213-8 (alk. paper)
1. Labor market—Europe—Congresses. 2. Manpower policy—Europe—Congresses.
I. Agell, Jonas. II. Keen, Michael. III. Weichenrieder, Alfons J. IV. Series.

HD5764.A6L267   2004
331.12′042′094—dc22   2004044989

10 9 8 7 6 5 4 3 2 1

Contents

Series Foreword

This book is a part of the CESifo Seminar Series. The series aims to cover topical policy issues in economics from a largely European perspective. The books in the series are products of papers and intensive debates that took place during seminars hosted by CESifo, an international research network of renowned economists organized jointly by the Center for Economic Studies at Ludwig-Maximilians-Universität in Munich and the Ifo Institute for Economic Research. All publications in this series have been carefully selected and refereed by members of the CESifo research network.

Hans-Werner Sinn

Introduction

Many explanations for the painful European unemployment experience, and for poor labor-market performance more generally, stress the role of institutions and public regulation. Many economists agree that highly regulated labor contracts, high tax burdens on labor, inappropriate collective bargaining arrangements, excessive firing costs, generous unemployment insurance, and other features of labor-market regulation create significant waste in the form of stagnant employment and productivity growth. Against this background, many have argued that substantial deregulation of the labor market is the main way to foster employment and productivity growth in Europe.

This volume brings together six studies in which leading contributors analyze specific dimensions of public regulation of the labor market in a way that we hope will be accessible to non-experts and to readers who are more interested in policy than in equations.

The papers reflect the wide range of policy interventions that may affect the labor market's performance and the variety of methodologies that can be used to examine them. The first three papers highlight empirical issues; the last three use the tools of applied theory to deal with important policy issues. This introduction tries to whet the reader's appetite by setting out some of the many ways in which these papers advance the policy debate.

Active Labor-Market Policies

Many hopes have been placed in active labor-market policies. Much of the attraction of these programs is based on the belief that it should be better to pay the unemployed to take up training or subsidized employment, or engage in active search, than to pay them to stay at home. On the other hand, however, subsidized employment may be crowding out regular employment, and the training effects of programs may be small relative to their costs.

The Swedish experience is particularly rich in possibilities for analyzing the effects of almost all varieties of active labor-market programs. From 1986 to 1995, Sweden spent a larger fraction of its gross domestic product on those programs than any other country, and labor-market economists have produced many studies of both microeconomic and macroeconomic effects. Econometric evaluation has also benefited hugely from the existence of a comprehensive longitudinal data set containing the event history of all unemployed individuals since 1991. In "The Effects of Active Labor-Market Policies in Sweden: What Is the Evidence?" Lars Calmfors, Anders Forslund, and Maria Hemström give an authoritative review of these studies and fit the pieces together to form a larger picture. Their reading of the studies on labor-market training programs in Sweden is that these programs were successful in increasing reemployment probabilities of participating individuals in the 1980s, but not in the 1990s, when Sweden faced the deepest recession since the 1930s. When it comes to subsidized employment, the survey of the empirical studies suggests that programs seem to have produced better results in terms of future employment the closer the programs are to regular work. Some programs that do not have this character seem even to have reduced future employment chances.

The probability of returning to ordinary employment also depends on the intensity of job search. Calmfors, Forslund, and Hemström document that active labor-market programs significantly reduce search activities during the treatment period and therefore create lock-in effects, even though in post treatment periods a slightly better labor-market performance may result.

Direct crowding out effects are present if the programs for subsidized labor reduce regular employment. Calmfors, Forslund, and Hemström conclude that crowding-out effects, according to econometric studies, seem well above 60 percent, meaning that for every 100 workers participating in a program there may be at least 60 fewer regular jobs. Crowding-out effects seem to be particularly large for young people.

The Swedish experience shows mixed results on whether the programs have decreased or increased wage pressure, while labor-market participation has obviously been boosted. Calmfors, Forslund, and Hemström hesitate, however, to confirm success of the programs in this latter respect: to the extent that program participation is only used to renew eligibility for unemployment benefits, effective labor supply may not have increased.

Calmfors, Forslund, and Hemström also compare the empirical results for Sweden on active labor-market programs with the results of studies using cross-section or panel data from the Organization for Economic Cooperation and Development countries. The conclusion is that, although these studies usually find that active labor-market programs reduce open unemployment, it is an open question whether or not total unemployment (open unemployment plus program participation) is reduced and regular employment is increased.

The effects of active labor-market programs on employment do not give a complete picture of the effects on social welfare. Nevertheless, the ample Swedish experience and the richness of detailed empirical results make the paper a must read for any policy maker engaged in improving labor-market outcomes. The paper suggests strongly that there are considerable limitations on how much labor-market performance can be improved through active labor-market policy.

Generosity and the Duration of Unemployment

A voluminous literature has explored how generous unemployment insurance affects the intensity of job search and the duration of unemployment. In theory, benefit generosity need not have very strong effects. Benefits can be expected to decrease the exit rate from unemployment at the start of an unemployment spell, but this disincentive effect might be countered by a sharply increased exit rate as a person approaches the end of the entitlement period. The existing evidence suggests that the incentive effect dominates the entitlement effect, and that an additional week of eligibility for unemployment benefits increases unemployment duration by perhaps one day.

In "Benefit Entitlement and the Labor Market: Evidence from a Large-Scale Policy Change" Rafael Lalive and Josef Zweimüller take a new look at these issues. They use Austrian data covering a period when unemployment benefits were significantly extended for elderly workers in certain regions. They adopt a very broad perspective, recognizing that the generosity of benefits may affect several behavioral margins, including firing decisions, early retirement, and equilibrium wage differentials. Lalive and Zweimüller make careful comparisons with control groups in other regions and other age groups, and they present their results in easy-to-understand diagrams and tables. They draw several interesting conclusions. Their general message is that Austria's extended benefits had a profound effect on the labor markets of the affected regions. They do not find that the increase in benefit entitlements had a very strong direct effect on unemployment duration: though the benefit program was accompanied by a tremendous increase in unemployment, most of this increase was driven by severe labor-market problems in the steel sector. But, Lalive and Zweimüller conclude, the benefit extension did have a significant effect on long-term labor-market participation, and it induced a strong increase in early retirement. There is also evidence that the benefit extension affected wage formation, and that this initiated general-equilibrium mechanisms that led to a greater dispersion of wages.

From a policy point of view, a main lesson is that policy makers are well advised to look beyond the short-term effects of unemployment benefits on job search and unemployment duration. The design of unemployment insurance can be expected to have important consequences for long-run labor-market outcomes, including labor-force participation and early retirement. Unemployment insurance can also have non-negligible general-equilibrium effects on wage inequality. These response margins were largely neglected in the earlier literature. At the same time, it is important to note that an overall welfare evaluation of generous unemployment benefits requires that one also account for some of the benefits from generosity. As Lalive and Zweimüller note, the Austrian program of extended benefits inflicted economic costs, but it also eased the transition period for workers in the steel sector, which had been severely battered by the international recession.

On the Merits of Being Credible

Stubbornly high levels of unemployment—especially relative to the United States—continue to be a pressing policy concern in many European Union countries. And Spain has had especially difficult experiences, with measured unemployment at times reaching 25 percent. Though unemployment has now fallen to about 11 percent, labor-market performance in Spain continues to lag behind that elsewhere in

Europe. In "Flexibility vs. Rigidity: Does Spain Have the Worst of Both Worlds?" Gilles Saint-Paul takes a close look at possible explanations, focusing on a comparison of the structure of unemployment in Spain, France, and the United States. Whereas much of France's higher unemployment relative to the United States can be explained by differences in the composition of the workforce, the explanation of Spain's poor performance seems to lie in Spain's managing to combine low rates of job finding (as in France) with relatively high rates of job loss (more like those in the United States)—the worst of both worlds. This poses something of a puzzle. That labor-market reforms in Spain during this period (especially the facilitation of temporary employment contracts) increased job loss seems clear enough; however, the effect on job finding that one would hope to see—with employers more at ease hiring workers, knowing that it is easier to dismiss them later if circumstances warrant—is not apparent. One explanation for this suggested by Saint-Paul is that employers may have feared a subsequent reversal of the policy, with it becoming harder to dismiss workers than it currently seems. This in turn reminds us of the general point that policy reforms, if they are to have the desired effect, must be credible—a point that is familiar in the macroeconomic literature but whose importance is only now coming to be fully appreciated in relation to microeconomic policies. The question this raises is how such credibility can be achieved. In the somewhat similar context of dealing with the problem of time consistency in relation to the taxation of investment income—firms' reluctance to incur sunk costs in view of the scope for ex post expropriation once they have done so—one approach has been to provide up-front benefits in the form of tax holidays or investment subsidies. But these policy measures bring their own problems (such as the ability to arbitrage low tax rates). In the labor-market context, the analogous policy response would be to offer employment subsidies—but these too have disadvantages (for example, the scope for abuse). An alternative would be to enter arrangements that impose some financial penalty on government if the terms of temporary contracts are subsequently revised, though how to make these arrangements credible is not clear. Perhaps the simplest approach is simply to stick with the policy long enough for the market to discount the possibility of reversal. Whether this has happened in Spain and whether indeed this accounts in some part for the improved performance of the labor market in the latter half of the 1990s are open questions.

Educating Students to Be More Equal

One of the clearest policy recommendations to have come out of the literature on the economics of education is that, though there may well be a strong case for public support of basic and secondary education, tertiary and higher education are best left to the market. This rests on the view that it is at the lower levels of education that the potential gains from public spending—in terms of alleviating the divergence between private and social returns, and increasing the real incomes of the poorest—are greatest. And this has become an extremely influential view, both in developed economies (with a movement toward enhanced private contributions to the cost of tertiary education) and in the developing world (with a stress on the provision of education, for instance, in the poverty reduction and growth programs supported by the International Monetary Fund and the World Bank).

Robert Dur and Coen Teulings provide a fresh, striking, and contrary view in "Are Education Subsidies an Efficient Redistributive Device?" They remind us that general-equilibrium effects matter. Focusing public support entirely on the development of basic abilities may simply lead to an increase in the supply of relatively unskilled workers, and so reduce their wages. On the other hand, more general support for education, by raising the relative supply of skilled workers, is likely to raise the wages of the unskilled relative to those of the skilled—so long as the types of workers are less than perfect substitutes (in which case their relative wages would be fixed by their unchanging relative productivities). General demand for redistribution should be reflected both in a higher subsidy to education and in more progressive taxation. And indeed Dur and Teuling argue that this is borne out in practice in the OECD countries: tax progressivity and the extent of education subsidies are positively correlated.

Dismissal Pay and Shirkers

For someone who loses his or her job, it may not matter whether or not workmates have lost theirs too (except in having someone to share their sorrows with). In practice, however, the two events—an individual dismissal and a general redundancy—are often treated differently in terms of the level of benefit entitlement. Specifically, payments for collective redundancy are generally higher. Lazlo Goerke, in "Mandated Severance Pay in an Efficiency-Wage Economy," draws attention to this stylized fact, and asks why. A key element in the explanation given—developed in a Shapiro-Stiglitz efficiency-wage model—is the supposition that even those who "shirk" when employed stand some chance of receiving dismissal pay. For in this case, dismissal pay tends to make shirking more attractive than it otherwise would be; that, in turn, raises the efficiency wage (since people must then be paid more not to shirk), and so it has adverse effects on employment and profitability. Payments in respect of large-scale layoffs do not have the same effect in making shirking more attractive, even though they too are assumed to be available irrespective of whether the worker shirked when employed. This may seem surprising—the shirker receives benefits whether unemployed on his own or in a group (at least in the simplest variant of Goerke's model). The important difference is that an individual worker can affect the chance of his own individual dismissal by choosing whether to shirk, but cannot affect the likelihood of a mass dismissal. This gives payments in the event of mass redundancy much more attractive properties than payments for individual dismissal. Redundancy pay lowers the efficiency wage, rather than increasing it, because, in effect, it in itself raises the expected return to having a job. It thus increases profits and employment—indeed, Goerke shows that it can improve the lot of firms, governments, and workers (both employed and unemployed). Seen in this light, the more pervasive nature of collective redundancy payments appears less of a puzzle.

Goerke's paper has clear and direct implications for the understanding and the design of important aspects of employment protection legislation. Beyond this, it illustrates two general points for policy design. First, detail matters in thinking about social insurance systems. Here the important detail is in the restrictions associated with individual dismissal pay, in terms of the reasons for the dismissal and hence its availability to shirkers. Mandated payments by employers to individuals dismissed individually and en masse may appear to be the same thing in two different guises, but in practice they can be quite different things. The second (and related) general point is that the appropriate policy response to problems of asymmetric information depends critically on the information that the government has available to it and chooses to act upon. Suppose, for example, that the government is perfectly capable of telling (and proving) whether an individually dismissed worker has shirked, and that it chooses to deny dismissal pay to shirkers. Then the provision of dismissal pay has no effect on incentives to shirk, and the difference between dismissal and redundancy pay vanishes.

Redistribution and Globalization

Redistribution toward the poor may be accomplished by a variety of measures. In "Some Macroeconomic Consequences of Basic Income and Employment Subsidies" Thomas Moutos and William Scarth compare different kinds of transfer to low-skill workers that in all cases are financed by an increase in the tax on capital. The main focus of the paper is how moving from inelastic capital supply (in a closed economy) to a perfectly elastic supply (in the globalized economy) will affect the possibilities to redistribute from capital to labor in a small country.

Clearly, in a first-best situation, redistribution will be bound to fail, since with a perfectly elastic capital supply all the incidence of the tax must fall on labor. But what happens in a second-best economy, in which there are pre-existing distortions? To answer this question, Moutos and Scarth consider an efficiency-wage model of unemployment. The message of their analysis is that redistribution may indeed survive in such a second-best world if this redistribution at the same time fixes an allocative problem.

In the efficiency-wage model, the problem is that the marginal productivity of labor is above its social marginal cost. A policy that reduces this gap also fosters employment, and in an open economy this can even lead to an inflow of capital as additional labor makes capital more productive. Moutos and Scarth argue that a tax cut for labor that is financed by a tax increase on capital does exactly this job. Conversely, they find that employment subsidies (as well as basic income schemes) will not have the desired effects on redistribution. One problem of employment subsidies that are paid to employers is that along with wages they drive up wage-related unemployment benefits, and therefore they are bad instruments for dealing with the pre-existing distortion.

The initial versions of the papers in this volume were presented and discussed at a CESifo/ISPE conference held in Munich in late 2001. A follow-up meeting, with revised versions, took place at Lake Como, Italy, in June 2002. We are highly indebted to the authors for their continuing patience toward referees and editors, and for their responsiveness to comments. We are also indebted to the staff at CESifo for organizing excellent meetings, the atmosphere of which, we hope, is reflected in this volume.

Jonas Agell
Michael Keen
Alfons J. Weichenrieder

Labor Market Institutions and Public Regulation

1

The Effects of Active Labor-Market Policies in Sweden: What Is the Evidence?

Lars Calmfors, Anders Forslund, and Maria Hemström[1]

During the last decade there has been an increasing international interest in active labor-market policies, i.e., measures to raise employment that are directly targeted at the unemployed. According to conventional definitions, these policies comprise (i) job broking activities with the aim of improving the matching between vacancies and unemployed, (ii) labor-market training, and (iii) subsidized employment (job creation). Recommendations to expand the use of these policies have become standard from international bodies, such as the OECD and the EU Commission (e.g., OECD 1994; European Commission 2000). In 1997, the European Council agreed on an employment strategy that includes active labor-market policy as a key ingredient,[2] and many member states have followed these recommendations.[3]

The recent interest in active labor-market policies motivates a thorough evaluation of how successful the active labor-market programs (henceforth denoted ALMPs) in various countries have been. Sweden is then a case of particular interest, as this is the country where the focus on active labor-market policy has been the greatest. Partly this reflects an old tradition; partly it was the response to a sudden and steep increase in unemployment in the early 1990s. At their peak in 1994, ALMPs in Sweden encompassed more than 5 percent of the labor force and expenditures accounted for more than 3 percent of GDP.

The Swedish case is interesting from the point of view of evaluation because a large number of studies of the effects of ALMPs have been made. Recent studies have been able to draw on an internationally unique data material: the National Labor Market Board (Ams) provides a longitudinal data set with the event history of all unemployed individuals registered at the public employment offices since 1991. This makes it possible to trace the effects of participation in ALMPs for a very large number of persons over long periods. The Swedish experiences are of great interest also because they illustrate clearly the interdependence between "passive" unemployment support and "active" measures, which has been the subject of much recent policy discussion (see, e.g., European Commission 2000).

This paper surveys the evidence on the employment effects of Swedish active labor-market policy. The focus is on how ALMPs affect regular employment, i.e., employment excluding participation in programs. The motivation for this focus is that employment generation is widely considered to be the primary aim of active labor-market policy, even though there are also other goals, such as social-policy aims of mitigating the consequences of open unemployment and contributing to a more even income distribution, as well as additional macroeconomic aims of, for example, raising productivity growth. The results from studies of Sweden will be compared with the evidence from macroeconomic studies based on cross-country or panel data for the OECD countries. Such a comparison is highly relevant, because the latter studies, originating with Layard et al. (1991), have usually been interpreted to give strong empirical support for the effectiveness of active labor-market policy as a means of raising employment.

Section 1 gives a background picture of how ALMPs have been used in Sweden. Section 2 identifies a number of theoretical mechanisms. Section 3 surveys Swedish microeconometric studies of the effects on the individuals participating in ALMPs. Section 4 surveys Swedish macroeconomic studies of the general-equilibrium effects. Section 5 reviews the studies based on cross-country or panel data for OECD countries. Section 6 sums up the results and draws policy conclusions.

1   Active Labor-Market Policy in Sweden

There is a long tradition of active labor-market policy in Sweden. In the beginning of the twentieth century, municipal employment offices were established (Thoursie 1990). In the depressions of the interwar years, the government organized relief works and special youth jobs. In 1948, the foundations of modern labor-market policy were laid when the National Labor Market Board was instituted.

1.1   The Thinking behind Labor-Market Policy
The thinking behind Swedish labor-market policy was, at least before the 1990s, guided mainly by the principles laid out by two trade union economists, Gösta Rehn and Rudolf Meidner, in the late 1940s and the early 1950s.[4] They saw active labor-market policy as a necessary ingre-

dient in a policy mix designed to combine low inflation, full employment, and wage compression. They worried that an anti-inflationary demand-management policy would cause unemployment in low-productivity sectors. To avoid that, they recommended labor-market re-training and other mobility-enhancing measures, so that workers threatened by unemployment in low-productivity sectors could be transferred to high-productivity sectors, relieving labor shortages there.

The original focus in postwar Swedish labor-market policy was thus on increasing labor mobility. However, in the period 1960–1990 the emphasis gradually shifted in the direction of counteracting all types of unemployment. In the late 1960s and the early 1970s, the objective of eliminating remaining "islands of unemployment" through selective job-creation programs became more important (Meidner 1969). Gradually, it also became a more important aim to hold down unemployment in general in recessions. This development seems to be explained by generally rising ambitions in employment policy (Lindbeck 1975; Calmfors and Forslund 1990).

The motive of holding down open unemployment in general came to dominate completely in the 1990s. In the early 1990s, Sweden entered its deepest recession in the postwar period, with regular employment falling by 13 percent between 1990 and 1994. In this situation, placement in ALMPs became the main short-run policy instrument to counteract the rise in open unemployment. Policy was also to a large extent guided by the social-policy objectives of providing income support for the unemployed: formally, unemployment compensation could not be had for more than 14 months for the majority of the work force, but eligibility could be renewed through participation in ALMPs. There is ample evidence that program placements were systematically used to this end (e.g., Carling et al. 1996; Sianesi 2001).

An important side objective of Swedish active labor-market policy has always been to mitigate the moral hazard problems of a generous unemployment insurance: by making payment of unemployment compensation conditional on accepting regular job offers or placement offers in ALMPs from the public employment offices, active labor-market policy has been used as a work test for the recipients of unemployment compensation.

1.2 The Various Programs

Originally, *labor-market training* consisted mainly of vocational training programs, but over time schemes containing more general education have become more important. In recent years, *education in the Swedish language for immigrants* has been a part of labor-market training. *Computer activity centers*, which were introduced in 1995, represent another innovation; in addition an IT program (*Swit*) was launched by the government in 1998 in cooperation with the Confederation of Swedish Industries. The duration of training programs has usually been six months. Participants have received training grants equivalent to unemployment compensation. In the second half of the 1980s, it became possible for unemployed individuals to requalify for unemployment compensation through participation in training programs. In 2000, this possibility was abolished for all labor-market programs.

There have been many types of subsidized employment schemes over the years. The classical measure was *relief works*. They consisted of temporary jobs (around six months), which were usually arranged in the public sector, but to some extent also in the private sector, and where employers obtained a subsidy for employing individuals selected by the public employment offices. The participants were paid wages according to collective agreements. Relief works were used up to 1998, when they were abolished.

In the 1990s, relief works were largely replaced by *work-experience schemes*. These consisted of activities that "would otherwise not have occurred" and were often arranged by various non-profit organizations. The aim was to organize activities that would not crowd out regular employment. Participants in work-experience schemes received unemployment compensation. *Recruitment subsidies* and (more recently) *employment subsidies* are programs that are more similar to regular employment. Both programs have entailed wage subsidies to employers for hiring unemployed (mainly long-term unemployed). Participants have been paid regular wages according to collective agreements.

Another type of subsidized employment is *self-employment grants*. These grants, which consist of unemployment benefits for up to six months, are given to unemployed persons to start their own businesses after scrutiny by the employment offices. These have also arranged entrepreneurial training for the participants.

Other programs can be characterized as *work-practice programs*. In our survey of empirical results, we include these in job-creation activities, but work-practice programs are supposed to have also a training content. Various types of *youth schemes* belong to this category. The first youth program was *youth teams*, introduced in 1984. They were followed by *"schooling-in slots."* During 1992, *youth practice* was introduced. This program expanded rapidly. The program was targeted at those below the age of 25. As was the case for work-experience schemes, there were clear instructions to avoid displacement effects.

Other examples of work-practice programs were *practice for immigrants* and *practice for academic graduates*, which were similar in spirit to youth practice, but with different target groups. Yet another work-practice program was *work placement schemes*, which replaced practice for immigrants, practice for academic graduates, and youth practice in 1995.

Resource jobs, introduced in 1997, entailed subsidies to employers for temporarily (six months with an option to prolong it by three months) hiring unemployed persons. The participants were mainly supposed to work, but were in addition supposed to take part in training and to actively search for jobs. The wage rate was capped at what roughly corresponds to 90 percent of the participant's previous income.

Trainee replacement schemes involved subsidies during at most six months to employers, who paid for training for an employee and hired a replacement (who received a wage according to collective agreements). Hence, trainee replacement schemes can be classified as both training and job creation.

The only program that has been used over the entire period under study is labor-market training. All other programs have been instituted during the period and/or ended during it. Relief works were abandoned in 1998; recruitment subsidies were used between 1981 and 1997; work-experience schemes were used between 1993 and 1998, work placement schemes between 1995 and 1998, trainee replacement schemes between 1991 and 1997, resource jobs between 1997 and 1999, and practice for academic graduates and practice for immigrants between 1993 and 1995. Self-employment grants were introduced in 1984, youth programs in 1984, computer activity centers in 1995, and employment subsidies in 1997.

Finally, a reform took place in 2000, when an *activity guarantee* was introduced. This program is targeted at persons who are or are at risk of becoming long-term unemployed (or, more precisely, long-term registered at the public employment service). Participants are given some full-time activity (e.g., job search) until they find a job or enroll in regular education. This reform was made in connection with the abolition of the earlier possibility to renew benefit eligibility by participating in ALMPs.

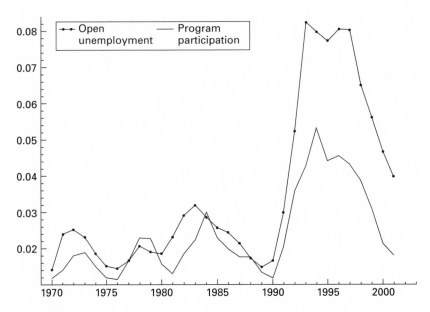

Figure 1.1
Open unemployment and program participation (shares of labor force), 1970–2001.
Sources: Unemployment and labor force: Statistics Sweden, Labour Force Surveys; Program participation: National Labour Market Board.

1.3   The Empirical Picture

Figures 1.1–1.3 illustrate how the program volumes have developed over time.

Figure 1.1 shows open unemployment and total participation in ALMPs. The picture is one of a slow trend-wise growth in the size of ALMPs in the 1970s and the 1980s, but there is also a cyclical pattern. The large expansion in the 1990s in connection with the steep rise in unemployment also stands out. Towards the end of the 1990s, when unemployment came down, the program volumes were reduced again.

Figure 1.2 depicts *total unemployment* (the sum of open unemployment and participation in ALMPs) and the *accommodation ratio* (the ratio between program participation and total unemployment). In the 1970s and the 1980s, the accommodation ratio was approximately 0.4–0.5, but it fell in the 1990s. Although programs expanded strongly then, they did not increase proportionally to the rise in unemployment. In 2000, the accommodation ratio was around 0.2.

Figure 1.3 shows the development of various program types. In the 1970s and the 1980s, training encompassed more persons than sub-

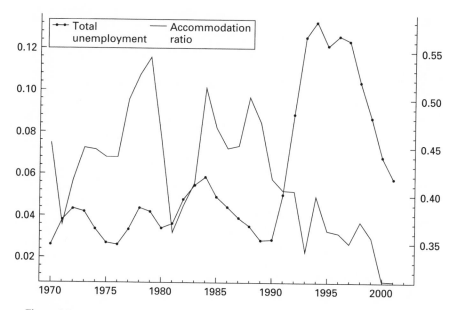

Figure 1.2
Accommodation ratio (right-hand scale) and total unemployment, 1970–2001. Total unemployment is defined as the sum of open unemployment and total participation in ALMPs. Accommodation ratio is defined as ratio of program participation to total unemployment. Sources: Participation in ALMPs: National Labour Market Board. Unemployment and the labor force: Statistics Sweden.

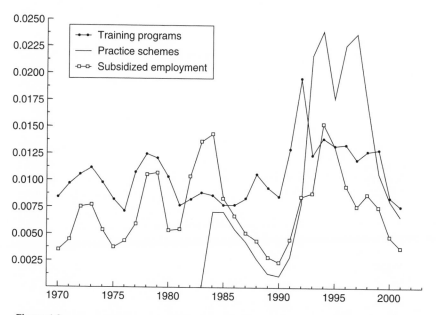

Figure 1.3
Participation in different kinds of labor-market programs, 1970–2001. The programs are generally classified as in the main text. Trainee replacement schemes and resource jobs are classified as subsidized employment. Source: National Labour Market Board.

Table 1.1
Swedish ALMPs in an international perspective. Source: OECD Employment Outlook, various issues.

	Expenditures on ALMPs (percent of GDP)			Expenditures on ALMPs (fraction of total unemployment expenditures)			Allocation of expenditures on ALMPs in 1986–2000			
	1986–90	1991–95	1996–2000	1986–90	1991–95	1996–2000	Public employment services and administration	Labor market training	Youth measures	Subsidized employment
Austria	0.26	0.28	0.38	0.21	0.18	0.23	0.39	0.37	0.04	0.16
Belgium	1.06	0.99	1.13	0.27	0.26	0.31	0.19	0.14	0.00	0.67
Denmark	0.82	1.15	1.19	0.17	0.19	0.25	0.10	0.48	0.21	0.21
Finland	0.82	1.39	1.11	0.37	0.27	0.29	0.12	0.32	0.04	0.50
France	0.50	0.85	1.04	0.2	0.3	0.37	0.20	0.42	0.13	0.25
Germany	0.72	1.16	1.03	0.36	0.35	0.31	0.25	0.37	0.05	0.33
Greece	0.16	0.23	0.29	0.29	0.34	0.39	0.45	0.08	0.03	0.44
Ireland	1.06	0.70	1.37	0.26	0.29	0.36	0.15	0.26	0.23	0.35
Italy	—	0.89	0.44	—	0.47	0.36	0.16	0.03	0.42	0.35
Luxembourg	0.16	0.12	0.18	0.17	0.16	0.21	0.23	0.12	0.38	0.27
Netherlands	0.56	0.85	0.95	0.16	0.22	0.25	0.30	0.43	0.05	0.21
Portugal	0.26	0.41	0.37	0.45	0.36	0.30	0.33	0.10	0.26	0.26
Spain	0.71	0.59	0.54	0.22	0.17	0.25	0.16	0.18	0.11	0.52
Sweden	1.10	1.79	1.30	0.59	0.47	0.41	0.19	0.42	0.08	0.31

United Kingdom	0.50	0.38	0.21	0.26	0.22	0.20	0.46	0.29	0.01	0.18
EU average	**0.62**	**0.79**	**0.80**	**0.28**	**0.28**	**0.35**	**0.24**	**0.27**	**0.14**	**0.33**
Australia	0.25	0.45	0.46	0.19	0.21	0.28	0.40	0.17	0.04	0.33
Canada	0.52	0.57	0.45	0.24	0.23	0.30	0.38	0.47	0.03	0.07
Japan	0.09	0.10	0.26	0.22	0.27	0.38	0.27	0.20	0.00	0.49
New Zealand	0.81	0.77	0.56	0.43	0.31	0.29	0.18	0.47	0.04	0.27
Norway	0.64	1.28	0.34	0.52	0.72	0.37	0.32	0.32	0.11	0.20
Switzerland	0.08	0.18	0.48	0.32	0.15	0.32	0.61	0.20	0.00	0.14
United States	0.20	0.17	0.14	0.3	0.26	0.34	0.37	0.34	0.17	0.06
OECD average	**0.54**	**0.70**	**0.66**	**0.29**	**0.29**	**0.34**	**0.28**	**0.28**	**0.11**	**0.30**

sidized employment. The only exception was the recession in the first half of the 1980s. The steep increase in unemployment in 1991–92 was first met by a large expansion of training programs, but later there were large increases in schemes of subsidized employment and practice. Recently, training programs have again become relatively more important.

1.4   Swedish ALMPs in an International Perspective

Table 1.1 provides an international perspective. In 1986–1990 and in 1991–1995, Sweden spent more on active labor-market policy than any other country. The difference is especially marked in 1991–1995, when expenditures in Sweden amounted to 1.79 percent of GDP, one percentage point higher than the EU average. Expenditures in Sweden were reduced in 1996–2000, when unemployment fell, but still amounted to as much as 1.3 percent of GDP, which was well above the EU and OECD averages. In this period, Ireland, however, spent slightly more on active labor-market policy.

The table also shows that Sweden had the largest share of active expenditures (relative to total expenditures on the unemployed) in 1986–1990, when it was 59 percent, more than double the EU and OECD averages. The share subsequently fell, but it remained substantially above the EU and OECD averages.

What finally stands out is the larger emphasis in Sweden than in most other countries on labor-market training: 42 percent of the expenditures on ALMPs in Sweden have been on training, compared to EU and OECD averages of 27 and 28 percent, respectively. Only a few countries (New Zealand, Canada, Denmark, and the Netherlands) have spent larger fractions of active expenditures on training than Sweden.

2   A Theoretical Framework

ALMPs can have a number of effects on employment. Some of the effects are intended, whereas others are unintended. To sort them out, we use a modified version of the Layard et al. (1991) theoretical framework for analyzing equilibrium real wages and unemployment, as set out by Calmfors (1994).

In figure 1.4, a downward-sloping *employment schedule* shows how regular labor demand (labor demand excluding participation in ALMPs) depends negatively on the real wage. An upward-sloping

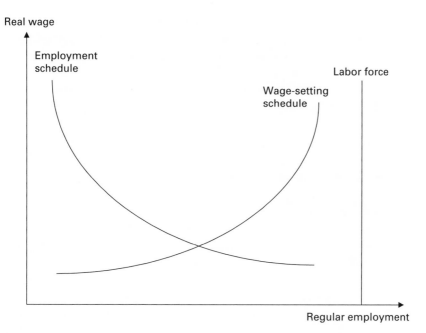

Figure 1.4
Wage setting and employment.

wage-setting schedule shows how wage pressure depends positively on regular employment. (The underlying assumption is that higher regular employment is associated with a higher probability of finding a job if an employee is separated from his present job. This gives employees a better outside option when bargaining with the present employer, which makes it possible to obtain a higher wage.) The intersection of the two curves gives the equilibrium levels of real wages and regular employment. In addition, a vertical line shows the labor force. By deducting participation in ALMPs from the labor force, and comparing the outcome with regular employment, one obtains open unemployment.

The analytical framework in figure 1.4 can be motivated in several ways. The simplest possibility is to view the employment schedule as an ordinary stock demand for labor, following from the usual marginal productivity condition. The wage-setting schedule may be viewed as the (steady-state) outcome of either collective wage bargaining or unilateral employer decisions on wages in an efficiency-wage framework. However, for some applications it is more worthwhile to see the employment schedule as a (steady-state) reduced form derived from a framework where vacancies and unemployed need to be matched along the lines of Pissarides 1990 and Mortensen and Pissarides 1994. In this case, it is convenient to regard wage setting as the outcome of agreements between employers and individual employees.

With the help of the above framework, we shall analyze various effects of ALMPs. Following Calmfors (1994), we distinguish (i) effects on the matching process, (ii) effects on the competition for jobs, (iii) productivity effects, (iv) effects on the allocation of labor between sectors, (v) direct crowding-out effects on regular labor demand, and (vi) accommodation effects on wage setting.

2.1 Effects on the Matching Process[5]

The aim of the job-broking and counseling activities for the unemployed by the public employment offices is to make the matching process more efficient, i.e., to increase the number of successful matches at given numbers of vacancies and job seekers. This is often regarded as the primary function of active labor-market policy.

A more efficient matching process shifts the employment schedule in figure 1.4 to the right, which tends to raise both employment and the real wage. The explanation is that an increase in matching efficiency increases the probability of filling a posted vacancy at any point of time. Hence, the expected return to posting vacancies increases, and therefore more vacancies are posted. This results in higher employment.

An increase in matching efficiency also shifts the wage-setting schedule to the right, which works in the direction of reducing the real wage and increasing employment. The reason is that the higher is matching efficiency, the better is the firm's bargaining position vis-à-vis the employee, because a vacancy can then be more quickly filled if the employee quits because of disagreement over the wage. Hence, a higher matching efficiency means that the firm is able to negotiate a lower real wage at each level of employment.[6]

As a higher matching efficiency will shift both the employment and wage-setting schedules to the right, this effect must increase employment, whereas the effect on the real wage is ambiguous.

One should indeed expect active labor-market policy in the form of job broking and counseling activities as well as completed labor-market training to increase matching efficiency. This is the desired *treatment effect*. But there may also be a *locking-in effect* of training or job-creation programs working in the opposite direction if the participants do not exit from the programs before they are completed. This effect tends instead to shift the employment and wage-setting schedules to the left. The consequence is then a tendency to lower regular employment (whereas the impact on the real wage is still unclear). Whether or not the treatment effect dominates the locking-in effect is an empirical issue.

2.2   Effects on the Competition for Jobs

Quite apart from their effect on matching efficiency, ALMPs may affect the degree of competition for the available jobs by making participants more competitive. This may result from several mechanisms (Layard et al. 1991; Nickell and Layard 1999). Participation in an ALMP may help to maintain the motivation to seek actively for work, i.e., counteract the discouraged-worker effect of unemployment. The competition for jobs is also stimulated if ALMPs help to preserve or increase the skills of the unemployed. And employers may in general perceive participants in ALMPs as more attractive than the openly unemployed.

As a result, ALMPs may have a positive effect on labor force participation. In figure 1.4, the labor-supply schedule, showing the size of the work force, is then shifted to the right. The wage-setting schedule is also shifted to the right. The reason is that there are more workers competing for the same number of jobs: a certain level of regular employment is thus associated with a lower job-finding probability, which worsens the outside option of employees in wage bargaining.

So, ALMPs may exert a positive employment effect by increasing the competition for the available jobs. But just as with matching efficiency, this requires that the earlier discussed treatment effects are stronger than the locking-in effects.

2.3   Effects on the Productivity of Job Seekers

Another desired effect of ALMPs is to increase the productivity of job seekers (Calmfors 1994). This is the aim of labor-market training as well as of various work experience programs, but such an effect may also arise because of on-the-job training in a pure job-creation scheme.

An increase in the productivity of job seekers shifts the segment of the marginal product curve that applies to job seekers (non-employed workers), i.e., the segment to the right of the intersection with the wage-setting schedule, in figure 1.4 upwards. Everything else equal, this results in an increase in regular employment. But an increase in the productivity of job seekers may also cause their *reservation wages* to increase. If this occurs, the wage-setting schedule is also shifted upwards in this segment, which tends to offset the positive effect on regular employment. If the wage-setting schedule is shifted upwards by as much as the employment schedule, the net effect on regular employment is zero. Whether or not such effects are important is an empirical issue.

2.4   Effects on the Allocation of the Work Force

A fourth intended effect of ALMPs can be to change the allocation of the work force between different sectors. According to the Rehn-Meidner model (see subsection 1.1), the original goal of active labor-market policy in Sweden was to transfer labor from stagnating low-productivity sectors with high unemployment to expanding high-productivity sectors with low unemployment through training programs and other mobility-enhancing measures. Such policies will reduce wage pressures substantially in low-unemployment sectors, whereas wage pressures will increase only a little in high-unemployment sectors if the sector-specific wage-setting schedules are convex (Calmfors 1995; Fukushima 1998). The result will be a rightward shift of the *aggregate* wage-setting schedule.

2.5   Direct Crowding Out (Displacement)

An unintended side effect of ALMPs is that they may crowd out regular labor demand (see, e.g., Dahlberg and Forslund 1999). This is likely to apply mainly to schemes of subsidized employment. Such crowding out (displacement) presupposes that the unemployed who are hired are substitutes—and not complements—to other employees in production, so that the hiring of unemployed workers lowers the marginal product of regular employees.

In terms of figure 1.4, direct crowding out means that the employment schedule (the regular labor demand schedule) is shifted to the left. This tends to reduce both the real wage and regular employment.

Direct crowding out should be seen in association with the competition effects in subsection 2.2. Even if there is complete crowding out, there may be a positive employment effect to the extent that employment of long-term unemployed (outsiders) crowds out employment of insiders, so that the latter group meets more competition. The crowding out may thus be necessary to reach the desired competition effects.

2.6 Accommodation Effects on Wage Setting

Participation in ALMPs may also give rise to unintended side effects on wage setting because the welfare of the unemployed is affected. There are several possible effects:

• Participation in ALMPs may imply higher incomes for job seekers than would otherwise be the case, if compensation there is higher than the unemployment benefit (Calmfors and Nymoen 1990; Calmfors and Forslund 1991).

• Participants in ALMPs may experience a higher degree of psychological well-being than the openly unemployed, because program participation is considered more meaningful (Korpi 1997).

• If program participation is expected to improve future labor-market prospects, it will increase the expected future welfare of participants (Calmfors and Lang 1995).

• If program participation means that the participants renew their eligibility for unemployment compensation (the earlier Swedish system) or is used as a supplement to extend the period of income support beyond the maximum unemployment benefit period (the present activity guarantee in Sweden), this will also raise the future expected incomes of the unemployed.

All the above effects reduce the welfare difference between having and not having a job. Hence, they increase wage pressure. In terms of figure 1.4, the wage-setting schedule is shifted upwards. This means higher real wages and lower regular employment. This can be seen as an *accommodation effect*, which leads to *indirect crowding out* of regular jobs.

However, there may also be a "control effect" working in the opposite direction (Jackman 1994). Participation in ALMPs and active job search on part of the unemployed are requirements to receive unemployment compensation. So for some unemployed individuals, program participation means a welfare loss because they can no longer allocate their time freely. Judging from the reactions of some of the unemployed, the activity guarantee in Sweden may to some degree work in this way (see subsection 1.2). To the extent that this is the case, the above effects are reversed, and the wage-setting schedule tends to be shifted downwards.

2.7 The Effects of ALMPs

Our analysis is summarized in table 1.2, which shows the expected direction of the various effects. We have put question marks where

Table 1.2
The expected effects of ALMPs—a summary of the theoretical discussion.

	Wage given employment (wage pressure)	Regular employment given wage	Net effect on regular employment
Matching	− (?)	+ (?)	+ (?)
Competition	− (?)	0	+ (?)
Direct displacement	0	−	−
Accommodation	+ (?)	0	− (?)
Productivity of job seekers	(+)	+	+/(0)
Allocation of labor force	−	0	+

the expected effects may theoretically be counteracted by other effects. This applies to matching efficiency and the competition for jobs, where treatment and locking-in effects work in opposite directions. It applies also to the accommodation effects on wage setting, where the wage-rising effects may be counteracted by control effects. We have indicated with parentheses that the positive productivity effects may be offset by increased reservation wages.

The net employment effect of ALMPs is obviously an empirical issue. The rest of the paper is devoted to a survey of the empirical research on the employment effects of ALMPs in Sweden. These studies are in principle of two types: microeconomic and macroeconomic. The microeconomic studies evaluate the effects of participation in ALMPs for the participating individuals, whereas the macroeconomic ones examine the aggregate general-equilibrium effects.

The microeconomic studies can benefit from data sets with a large number of observations. By examining whether participation in ALMPs implies larger employment chances as compared to non-participation, these studies can give indications of the effects on matching efficiency, the competition for jobs, the productivity of the participants and the allocation of labor. Knowledge on these effects can also be obtained by examining how program participation affects the mobility of job seekers, their search behavior and the attitudes of employers.

The microeconomic studies of the effects on individuals do not by definition capture the effects of ALMPs on non-participants. These general-equilibrium effects can only by examined in macroeconomic studies. This applies, for example, to the direct crowding out effects

and the accommodation effects on wage setting. Only the macroeconomic studies can give the full picture of the effects of ALMPs on
employment and wages. But a problem with these studies is that the
number of observations is often small.

The two types of studies complement each other. The two subsequent sections summarize the studies of these types that have been
made in Sweden.

3 Microeconomic Studies

This section surveys the evidence from microeconometric studies of
the effects of ALMPs on the participants. We focus on the effects on
regular employment, but look also at the effects on income (since
income depends positively on employment).

The issue is how the labor-market outcome of participants compares
to the outcome that would have prevailed had they not participated
in an ALMP. The crucial element in such an evaluation is to find a
comparison group whose outcome equals the counterfactual needed
to establish the treatment effects. Evaluations are plagued by potential
problems of *sample selection bias*. There is a large literature on this evaluation problem, which was initiated by Heckman (1979) (see, e.g.,
Heckman et al. 1999). However, the set-up of the Swedish labor-
market policy differs from the one usually considered in the evaluation
literature. As was discussed in subsection 1.2, there is a wide array of
continuously ongoing programs for the unemployed. All unemployed
may, theoretically, participate and most long-term unemployed do
so repeatedly during their unemployment spell(s). Therefore, it is difficult to find a proper comparison group who neither has participated
nor will participate in an ALMP. The choice for an unemployed person
is to participate in a program now or *later*, rather than now or *never*
(see Carling and Larsson 2000a and Sianesi 2001a for further discus-
sions). As a consequence, the mere existence of programs may influence the behavior of non-participants also.

Also, the fact that most long-term unemployed will ultimately participate in (several) ALMPs makes it difficult to evaluate the long-term
effects. First, it is difficult to relate estimated effects to specific ALMPs.
Second, the number of openly unemployed who have never participated, and can therefore be used as a comparison group, will be very
small. This problem is genuine if treatment effects are not immedi-
ate and rapidly transient (Carling and Larsson 2000b). Third, as every

Table 1.3
Treatment effects of labor-market training (LMT).

Study	Program and timing	Sample	Dependent variable	Results
Edin and Holmlund 1991	LMT, 1981–1984	Register and survey data on 800 16–24-year-old unemployed in the Stockholm area, 1981	Reemployment probability in subsequent unemployment spells	Significant, positive effect
Axelsson and Löfgren 1992	LMT, 1981	Register and survey data on 2,000 participants. Random selection and representative sample	(i) Yearly income 1982 and 1983; and (ii) income growth 1981–82 and 1981–1983	Significant, positive effects
Korpi 1994	LMT, 1981–1984	Register and survey data on 800 16–24-year-old unemployed in the Stockholm area, 1981	Duration of employment	Insignificant effect
Harkman, Jansson, and Tamás 1996	LMT, 1993	Register and survey data on 3,000 20–54-year-old participants. Random selection and representative sample	Regular employment 6 months and 2.5 years after program	Positive effect only if potential selection is not considered
Harkman 1997	LMT, 1994	Register and survey data on 3,000 20–54-year-old participants. Random selection and representative sample	Regular employment 2 years after program	Significant, negative effect of training ≤100 days; no significant effect of training ≥100 days; the *difference* of 4% between short and long programs is significant
Regnér 1997	LMT, 1989–1991	Register data on 9,000 participants. Non-participating comparison group through matching. Random selection and representative sample	Yearly income 1990–1992	Significant, negative effect 1 year and insignificant effect 3 years after program
Harkman, Johansson, and Okeke 1999	LMT and computer activity centers, 1996	Register and survey data on 3,000 20–54-year-old participants. Random selection and representative sample	Regular employment 1 year after program	Positive effect of LMT only if potential selection is not considered; no significant effect of computer activity centers

Larsson 2000	LMT, 1992–93	Register data on 600 20–24-year-old participants. Non-participating comparison group through propensity score matching	(i) Yearly income; and probability to (ii) obtain a job; or (iii) proceed to regular education 1–2 years after program	Significant, negative effects
Johansson and Martinsson 2000	Swit, 1999	Register and survey data on 4,000 Swit participants. Comparison group = 7,000 participants in similar traditional IT training	Regular employment 6 months after program	Significant, positive effect
Okeke 2001	LMT, 1998–99	Register and survey data on a stratified subsample of participants. Non-participating comparison group through propensity score matching	Regular employment 6 months after program	Significant, large positive effect
Richardson and van den Berg 2001	LMT, 1993–2000	Register data on a 1% random subsample of all who became openly unemployed, 1/1/1993–6/22/2000 (5,000 individuals, of whom 665 participated in LMT). Bivariate duration model with individual heterogeneity	Unemployment duration	Significant, negative effect that vanished within two months after the training ended if unemployment duration is measured from the end of LMT; insignificant effect if unemployment duration is measured from the start of program participation.
Sianesi 2001b	LMT, 1994–1999	Register data on 30800 adult individuals, entitled to unemployment benefits, who registered with employment offices for the first time in 1994 (1387 in LMT)	(i) Employment rate; and (ii) benefit collection	(i) Significant, negative effect on employment rates up to 30 months, then insignificant effect; (ii) significant, positive effect on benefit collection. The comparison is between participation now and "waiting in open unemployment"

long-term unemployed is likely sooner or later to participate in an ALMP, the problem of sample selection bias is exacerbated: job seekers with large difficulties of finding a job tend to be over-represented among ALMP participants (Sianesi 2001b).

The evaluation literature on Swedish ALMPs since the mid-1980s must therefore be interpreted with caution. It is possible that these evaluations analyze the effect of participating at *a specific point in time rather than later* or in *a certain program rather than in another* instead of the effect of participation compared to non-participation as such.

The early Swedish evaluation literature proceeds from small and "special" data sets based on survey data and/or information from personal files kept at the employment offices. The research of the 1990s leans heavily on the event data base Händel (which comprises information on all registered job seekers since 1991) and sometimes combines this with register or survey data on employment and income. Statistics on search behavior and employer attitudes are based on survey data.

Subsection 3.1 looks at treatment effects of labor-market training (LMT), whereas subsection 3.2 focuses on the effects of subsidized employment. Subsection 3.3 summarizes the evidence on the effects of ALMPs on the search behavior of participants. Subsection 3.4 reviews the studies of effects on employers' attitudes.

3.1 Labor-Market Training

The research on the effects of labor-market training is summarized in table 1.3.

Although results vary a lot between studies, some conclusions can be drawn. The estimated effects of labor-market training differ between the 1980s and the 1990s. Evaluations of training acquired during the first half of the 1980s suggest positive effects on participants' employment and/or income. Evaluations of training that took place in the 1990s usually find instead insignificant or significantly negative effects.

Both Edin and Holmlund (1991) and Korpi (1994) estimated, using the same sample, the effects of labor-market training for young people in the early 1980s. Edin and Holmlund found that training increased the re-employment probability in subsequent unemployment spells. Korpi found that training increased the duration of subsequent employment.

Axelsson and Löfgren (1992) analyzed the impact of labor-market training in 1981 on the (growth and level of) incomes obtained one to two years later. Fixed-effect estimates, using the entire sample, indicated that the yearly incomes of participants increased by as much as 21 percent the first and 30 percent the second year following training. The authors also found that returns were higher the longer the training. But the estimated effects decreased considerably—but were still sizable—as the sample and/or methods were changed. The results further indicated that participants were, on average, more ambitious and motivated than non-participants. As the selection thus established was considered, estimates became unstable, divergent and sometimes implausible.

Regnér (1997) also analyzed the effect on yearly incomes. Irrespective of the method used, the effects were negative after one and insignificant after three years. However, specification tests yielded varying results, and models that were just about accepted by one test were rejected by another. But the qualitative conclusions remained basically the same.

Three different evaluations of labor-market training in the 1990s have been published by the National Labor Market Board. Harkman et al. (1996) estimated the effect of training in 1993 on the probability of having a regular job later on. The results differ depending on the method used. According to one method, training had no effect after six months, but a significant and positive effect after three years. However, as selection problems were considered, the authors found no significant effect on the probability of having a job at either time.

Harkman (1997) analyzed the effect of training undertaken in 1994 on the probability of having a job two and a half years later. Although selection problems were not considered, no effects of training in general were found. The analysis also compared the effects of short and long spells of training (with the limit set at 100 days). The short spells of training had a significant, negative impact on the employment probability, while long spells had a positive but insignificant effect. The *difference* in effect between short and long spells was, however, statistically significant, and amounted to 4 percent.

Harkman et al. (1999), finally, analyzed the effect of training in 1996 on the employment probability one year later. Besides "traditional" labor-market training, this evaluation looked also at the effect of training in computer activity centers. The results are hard to interpret, as participants (on average) have different prior unemployment and program participation experiences than non-participants. The analysis of the effect of a single program is further complicated by the fact that participants as a rule have participated in several programs earlier. One way to handle this problem is to consider only persons without earlier program participation. Such estimates indicate that computer activity centers had no significant effect, while participation in traditional training had a positive effect on the employment probability one year after program completion. But these results must be interpreted cautiously because the effect is measured from the time of program completion. This implies that the estimated effect will be positively biased.[7]

Larsson (2000) estimated the effect of labor-market training of young people in 1992–93. Her results convey a very discouraging picture. The effects on both future income and employment were significantly negative.[8] In addition, the transition probability to regular education was lower among participants in training than among nonparticipants.

Johansson and Martinsson (2001) studied a program called Swit, which was a joint project between the Swedish government and the Confederation of Swedish Industries. The program was initiated as an experiment during a two-year period (1997–1999) with the aim of providing the Swedish industry with IT-skilled personnel. The set-up was non-traditional and combined traditional education and practice at host companies. The employment effects were compared with the effects of more conventional IT training run by the National Labor Market Board. The results indicated that Swit participants had a 20 percent higher probability to find a regular job than did participants in conventional IT training.

Okeke (2001) studied the effect of participation in training in 1998–99. According to the study the effects on participants' employment were large, positive, and significant. But once again the results are hard to interpret, as it is not clear from the presentation how the control group was selected, but the procedure used might imply a positive bias.[9]

Richardson and van den Berg (2001) analyzed the effect of training undertaken in 1993–2000. They found a significant negative effect on the duration of unemployment when the duration was measured from the end of the program. When duration instead was measured from the start of the program, the effect was insignificant. This suggests that a negative locking-in effect of labor-market training more or less offsets a positive treatment effect once the program had been completed.

Sianesi (2001b) estimated the effect of participating in training in the period 1994–1999. The comparison made in the study is between "participation now" and "waiting in open unemployment." She found that the effect on the participants' employment rate was significantly negative until 30 months after the end of the program; later the effect was insignificant. Also, the probability of collecting unemployment benefits in the future was significantly higher for participants than for nonparticipants.

Another observation refers to the differences between short-run and long-run effects of labor-market training. The short-run effects are often insignificant or even negative. However, with a time horizon of a few years the estimated effects are more positive (1980s) or are, at least, no longer negative (1990s). A conceivable explanation is that training increases the reservation wages of participants (see subsection 2.3). However, Richardson and van den Berg (2001) found a different pattern. According to their study, the treatment effect of training vanishes after two months. The authors suggest that the short-run treatment effect could be due mainly to extra placement efforts on the part of employment officers.

There is some evidence to suggest that income and employment effects are more favorable with longer training periods. But here the amount of research is very small.

3.2 Subsidized Employment

There are a number of studies on the effects of subsidized employment, of which a few look also at the effects of labor-market training. However, given the amount of different subsidized employment programs, less is known about the specific effect of single programs than about labor-market training. The studies of subsidized employment programs are surveyed in table 1.4.

Some of the studies listed in table 1.4 have tried to evaluate the effects on subsequent employment of participation in various programs as compared to open unemployment, whereas other studies have tried only to compare various programs with each other (but not with open unemployment) or to study the effect of participating in a program at a given point of time rather than later. The latter studies avoid the problem that most long-term unemployed will sooner or later end up in a program, which makes it hard to find a comparison group of non-participants. (See the discussion in the introduction to section 3.)

Table 1.4
Treatment effects of subsidized employment.

Study	Program and timing	Sample	Dependent variable	Results
Sehlstedt and Schröder 1989	Recruitment subsidies and relief work, 1984	Register and survey data on unemployed 20–24-year-olds, 1984	Labor market situation, 1987	Significant, positive effect of recruitment subsidies if part of an "action plan". No significant effect of relief work
Edin and Holmlund 1991	Relief work, 1977–1984	Register and survey data on 800 unemployed 16–24-year-olds in Stockholm area, 1981; and register data on 300 displaced workers in northern Sweden, 1977	Job finding probability in (i) the contemporary; and (ii) subsequent unemployment spell(s)	Significant, negative effect in the contemporary unemployment spell, but significant, negative effect on subsequent unemployment spells
Korpi 1994	Relief work, 1981–1984	Register and survey data on 800 16–24-year-old unemployed in the Stockholm area, 1981	Duration of employment	Significant, positive effect
Axelsson, Brännäs, and Löfgren 1996	LMT, work experience schemes, relief work, and youth practice, 1993	Register data on 10,000 unemployed 20–54-year-olds, 1993	Employment within 30 days after program	LMT, work experience schemes, and relief work are equivalent alternatives, but youth practice is better
Harkman, Johansson, and Okeke 1999	Recruitment subsidies, trainee replacement schemes, work placement schemes, relief work, and work experience schemes, 1996	Register and survey data on 3,000 20–54-year-old participants. Random selection and representative sample	Employment 1 year after program	Large significant, positive effects of recruitment subsidies, and significant, positive effects of trainee replacement and work placement schemes as well. No significant effects of relief work and work experience schemes
Carling and Gustafson 1999	Self-employment grants and recruitment subsidies, 1995–96	Register data on individuals with self-employment grants (9,000) or recruitment subsidies (14,000) in 1995 or 1996	The duration of employment	Significantly better employment results for self-employment grants than for recruitment subsidies

Study	Program	Data	Outcome	Results
Okeke 1999	Self-employment grants, 1994	Register and survey data on 7,000 enterprises (entrepreneurs)	Enterprise survival rate, 1997	No significant difference between enterprises with and without self-employment grants
Larsson 2000	Youth practice, 1992–93	Register data on 600 20–24-year-old participants. Non-participating comparison group through propensity score matching	(i) Yearly income (ii) employment (iii) regular education 1–2 years after program	Significant, negative effect on yearly income and employment; no significant effect on education
Okeke and Spånt Enbuske 2001	Self-employment grants, 1995	Register and survey data on 8,000 entrepreneurs	(i) Enterprise survival rate; and (ii) probability to earn a living through the enterprise, 1998	No significant difference between enterprises with and without self-employment grants. Self-employment grants have, according to self-reported averages, a positive effect on the probability to earn a living through the enterprise
Carling and Richardson 2001	Work experience schemes, LMT, work placement schemes, relief work, computer activity centers, recruitment subsidies, self-employment grants, trainee replacement schemes, 1995–1997	Register data on 25,000 individuals who became unemployed and began their first program in 1995–1997	Unemployment duration	Significantly better results for recruitment subsidies, self-employment grants, trainee replacement schemes, and work placement schemes than for LMT, computer activity centers, work experience schemes, and relief work
Sianesi 2001b	"Work practice" (work experience *plus* work placement schemes), LMT, relief work, recruitment subsidies, and trainee replacement schemes, 1994–1999	Register data on 30,800 25–54-year-olds who became unemployed for the first time in 1994 and were entitled to unemployment benefits. Comparison group through propensity score matching	Employment rate over time	Significantly better employment results for recruitment subsidies and trainee replacement schemes than for LMT, "work practice" and relief work. Subsidies are also better than "waiting in open unemployment."

Sehlstedt and Schröder (1989) found that recruitment subsidies improved the labor-market situation of young people, provided that program participation constituted a part of a larger "plan" designed to improve their labor-market prospects. But the effect of relief work was not significant.

Edin and Holmlund (1991) analyzed, in addition to labor-market training (see subsection 3.1), the employment effects of relief work, using a sample of young people and displaced workers. One result was that relief work participants found regular employment at a slower pace than non-participants. But re-employment probabilities in subsequent unemployment spells were significantly higher for former relief-work participants than for non-participants. When Korpi (1994) used the same sample of youth to analyze the effects of relief work on the duration of employment, he found a significant positive effect.

Axelsson et al. (1996) analyzed the relative efficiency of labor-market training, work-experience schemes, relief work, and youth practice in terms of the employment probability within thirty days after the program ended. There were no significant differences between labor-market training, work-experience schemes and relief work, while youth practice had a significantly larger impact on the short-run probability of leaving unemployment.

Harkman et al. (1999) analyzed (in addition to labor-market training and computer activity centers (see subsection 3.1)) the effect of job-creation schemes in 1996 on the probability of having a job one year later. Also here the results must be interpreted with caution because of the risk of biased estimates (see subsection 3.1). Another problem is that the number of first-time participants in other forms of subsidized employment than work-experience schemes and work placement schemes was small. With these caveats, the results suggest that recruitment subsidies had the most favorable effects. Also work placement schemes and trainee replacement schemes seem to have had positive effects, while this was not the case for work-experience schemes and relief work.

Three evaluations of self-employment grants were published in 1999–2001. Okeke (1999) analyzed the enterprise survival rate, which we interpret as an indicator of the employment effect. She found no significant difference in the survival rate between enterprises started with and enterprises started without self-employment grants three years after the start-up. This can be interpreted as a positive result if one assumes that enterprises started by unemployed (as an alternative to unemployment) have worse prospects than enterprises started by employees who choose voluntarily to leave their employment to exploit supposedly profitable opportunities. However, potential selection bias was not considered, and the estimates should therefore be interpreted with caution.

In a more comprehensive analysis, Carling and Gustafsson (1999) found that the outflow to unemployment was half as large among those who had obtained self-employment grants as among those who had benefited from recruitment subsidies during 1995–1997. This also supports the favorable impression of self-employment grants, as other evaluations (discussed earlier in this section) indicate that recruitment subsidies have had positive effects.

Okeke et al. (2001) compared the rate of survival in 1998 for firms started with and without self-employment grants in 1995. The difference in survival was insignificant, but a larger fraction of those who had received self-employment grants reported that they could make a living from the returns from their firms three years after the launching of the firm.

Larsson (2000) analyzed the effects of youth practice and labor-market training (see subsection 3.1) in 1992–93. The results of youth practice were very similar to those of labor-market training: incomes were 20–30 percent and employment probabilities 18–37 percent lower among former participants than among non-participants one or two years after the program.[10] But, in contrast to labor-market training, youth practice had no decreasing effect on the transition rates to regular education.

Carling and Richardson (2001) analyzed the relative efficiency of eight different programs in terms of employment probabilities. The results indicate that the programs in which participants conduct regular work (recruitment subsidies, self-employment grants, and trainee replacement schemes) or at least obtain practice at a regular workplace (work placement scheme) achieve the best results. Training (both ordinary labor-market training and training at computer activity centers) and job-creation programs that do not constitute regular work (work-experience schemes and relief work) perform less well in terms of subsequent regular employment. The same ranking holds for different subgroups of unemployed and is not affected by the timing of program entry. This suggests that the results are not due to selection bias.

Sianesi (2001b) compared the effects of participation in six different programs (including labor-market training; see subsection 3.1) in

1994–1999. She found that it was (significantly) better to "wait in open unemployment" than to participate in "work practice" (work placement schemes and work-experience schemes) or relief work in terms of subsequent probability of employment. Trainee replacement schemes and recruitment subsidies, however, were equally good and better, respectively, compared to waiting in open unemployment. A mirror image of this was that both work practice and relief work had a significant, positive effect on the probability to receive future unemployment compensation.[11] This indicates that the possibility to renew unemployment benefit eligibility may have been an important reason for program participation. Another aspect of this is that the most negative effects of program participation arose for those who started a program close to the time of benefit exhaustion (Sianesi 2001a).

3.3 Search Activity

The probability to obtain a job is influenced by the job applicants' search activity. It is therefore of interest to study whether or not ALMPs influence search activity. This is the topic of a number of survey studies, which have examined the difference in search behavior between program participants and openly unemployed. The studies are summarized in table 1.5.

Edin and Holmlund (1991) found that unemployed youths devoted fully seven hours a week to job search in the beginning of the 1980s. The corresponding figure for relief work participants was less than one hour. The same survey indicated that the number of search methods used was significantly higher among the unemployed (3.1 per week) than among relief workers (0.6 per week). The results of Sehlstedt and Schröder (1989) for youth search behavior in the mid 1980s convey a similar picture.

Ackum Agell (1996) and Regnér and Wadensjö (1999) studied search behavior among adults. Ackum Agell (1996) found that the unemployed are more active job seekers than program participants. The percentage of active seekers is much (and significantly) higher among the unemployed (95) than among program participants (57), and program participants use fewer search methods. Among the unemployed, 30 percent reported that they did not search at all during the survey week; the corresponding percentage for program participants was 68. This difference was statistically significant.

Regnér and Wadensjö (1999) found that the percentage actively searching jobs or being in contact with the public employment service

Table 1.5
Search activity.

Study	Program and timing	Sample	Dependent variable	Results
Sehlstedt and Schröder 1989	Relief work, 1984–85	Register and survey data on 500 20–24-year-old unemployed, 1984	Search activity and number of search methods	Significant, negative effect
Edin and Holmlund 1991	Relief work, 1977–1984	Register and survey data on 800 16–24-year-old unemployed in the Stockholm area, 1981	Search activity and number of search methods	Significant, negative effect
Ackum Agell 1996	LMT and job creation programs (work experience schemes, relief work, and trainee replacement schemes), 1993–94	Survey data on 4,000 20–54-year-old unemployed, 1991	Search activity and number of search methods	Significant, negative effect
Regnér and Wadensjö 1999	Program participation in 1998	Survey data on 700 19–65-year-olds, unemployed during the spring of 1998 ("stock sample") and 1,300 25–60-year-olds leaving unemployment during the spring of 1998 ("flow sample")	Search activity and search methods	Compared to the openly unemployed, program participants search less actively while in programs, but more actively after program completion

was significantly higher among the openly unemployed (72 and 79, respectively) than among program participants (53 and 63, respectively) during the four weeks preceding the interview. But the authors also found that persons who had participated in a program during the preceding twelve months searched significantly more than those who had not participated in any program during the same period.[12] This suggests a negative locking-in effect on search effort during program participation, but a positive treatment effect after completion of the program.

Ackum Agell (1996) emphasized that participants have less time to search for work than do non-participants. Also, it can be socially beneficial that participants do not look for work if the program forms part of a comprehensive plan to improve their labor-market prospects. But this conclusion no longer holds if placement in ALMPs is used to renew eligibility for unemployment insurance. Either way, the studies of search activity do suggest that ALMPs cause temporary locking-in effects.

3.4 Employer Attitudes

Employer attitudes towards different categories of job applicants is another factor that influences the possibility of finding a job. Several survey studies have examined the effect of ALMPs in this respect. The studies are summarized in table 1.6.

Agell and Lundborg (1995, 2002), in two survey studies, undertaken in 1991 and 1998, asked personnel managers about their attitudes to unemployed job seekers with and without prior participation in ALMPs. The percentage who considered a long-term unemployed potentially less productive than a similar job applicant without an unemployment history rose from 21 to 27 between 1991 and 1998. Eighteen percent of the respondents in the 1991 survey also considered applicants with prior participation in a labor-market program potentially less productive than a similar applicant without unemployment experiences. The questions in the 1998 survey were more specific about the effects of program participation. Almost 15 percent of the respondents considered a participant in labor-market training potentially less productive than a similar person without an unemployment history. The corresponding percentage for participants in relief work and work-experience schemes was 20. However, the differences between participants in various programs and the openly unemployed were never significant.

Table 1.6
Employer attitudes.

Study	Source of information	Sample	Dependent variable	Results
Agell and Lundborg 1995	Survey, 1991	Personnel managers at ~150 companies	Share who believe that (i) unemployed non-participants; and (ii) participants are potentially less productive than other job seekers	Openly unemployed 21%; program participants 18%
Behrenz 2001	Survey, 1995	Company representatives at ~800 companies	Share who automatically sort out (i) unemployed non-participants; and (ii) participants	Openly unemployed 4.2%; LMT participants 1.2%; participants in other programs 1.6%
Agell and Lundborg 2002	Follow-up survey, 1998	Personnel managers at ~150 companies	Share who believe that (i) unemployed non-participants and (ii) participants are potentially less productive than other job seekers	Openly unemployed 27%; LMT participants 15%; participants in work experience schemes/relief work 20%
Klingvall 1998	Survey, 1998	Employers at ~280 workplaces	Share who consider hiring various categories	Openly unemployed 2%; LMT participants 30%; participants in other programs 20%
Agell and Bennmarker 2002	Survey, 1999	Personnel managers at 885 workplaces	How long a spell of unemployment or training/unemployment is needed before a job applicant is considered less suitable	Labor market training increases the time required for stigma from unemployment to arise

In a survey reported by Klingvall (1998) only some 3 percent of the responding employers stated that they would consider hiring an openly unemployed job applicant, while 30 (20) percent stated that they would consider hiring a job seeker who had participated in labor-market training (any other labor-market program). The differences were statistically significant.

Also the results in the survey reported by Behrenz (2001) suggests that employers consider open unemployment more negative than participation in labor-market programs: 4.2 percent of about 800 respondents said that they automatically discard applications from openly unemployed job seekers; the corresponding percentages for participants in labor-market training and participants in other programs were 1.2 and 1.6, respectively. The differences between the figures for program participants and openly unemployed were significant; the difference between training and other programs was not.

Agell and Bennmarker (2002), in survey questions answered by personnel managers at 885 workplaces, found that participation in labor-market training prolonged the time required for a stigma from unemployment to arise.

The survey studies of employer attitudes are the studies giving the most favorable results for the effects of ALMPs on individuals. Although questions and estimated effects differ, these studies suggest that employers judge former ALMP participants more favorably than unemployed who have not participated in programs. This evidence also suggests that labor-market training is preferred to the other programs. It is notable that this favorable view of labor-market training has no counterpart in the econometric results reported in subsection 3.1. It is not clear exactly what this discrepancy reflects; perhaps it can be explained by the fact that the survey studies of employer attitudes do not control for other factors or potential selection, as the econometric studies do.

4 Macroeconomic Studies

In this section we survey the macroeconomic studies of the total (general-equilibrium) effects of ALMPs in Sweden, using our earlier classification in table 1.2.

There are some general methodological problems in the macroeconomic studies. It may be difficult to obtain precise estimates of effects because the number of observations that can be used in the econometric analyses is often small. Another problem is two-way causality. It is not only the case that ALMPs may affect (un)employment, but changes in the labor-market situation may also trigger political decisions to adjust the volume of ALMPs. This may give rise to simultaneity bias and identification problems. We will repeatedly return to how this issue has been handled in various studies below.

4.1 Beveridge Curves, Matching Functions, and Migration Relationships

A first type of macroeconomic studies directly shed light on the efficiency of the matching process. These are studies of *Beveridge curves*, *matching functions* and *geographical mobility*.

Somewhat surprisingly, only two studies of Sweden have looked at the effects of ALMPs on matching in a *Beveridge-curve* context (Jackman et al. 1990; Calmfors 1993). Neither of these studies show any effects of ALMPs on matching efficiency.[13] But the main conclusion is that we largely lack knowledge of the Beveridge-curve effects as none of the studies covers the 1990s.

There are two studies of *matching functions*, which relate the number of hirings to the numbers of vacancies and unemployed, on Swedish data. Edin and Holmlund (1991) found that program participation contributes to matching, but that the effect is only half that of open unemployment.[14] This suggests that locking-in effects dominate treatment effects of these programs in the short run. Hallgren (1996) found that subsidized employment had a significant negative impact on matching, whereas the opposite was true for labor-market training. But again the main conclusion is the lack of empirical knowledge.

Geographical mobility is one important dimension of the matching process. Hence, the effects of ALMPs on this variable may serve as a proxy for the effects on matching. Several studies have been made. They are summarized in table 1.7.

McCormick and Skedinger (1991) found that increased program volumes at the regional level give rise to higher unemployment. The results may be interpreted in several ways, but the authors conclude that ALMPs have reduced geographical mobility.

Nilsson (1995), Westerlund (1997), and Heiborn (1998) all estimated models of migration between the Swedish counties. Nilsson found some evidence of locking-in effects: increased program participation in a county led to a significant decrease in out-migration. Some of Westerlund's estimates also pointed to locking-in effects, while others

Table 1.7
Effects of ALMPs on geographical mobility.

Study	Data	Results
McCormick and Skedinger 1991	24 counties, 1968–1985	Locking-in effects
Nilsson 1995	24 counties, 1966–1993	Locking-in effects
Westerlund 1997	24 counties, 1970–1989	Locking-in effects or insignificant results
Heiborn 1998	24 counties, 1964–1993	Mixed results
Westerlund 1998	24 counties, 1970–1989	Mixed results
Widerstedt 1998	541 males, 1981–1991	No effects
Fredriksson 1999	24 counties, 1968–1993	Small locking-in effects

gave insignificant results. Heiborn's results were not stable over different specifications, so it is hard to draw any firm conclusions from her study.

Westerlund (1998) studied the effects of mobility grants, labor-market training, and relief work on mobility across county borders. Mobility grants had a marginally significant positive effect on total migration, while training and relief work gave significant locking-in effects. Looking separately at migration of the unemployed and the employed, all programs had a positive effect on the mobility of the unemployed and a negative effect on other (potential) movers.

Widerstedt (1998) estimated models of individuals' mobility probabilities, but found no significant effects of ALMPs.

Fredriksson (1999) looked at regional adjustments to employment shocks at the county level. The main finding was that the bulk of the adjustment burden falls on mobility: ALMPs lower mobility marginally, and, hence, locking-in effects seem to dominate.

The results concerning geographical mobility are thus mixed. But most of the evidence suggests that ALMPs have reduced mobility. However, none of the studies have considered the job broking activities of the employment offices. In addition, most of the studies do not distinguish between subsidized employment and labor-market training.[15]

4.2   Direct Crowding Out (Displacement)

As discussed in subsection 2.5, subsidized employment is likely to cause direct displacement. The studies of this fall into two categories: *survey* studies and *econometric* studies of labor demand.

4.2.1 Survey Studies

In a number of surveys, employers, program participants and employment officers have been asked whether (i) they believe that the work performed by program participant(s) would have been performed by *anyone* in the absence of the program (*substitution effects*); and (ii) in some cases, if this question was answered in the affirmative, whether the same person(s) would have been employed (*deadweight effects*).

Such surveys suffer from a number of problems. First, participants may have an exaggerated view of their importance for the activity concerned. This could lead to an upward bias in the estimated displacement. Second, both employers and employment officers have incentives to avoid the impression that programs are abused, which could give a bias in the opposite direction. Third, respondents are not likely to be able to evaluate the extent to which programs crowd out employment in other workplaces than that associated with the program.

A number of survey studies are summarized in table 1.8. Although the results vary considerably, all studies but one indicate that direct displacement occurs. In most cases the estimated displacement is substantial.

A way to summarize the information in table 1.8 is to compute the average displacement for each program according to the studies shown. The results are reported in table 1.9, where the programs have been ranked according to the size of the average displacement effect.[16] There is a clear tendency that the closer to the regular labor market a program is, the larger is the estimated displacement. For recruitment subsidies, trainee replacement schemes, general employment subsidies, and targeted employment subsidies, the estimated displacement effects are between 39 and 84 percent.

In addition to the studies in table 1.8, a number of earlier studies (Peterson and Vlachos 1978; Ams 1981; Ams 1983; Ams 1985; RRV 1989) used survey methods to estimate the total employment effects of temporary or permanent wage subsidies. The identified employment effects were generally small. So, these studies, too, suggest substantial displacement.

4.2.2 Econometric Studies of Direct Displacement

The econometric studies identify the relationship between programs and regular employment by comparing actual employment with the employment that would have been realized in the absence of programs.

Table 1.8
Survey studies of direct displacement.[a]

Study	Method	Program	Results
Sehlstedt and Schröder 1989	Interviews with participants and supervisors	RS for youth	Participants: 49%; Supervisors: 23%
LO 1993a, 1993b, 1994a, 1994b	Questionnaires to participants	WES	20–39%
Temo 1993, 1994, 1995[b]	Telephone interviews with participants, employers and employment officers	WES	Participants: 17% 1993, 12% 1994; Organizers: 3–7%
NUTEK 1994	Questionnaires to participants and employers	WES	About 30% according to both participants and employers
Ams 1995	Questionnaires to organizers	RS	36% (of which slightly more than half would have recruited the same person).
Hallström 1995	Interviews with participants	WES	20–25%
Anxo and Dahlin 1996	Questionnaires to employers	TES, GES	84% (GES); 69% (TES)
Ams 1997	Questionnaires to participants	RW, WPS, MYP, WES, TRS, RS	RW: 24%; WPS: 16%; MYP: 10%; WES: 8%; RS: 48%; TRS: 42%
Ams 1998a	Questionnaires to participants	WES, TRS, RS, MYP, RW, WPS	WES: 13%; TRS: 51%; RS: 40%; MYP: 14%; RW: 27%; WPS: 21%
Ams 1998b	Questionnaires to participants and employers	RS, RW, WES, TRS, WPS, TPJ, RJ, MYP	RS: 35%; RW: 14%; WES: 0%; TRS: 32%; WPS: 8%; TPJ: 1%; RJ: 1%; MYP: 3%
Johansson 1999	Questionnaires to participants and employment officers	RJ	Participants: 16%, 26%[c]; Employment officers: 11%[d]

a. The following abbreviations are used in the table. GES: general employment subsidy. MYP: municipal youth programs. RJ: resource jobs. RS: recruitment subsidy. RW: relief work. TES: targeted employment subsidy TPJ: temporary public jobs. TRS: trainee replacement schemes. WES: work experience schemes. WPS: work placement schemes.
b. The Ministry of Labour commissioned the study and the results were reported in Ams 1997.
c. This refers to answers to the question whether the participant believes that the employer actually could have afforded to hire someone in the absence of the program.
d. The fraction that answered "Yes, in most cases."

Table 1.9
Average direct displacement effects according to the studies in Table 1.8.

Program	Average displacement effect (%)	Number of studies
Temporary public jobs (TPJ)	1.0	1
Municipal youth programs (MYP)	9.0	3
Resource jobs (RJ)	14.3	3
Work placement schemes (WPS)	15.0	3
Work experience schemes (WES)	15.6	11
Relief work (RW)	21.7	3
Recruitment subsidies (RS)	38.5	6
Trainee replacement schemes (TRS)	41.7	3
General employment subsidy (GES)	69.0	1
Targeted employment subsidy (TES)	84.0	1

Most of the studies have estimated traditional labor demand schedules augmented with measures of the volume of programs.

A fundamental problem for econometric studies of direct displacement is that the relation between programs and employment goes both ways: employment may depend on program participation, but the size of programs is also likely to depend on (un)employment. This *simultaneity problem*, discussed in the introduction to section 4, may give rise to biased estimates of the effects of ALMPs. The problem is considered in different ways and to a various extent in the studies.

The econometric studies of displacement are much fewer than the survey studies. The results are summarized in table 1.10.

A first econometric study of direct displacement was carried out by Gramlich and Ysander (1981) using aggregate data for the period 1964–1977. Their results were that relief work in road construction crowded out 100 percent regular employment, whereas there was no significant effect of relief work in health and welfare.

Forslund and Krueger (1997) used panel data for counties for a period encompassing the 1980s. Their results were similar to those of Gramlich and Ysander. Forslund and Krueger found significant displacement (36–69 percent) in the construction sector, but no significant effects for health and welfare. The authors handled the simultaneity problem in two ways. First they ran vector autoregressions to check whether relief work "explains" employment or if it is the other way around. Second, they estimated "displacement equations" for a sector

Table 1.10
Econometric studies of direct displacement. Only results that are significantly different from zero are shown. Where the authors have estimated several models, we show the results preferred by the authors. For abbreviations, see table 1.8. Here, LMT denotes labor-market training.

Study	Program, data	Results
Gramlich and Ysander 1981	RW; aggregate time-series data 1964–1977.	Road construction: 100%; health and welfare: 0%
Forslund 1996	WES, LMT, RW, youth programs, TRS; panel of the Swedish munici-palities 1990–1994.	WES: 0%; LMT: 0%; RW: 84%; youth programs: 76%
Forslund and Krueger 1997	RW; panel of the Swedish counties 1976–1991, 1980–1991.	Construction workers: 69%; health and welfare 0%
Löfgren and Wikström 1997	WES, LMT, RW, youth programs, TRS; panel of the Swedish munici-palities 1990–1994.	WES: 0%; LMT: 0%; RW: 0%; youth programs: 94%; TRS: 0%
Dahlberg and Forslund 1999	RW, LMT, subsidized employment; panel of the Swedish municipalities 1987–1996.	RW: 66%; LMT 0%; subsidized employment: 65%
Edin, Forslund, and Holmlund 1999	Youth programs; panel of the Swedish municipalities 1990–1994.	76%

where there should be no displacement.[17] The results indicated that the effect is from relief work to employment and not the other way around.

Forslund (1996) and Dahlberg and Forslund (1999) used data at the municipal level. They distinguished between subsidized employment, relief work, and labor-market training.[18] Subsidized employment and relief work were found to give displacement effects of around 65 percent, while there were no significant effects of training. Dahlberg and Forslund treated the simultaneity problem in several ways, including IV (instrumental variables) estimations.

Sjöstrand (1997) claimed in a comment to Forslund (1996) that the analysis of the latter was built on a mis-specified model and that one finds no displacement effects with a correctly specified model. Löfgren and Wikström (1997) reviewed Forslund 1996 and Sjöstrand 1997 and found shortcomings in both studies. With the preferred specification of Löfgren and Wikström, only youth programs gave rise to displacement (94 percent).

Edin, Forslund, and Holmlund (1999) analyzed the effects of youth programs on youth employment and found large displacement effects

(76 percent evaluated at the means of the variables). The simultaneity problem was handled mainly by means of IV methods.

Generally, the econometric studies give higher estimates of displacement than the survey studies. Typical percentages are well above 60. One possible explanation for the difference in results is that displacement is partly the result of distorted competition. Such effects are clearly difficult to assess for the respondents in survey studies. Another difference between the two types of studies is that many of the econometric investigations do not distinguish between different programs. Hence, the effects are averages over several programs. As an example, both work-experience schemes and youth practice were included in "subsidized employment" in Dahlberg and Forslund 1999. The average displacement effect for subsidized employment in this study was 65 percent. This percentage would, for example, be consistent with youth programs crowding out significantly more than 65 percent and work-experience schemes crowding out significantly less.

Most of the studies of displacement effects have tried to handle the simultaneity problem discussed in the introduction to section 4 through various methods. The fact that the studies have not found displacement effects of labor-market training (although the size of training programs can be expected to change in response to the employment situation in a similar way as subsidized employment) also suggests that the relationships found reflect the effect of programs on employment rather than the other way around.

4.3 Labor-Force Participation

The effects of ALMPs on labor-force participation is yet another area where research efforts have been modest. We are aware of only three studies that deal directly with the issue: Wadensjö 1993, Johansson and Markowski 1995, and Johansson 2001. All studies indicate strong positive effects of ALMPs on labor-force participation.

One can also obtain indirect evidence on the labor-force effects of ALMPs from studies of direct displacement. If ALMPs have a positive effect on labor-force participation, the estimated crowding-out effects should be larger when employment is measured relative to the labor force than when they are measured relative to the population. This was indeed the case in Löfgren and Wikström 1997 and in Dahlberg and Forslund 1999.

However, the results on labor-force participation should be interpreted with caution. If program participation has been used as a means to renew eligibility for unemployment benefits, the increase in labor-force participation has not necessarily meant an increase in *effective* labor supply.

4.4 Wage Setting

For a number of reasons discussed in section 2, ALMPs may affect wage setting. The mechanisms involve effects on matching, the competition in the labor market, the welfare and productivity of job seekers, and the allocation of the labor force across sectors. The net effect is theoretically unclear. Estimates of *wage-setting schedules* can throw light on this issue. A large number of such studies have been undertaken. In all cases, real wage equations including measures of unemployment and the volume of labor-market programs as explanatory variables have been estimated. The main results are summarized in table 1.11.

The table shows mixed results. Many studies find that larger ALMPs increase wage pressure, but many studies do not find any significant effect. Only three studies (OECD 1993; Okeke 1998; Thomas 2000) suggest that ALMPs may reduce wage pressure. Most studies do not distinguish between different programs. No consistent pattern emerges from the three studies (Löfgren and Wikström 1991; Forslund 1992; Edin, Holmlund, and Östros 1994) that estimate separate effects of labor-market training and relief work.

Most of the studies cover periods ending before the deep recession of the 1990s. As both unemployment and ALMPs reached peaks during this recession, it is uncertain to what extent the results from earlier studies apply to the 1990s. To the extent that compensation levels in programs were lowered and the expected treatment effects on the probability of finding a job or on future income deteriorated, one should expect less unfavorable (or more favorable) wage effects of ALMPs. However, Johansson et al. (1999), Rødseth and Nymoen (1999), and Forslund and Kolm (2000) did not find any significant changes in the wage-setting behavior between earlier periods and the 1990s.

Simultaneity problems of the same kind as for studies of displacement effects may be present also in the estimation of wage effects. However, because it probably takes time for wage changes to influence employment and for employment changes to trigger changes in program volumes, the problem is likely to be less severe in this case. A more serious problem may be that program participation covaries

Table 1.11
Effects of ALMPs on the real wage.[a]

Study	Effect of ALMPs	
	Short run	Long run
Newell and Symons 1987	0	0
Calmfors and Forslund 1990, 1991	+	+
Calmfors and Nymoen 1990	+	+
Holmlund 1990	NA	+
Löfgren and Wikström 1991[b]	+/0	0/+
Skedinger 1991[c]	+	+
Forslund 1992[d]	+/−	+/−
OECD 1993[e]	−	−
Edin, Holmlund, and Östros 1994[f]	0/0/0	0/0/0
Forslund and Risager 1994[g]	0	0
Forslund 1995	0	+
Blomskog 1997[h]	NA	+/−/0
Okeke 1998[i]	NA	−
Johansson, Lundborg, and Zetterberg 1999[j]	+/+	+/+
Rødseth and Nymoen 1999	0	+
Forslund and Kolm 2000	0	0
Thomas 2000	−	NA

a. A "+" sign indicates a significantly positive effect, a "−" sign a significantly negative effect and "0" no significant effect.
b. The first effect refers to relief work, the second to labor-market training.
c. Data pertain to different groups of employees in mining and manufacturing 1971–1988. The program studied is relief work.
d. The data refer to twelve unemployment insurance funds. The first effect refers to relief work, the second to labor-market training.
e. The regression covers the period 1985–1990 for a cross-section of 19 OECD countries. A number of effects were assumed to be equal across countries, whereas the effect of ALMPs was estimated separately for each country.
f. The estimates pertain to individual wages for workers in engineering 1972–1987. The effects refer to total programs, labor-market training and relief work, respectively. The results in the table are IV estimates. OLS estimates gave significant, wage-reducing effects of total programs and labor-market training both in the short run and in the long run, and of relief work in the long run.
g. Separate estimates for industry and the rest of the business sector.
h. Different results in different model specifications.
i. The estimated models are "wage curves" on micro data. Okeke did not consistently find that ALMPs have contributed to less wage pressure. The shown negative effect was, however, found in most specifications.
j. Effects were estimated for the periods 1965–1990 and 1965–1998, respectively.

Table 1.12
Effects of ALMPs in reduced-form estimates.

Study	Period	Results
Ohlsson 1993, 1995	Vector autoregressions, aggregate time-series data, 1969–1990	Job-creation schemes crowd out regular employment and lower open unemployment. No significant effects on wages.
Skedinger 1995	Vector autoregressions, aggregate time-series data, 1979–1991	Youth programs crowd out regular youth employment (110% in short run).
Forslund 1995	Reduced form, aggregate time-series data, 1960–1993	No effect on open unemployment of aggregate ALMPs.
Calmfors and Skedinger 1995	Reduced form, panel data for counties, 1966–1990	Job-creation schemes crowd out regular employment; unstable results for labor-market training.

with long-term unemployment, so that adverse wage-setting effects of ALMPs could reflect that higher long-term unemployment reduces the competition for jobs that insiders meet (see subsection 2.2).

4.5   Reduced-Form Estimates

A last type of studies is *reduced-form* estimates of the effects of ALMPs on (un)employment, i.e., estimates of the total net effects through all channels discussed in section 2. Put differently, these estimations examine how the intersection between the wage-setting and employment schedules in figure 1.4 is affected by the size of ALMPs. The results from four reduced-form studies are summarized in table 1.12.

Ohlsson (1993, 1995) estimated vector autoregressions (VARs) on aggregate quarterly time-series data. The estimated model was used to study the effects of an expansion of subsidized employment. The result was displacement in the order of magnitude of 50 percent during the first quarter. During later quarters the estimates are too imprecise to warrant any conclusions. Ohlsson also looked at the effects of both subsidized employment and labor-market training on wage setting, but found no significant effects. This was also the case for the effects of training on unemployment.

Skedinger (1995) estimated VARs to analyze the effects of subsidized employment for youth on regular youth employment. The results imply more than total displacement as soon as after one quarter. The effect becomes smaller over time (partly because program volumes decline), but is statistically significant during the first five quarters.[19]

Forslund (1995) estimated a reduced-form unemployment equation. The results indicated that ALMPs lead to lower open unemployment in the short run, but not in the long run. This would indicate complete displacement in the long run.

Calmfors and Skedinger (1995) studied the relationship between total unemployment on the one hand and subsidized employment and labor-market training on the other hand using a panel of the 24 counties between 1966 and 1990. The authors tried to handle the simultaneity problem through instrumental variables methods (one assumption being that the composition of the political majority in a county influences the volume of ALMPs, because the Social Democrats have generally been more in favor of these programs than the Liberal and Conservative parties). Subsidized employment was found to cause large displacement effects (of the order of magnitude of 60–90 percent), whereas the results for training were very unstable.

To summarize, the reduced-form studies suggest that subsidized employment schemes tend to reduce regular employment, but also that they probably contribute to lower open unemployment.

4.6   Conclusions from the Macroeconomic Studies

Just as in the case of microeconomic studies, the overall picture from the macroeconomic studies of ALMPs in Sweden is rather disappointing. There is little evidence that ALMPs make the matching process more efficient; rather the studies of geographical mobility suggest the opposite. There is evidence of large direct displacement effects of those subsidized employment schemes that most closely resemble regular employment, but not of labor-market training. Some evidence indicates that programs tend to raise wage pressure, whereas other evidence does not point in this direction. Reduced-form estimates seem to show that programs (at least subsidized employment) tend to reduce regular employment, even though they may help reduce open unemployment. The most favorable effects of ALMPs refer to labor-force participation, which seems to be increased by an expansion of programs.

5   Reduced-Form Studies on OECD Data

Beginning with the influential study by Layard et al. (1991), a large number of studies have tried to explain unemployment differences among OECD countries by differences in labor-market institutions. The earlier studies explained cross-country variations in unemployment

Table 1.13
Effects of ALMPs on (un)employment in cross-section and panel data studies of the OECD countries.

Study	Countries and period	Effect on	Results[a]
Layard, Nickell, and Jackman 1991	20 OECD countries; 1983–1988; cross-section data	Open unemployment	− (−1.53)
		Total unemployment	0 (−0.53)
OECD 1993	19 OECD countries; 1983–1988; cross-section data	Open unemployment (Layard et al. measure of ALMPs)	—
		Open unemployment (ALMP expenditures as fraction of mean wage multiplied by labor force	0
Heylen 1993	18 OECD countries; second half of 1980s; cross-section data	Real-wage sensitivity to unemployment variations[b] (effect of expenditures on total ALMPs, employment service and labor market training, respectively)	—
		Real-wage sensitivity to unemployment variations (effect of job creation measures)	0
Zetterberg 1995	19 OECD countries; 1985–1991; panel data	Open unemployment (ALMP expenditures as fraction of total expenditures on unemployed)	− (−1.49)
		Total unemployment	− (−0.49)
Jackman, Layard, and Nickell 1996	20 OECD countries 1983–1988 and 1989–1994; panel data	Open unemployment	0 (−0.06)
		Long-term open unemployment	—
		Short-term open unemployment	0
		Total unemployment	+ (0.94)
Scarpetta 1996	17 OECD countries; 1983–1993; panel data	Open unemployment	− (−0.51)
		Total unemployment	+ (0.49)
		Employment as fraction of population	+

Study	Data	Variable	Result
Forslund and Krueger 1997	OECD countries; 1983–1988 and 1993; cross-section data	Open unemployment 1983–1988; (Zetterberg measure of ALMPs)[c]	− (−0.83)
		Total unemployment 1983–1988; (Zetterberg measure of ALMPs)[c]	0 (0.17)
		Open unemployment 1983–1988; (ALMP expenditure as fraction of GDP)	0
		Open unemployment 1993; (Zetterberg measure of ALMPs)[c]	+
Elmeskov, Martin, and Scarpetta 1998	OECD countries; 1983–1995; panel data	Open unemployment	− (−1.18)
		Total unemployment	0 (−0.18)
Nickell and Layard 1999	20 OECD countries; 1983–1988 and 1989–1994; panel data	Open unemployment	− (−0.18)
		Long-term open unemployment	−
		Short-term open unemployment	0
		Total unemployment	+ (0.82)
		Employment as fraction of population	0
Blanchard and Wolfers 2000	20 OECD countries; 1960–1995; panel data with five-year averages	Open unemployment	− (−1.43)
		Total unemployment	− (−0.43)
Fitoussi, Jestaz, Phelps, and Zoega 2000	19 OECD countries; panel data 1960–1998, cross-section data 1983–1988	Sensitivity of open unemployment to shocks	−
Okeke 2000	20 OECD countries 1986–1998, panel and cross-country data	Employment including ALMP participation; (Layard et al. measure of ALMPs)	+/0

a. The minus and plus signs indicate the signs of the effects on the respective variables. A zero indicates a non-significant effect. Numbers in parentheses indicate the calculated effect on the variable in question of an increase in the participation in ALMPs by 1 percentage point of the labor force.

b. According to conventional theory, the sensitivity of the real wage to variations in unemployment is negatively related to equilibrium unemployment (Layard et al., 1991; Nickell and Layard, 1999).

c. See the entry for Zetterberg 1995 above in the table.

rates with cross-country variation in labor-market institutions. Later studies have used panel data to exploit both cross-sectional and time-series variations. Most of these studies have examined the influence of ALMPs. As these studies have usually been interpreted to give very favorable results for ALMPs, it may be of some interest to compare them with the studies of Sweden that we have surveyed.

5.1 Main Results

The results in the studies of the OECD countries cannot be directly compared with those in the studies of Sweden. The reason is that the former studies use measures of expenditures on ALMPs (the only comparable measures available for all OECD countries), usually spending per unemployed person as a fraction of GDP per participant in the labor force (which was introduced by Layard et al. (1991)), as explanatory variables, and open unemployment as the dependent variable. This does not allow direct estimates of how total (and open) unemployment is affected by program participation, i.e., of how much displacement occurs. To derive these effects, the results in the studies on OECD data have to be recalculated using certain assumptions. The appendix describes how we did this. The results are shown in table 1.13.

Most of the studies reported in the table support the hypothesis that an expansion of ALMPs contributes to lower open unemployment. Two of the studies also show a larger effect on long-term than short-term open unemployment (Jackman et al. 1996; Nickell and Layard 1999). This is, of course, to be expected, as program placement can be used to interrupt long unemployment spells. However, looking at the calculated effects on total unemployment (the sum of open unemployment and program participation), the picture is different. Some studies indicate that total unemployment increases when ALMPs expand, others that it decreases. A couple of studies also find insignificant effects. One study (Okeke 2000) finds that ALMP spending according to some panel estimates contributes to higher employment (including subsidized employment), but that the effect is declining in the level of spending.[20]

5.2 Interpretation of the Results

There is reason to suspect that the problem of simultaneity bias in the studies reported above is quite serious. The reason is that the Layard et al. measure of ALMPs used in most of the studies, i.e., spending per unemployed person as a fraction of GDP, is likely to covary negatively with unemployment (OECD 1993; Forslund and Krueger 1997). Some of the studies have just neglected this problem. Others have tried to address it in various ways. OECD (1993) substituted ALMP expenditure as a fraction of the mean wage multiplied by the labor force, and Forslund and Krueger (1997) substituted ALMP expenditure as a fraction of GDP, for the Layard et al. measure. In both studies the introduction of the alternative measure resulted in insignificant estimates of the effects on open unemployment.

Elmeskov et al. (1998) used the average of the Layard et al. measure over the whole time period studied in order to reduce the problems of simultaneity, whereas Nickell and Layard (1999) divided ALMP expenditures by the number of unemployed persons in an earlier time period. According to the first study, ALMPs have an insignificant, negative effect on total unemployment, whereas they have a significant positive effect according to the second study.

On the whole, the conclusion seems to be that the results of ALMPs appear less favorable when simultaneity bias is addressed. One should also note that the reported results refer to unemployment as a share of the *labor force*. As was noted in subsection 4.3, results may be more favorable for ALMPs if unemployment is instead measured as a fraction of the population, as the programs may influence labor-force participation positively. Two of the studies on OECD data are consistent with such an effect. Nickell and Layard (1999) did not find any significant decreasing effect of ALMPs on employment as a fraction of the population at the same time as their results imply an increase in total unemployment as a fraction of the labor force. Scarpetta (1996) found that ALMPs contribute to a lower share of inactive persons in the population.

6   Conclusions

6.1   The Various Mechanisms of ALMPs
The empirical studies surveyed highlight the following mechanisms or complexes of mechanisms of active labor-market policy: (i) effects on the matching process and the competition for jobs, as well as on productivity and the allocation of labor, (ii) direct crowding out effects, (iii) effects on the wage pressure in the economy, and (iv) the net effect on regular employment (and open unemployment).

6.1.1   *Matching Efficiency and the Competition for Jobs*
The effects on matching efficiency and the competition for jobs are highlighted in both microeconomic and macroeconomic studies. These

effects are likely to be correlated with the effects on the productivity of job seekers and the allocation of labor (to the extent that ALMPs raise the productivity of the participants and re-allocate labor from low-demand to high-demand areas, matching efficiency and the competition for jobs are also likely to increase). On the whole, there is little support for the view that the active labor-market policy in Sweden in the 1990s had positive effects in these respects.

Macroeconomic studies of geographic mobility seem to imply that ALMPs have rather tended to lock in labor. Although the microeconomic studies of the effects of labor-market training on individuals in the 1980s found positive employment and income effects, this does not apply to the 1990s: the studies of the later period have instead usually found insignificant or negative effects. There are fewer studies of subsidized employment, and here the results vary more.

The most favorable results for the effects of ALMPs on individuals are obtained in survey studies of employer attitudes. But on the other hand, participants in ALMPs seem to search less actively for jobs than the openly unemployed while in programs (although one study indicates that they are searching more actively after program completion).

There is also some evidence that ALMPs in Sweden may have raised labor-force participation, which might potentially lead to more competition for jobs. But the number of studies is too small to warrant more definite conclusions. There is also the question to what extent such a "registered" increase in labor-force participation translates into effective supply rather than just raising the possibilities to collect benefits.

6.1.2 Direct Displacement

Both survey studies and econometric macro studies indicate that job-creation schemes have crowded out regular employment to a substantial degree. Labor-market training does not appear to have had such effects. The direct crowding-out effects are considerably larger in the econometric studies (often 60–70 percent) than in the survey studies (usually 15–40 percent).

6.1.3 Wage Pressure

The effect of ALMPs on wage pressure is the net of a number of effects that work in different directions: effects on matching efficiency, competition effects, accommodation effects, effects on reservation wages, and re-allocation effects. A large number of Swedish studies of the wage-setting relationship has examined this net effect. The results are not clear-cut. Many studies have found that an expansion of ALMPs has increased wage pressure. Nearly as many studies have found no significant effect at all. Fewer studies have found a wage-reducing effect. The conclusion is that Swedish ALMPs are unlikely to have reduced wage pressure, but it is unclear whether they have raised wages or had no effect at all.

6.1.4   Net Effect on Regular Employment and Unemployment

The net effect of ALMPs on (un)employment in Sweden has been studied in macroeconomic estimations of reduced-form equations. Most of the studies imply that an expansion of ALMPs reduces *open unemployment*. But the studies also suggest that the sum of direct and indirect crowding-out effects is large. The estimates do not support the view that an expansion of ALMPs reduces *total unemployment* (the sum of open unemployment and program participation). Some of the evidence rather suggests the opposite.

We compared Swedish reduced-form estimations with similar estimations on cross-country and panel data for the whole OECD area. The latter studies have often been interpreted to give a very favorable picture of the employment effects of ALMPs (see, e.g., Layard et al. 1991; Nickell and Layard 1999). This is, however, partly a misunderstanding, which derives from the fact that these studies have usually focused on the effect on open unemployment rather than on regular employment or total unemployment. If one recalculates the estimates in these studies to effects on total unemployment, the effects vary between studies, but the overall picture is similar to the one from the Swedish studies.

6.2   Relative Efficiency of Various ALMPs

What do the studies of Sweden say about the relative efficiency of different programs? A first issue concerns labor-market training versus subsidized employment. Here, the microeconomic studies of effects on individuals and the macroeconomic studies of general-equilibrium effects give inconsistent results. The microeconomic studies of labor-market training in the 1990s found no or negative employment effects. In contrast, some studies found positive effects of subsidized employment on later regular employment. But in the macroeconomic studies, there is a strong tendency that labor-market training gives more positive (or less negative) effects on regular employment than subsidized employment. Only the latter programs seem to cause direct crowding-out effects.

Another issue concerns the relative efficiency of various subsidized employment programs. The few available microeconomic studies suggest positive employment effects on the participating individuals of self-employment grants, recruitment subsidies, work placement schemes and trainee replacement schemes, whereas it has proved difficult to find such effects of relief work and work-experience schemes. But at the same time, there is much to suggest that these programs have large crowding out effects. Unfortunately, there is a strong tendency that the schemes close to regular jobs have both positive employment effects for the participating individuals and large negative crowding-out effects.

The empirical studies seem to be the most negative for youth programs. Here, there appear to be large crowding-out effects, at the same time as it is uncertain whether there are positive employment effects on the participating individuals.

6.3 Policy Conclusions

Which policy conclusions can be drawn from the unique Swedish experiment in the 1990s of using large-scale ALMPs to fight high unemployment? Should the Swedish policy be followed by other countries in similar circumstances? It is true that enough time may not yet have passed to allow a final verdict: this may require an analysis of to what extent the rise in unemployment in the early 1990s will lead to persistent effects, and of whether there are long-term employment effects of ALMPs on labor-force participation that have not yet worked themselves out. We do not rule out such effects. Notwithstanding these caveats, our conclusion is still that the labor-market policy followed in Sweden in the 1990s was not efficient. The Swedish experience shows clearly the limitations of ALMPs as a measure to fight unemployment. It is not a measure that should be relied on to the extent that was done in Sweden.

A main problem with ALMPs in Sweden in the 1990s was their size. This applies especially to labor-market training. It is a problem to expand training programs very rapidly in a situation when the appropriate infrastructure is not there. In such a situation, one should expect marginal returns to be decreasing, as is suggested by Björklund and Moffitt (1987), who found the average effect on the hourly wage to be decreasing with the volume of training. One should also expect training programs to be ineffective in a situation with very low demand, when unemployment duration is long under all circumstances, and when it is difficult to know where future labor shortages in the economy will appear. The upshot is that training programs should be kept rather small in a deep recession. There is certainly a strong case for not using ALMPs (especially training programs) as an income support measure (either as an alternative to unemployment benefits or as a means to re-qualify the participants for such benefits) as was done in Sweden, because this is likely both to distort the incentives for program participation and result in very large program volumes.

As to subsidized employment, we have pointed to the conflict between positive employment effects on the participating individuals and the macroeconomic crowding-out effects. This is a strong argument to target job-creation measures on the long-term unemployed (and those who are threatened to become long-term unemployed): then competition effects may affect regular employment positively, even if there are large crowding-out effects.

Our survey also questions the use of large-scale youth programs, as they seem to have large displacement effects, at the same time as it is unclear whether there are any positive employment effects for the participating individuals. Since those who have been unemployed for less than six months seem rarely to meet negative employer attitudes (Klingvall 1998), there appear to be no strong reasons to place young people in programs during their first half-year of unemployment. This is an argument for much smaller youth programs than were used in Sweden in the 1990s.

One cannot, of course, analyze the proper role of ALMPs without corresponding evaluations of alternative policy instruments. Indeed, subjecting only some policies to critical scrutiny, but not others, could lead to a worse policy mix. But it is safe to conclude that the Swedish strategy of using ALMPs as the main policy instrument to fight unemployment in the 1990s was not founded on systematic ex ante knowledge of the effectiveness of the programs, and that our ex post evaluation does not support the view that they were effective in maintaining regular employment. Rather, the policies that were pursued are likely to have reduced open unemployment at the cost of also reducing regular employment. It is a value judgment whether one should consider this to reduce or increase social welfare. But there is a lot to suggest that the Swedish example of the 1990s is not one to follow if one views high regular employment as the primary objective of labor-market policy.

Appendix

Many of the studies on data from a large number of OECD countries discussed in section 5 have estimated unemployment equations of the form

$$u = \alpha\gamma + \cdots,$$ (A1)

where

$$\gamma = b_r r / uy.$$ (A2)

u is open unemployment as a fraction of the labor force, γ is the measure of ALMPs, α is a parameter measuring the effect of ALMPs on open unemployment, b_r is the expenditure on ALMPs per program participant, r is program participation as a fraction of the labor force, and y is GDP per capita.

We are interested in computing du/dr and $d(u+r)/dr$ from the estimated equations. To do this, we substitute (A2) into (A1) and differentiate implicitly. This gives

$$\frac{du}{dr} = \frac{(b_r/y)\alpha u}{u^2 + (b_r/y)\alpha r}.$$ (A3)

To calculate du/dr we need information on b_r/y. In our calculations we set $b_r/y = 0.5$. This parameter value is motivated in the following way. For Denmark, Finland, Norway, and Sweden, Zetterberg (1995) provides information on γ. The database collected by Rødseth and Nymoen (1999) gives information on program participation and unemployment for the same countries. As $b_r/y = \gamma u/r$, we can compute this ratio. The average values for the period 1985–1991 are 0.41 for Denmark, 0.60 for Finland, 0.42 for Norway, and 0.44 for Sweden. As the effect on unemployment of ALMPs in (A3) is increasing in b_r/y, our "guesstimate" of 0.5 does not seem to imply that we have underestimated the effect systematically. Given this assumption, we can compute du/dr at given values of open unemployment and program participation. The effect on total unemployment (the sum of program participation and open unemployment) is

$$d(r+u)/dr = 1 + du/dr.$$

Zetterberg (1995) instead used the ratio between total ALMP expenditures and total expenditures on the unemployed (table 1.1) as the measure of ALMPs in his unemployment equations. This measure, which we label λ, can be written

$$\lambda = b_r r / (b_r r + b_u u), \tag{A4}$$

where, in addition to the previously explained variables, b_u is the expenditure per openly unemployed person. Here, we proceeded by assuming that the spending per program participant equals the spending per openly unemployed, i.e., $b_r = b_u$. Given this assumption, and given an estimated effect $\beta = du / d\lambda$, we have in this case that

$$\frac{du}{dr} = \frac{\beta u}{(u + r)^2 + \beta r}. \tag{A5}$$

In table 1.13, we have assumed throughout that $u = 0.07$ and $r = 0.03$.

Notes

1. Lars Calmfors is professor of international economics at the Institute for International Economic Studies, Stockholm University. Anders Forslund is a senior research fellow and deputy director of IFAU (the Swedish Office of Labor Market Policy Evaluation). Maria Hemström is a senior research fellow at IFAU. The authors are grateful for comments on previous versions from Jonas Agell, Susanne Ackum Agell, Jim Albrecht, Dan Andersson, Per-Anders Edin, Bertil Holmlund, Per Johansson, Katarina Richardson, Karl-Martin Sjöstrand, Alfons Weichenrieder, and Johnny Zetterberg.

2. See http://europa.eu.int/comm/employment_social/elm/summit/en/papers/guide2.htm.

3. This is evident from the national action plans on employment.

4. The main reference is Fackföreningsrörelsen och den fulla sysselsättningen 1951.

5. The exposition builds on Pissarides 1990, Mortensen and Pissarides 1994, and Romer 1996. See also Holmlund and Lindén 1993 and Fredriksson 1997 for direct applications to ALMPs.

6. One might think that an increase in matching efficiency should also have an effect working in the opposite direction because it will enable a quitter to find a new job more quickly. This is not, however, the case if employment is held constant. The probability for a job seeker to find a new job equals the aggregate number of matches divided by the aggregate number of job seekers in the economy. In a steady state with given employment (and thus a given number of job seekers), the number of matches is also given, if we assume—as is conventionally done—that the number of separations from jobs equals a fixed quit rate times employment. It follows that at a given aggregate employment level, the probability for a job seeker to find a job is independent of matching efficiency.

7. Larsson (2001) discusses the problems arising when effects are computed from the time of program completion rather than from the program start. The control group in the former case can be chosen in two ways: Program participants can be compared to either (i) non-participants who became unemployed at the same time as the participants and

were unemployed both at the program start and completion; or (ii) non-participants who at the time of program completion had been unemployed for as long as the participants at the time of the program start. Both procedures are likely to give a positive bias in the estimation of the treatment effect. In the first case, non-participants with a small job-finding probability tend to be over-represented in the sample (because they did not find a job during the program period). In the second case, the participants have a longer time to search for jobs, because they can search also while participating in the program.

8. However, the analysis in Fredriksson and Johansson (2002) shows that the procedures used in this study result in a negative bias in the estimated program effects because the control group is selected in such a way that all spells end in employment.

9. See the discussion in note 7, which is applicable also to Okeke's study.

10. However, there is likely to be a negative bias in the estimated program effects, as discussed in note 8.

11. Recruitment subsidies was the only program associated with a significantly lower probability of future receipt of unemployment benefits.

12. This conclusion was based on estimates in which search behavior was related to different individual characteristics. The outcome measure was a "search index" constructed from answers to questions about search time and search methods. Information about program participation at (i) the time of the interview and (ii) the twelve months preceding the interview are two of the variables used to explain individual search behavior.

13. The relevant relationship to look at is the one between vacancies and *total* unemployment (the sum of open unemployment and program participation). Calmfors (1993) estimates how this relationship is affected by a change in the accommodation ratio (the ratio between program participation and total unemployment). Jackman et al. (1990) study instead the relationship between vacancies and *open* unemployment, but their results are recalculated in Calmfors (1993).

14. The authors could not reject the hypothesis that relief work and labor-market training have the same effect (and that this effect is half that of open unemployment). However, when the effects of training and relief work were estimated separately, it could not be rejected that training and unemployment have the same effect.

15. *A priori*, it seems likely that subsidized employment would be associated with geographical locking-in effects. Regarding training, the case is not so clear: on one hand, training can be a substitute for geographical mobility, on the other hand, training may provide the trainee with skills that are valuable outside the home region.

16. The table should be interpreted with caution, as the averages derive from studies using different methods, and some programs have been subject to a large number of studies and others to only a few ones.

17. Forslund and Krueger estimated a displacement effect for the durable manufacturing sector, in which there were no relief works. Such estimates test whether or not the displacement results are only spuriously reflecting cyclical patterns in both employment and relief work.

18. Relief work was singled out as a separate category to allow comparisons with earlier work.

19. Holmlund (1995) criticized Skedinger's assumption that aggregate unemployment is exogenous, and showed that displacement falls to 40 percent if this assumption is

dropped. Skedinger's analysis was also criticized by Sjöstrand (1996a). See also Sjöstrand 1996b and Skedinger 1996a,b.

20. The model includes ALMP spending as both a linear and a squared term among the explanatory variables; the estimated coefficient for the linear term is positive, whereas the estimated effect of the squared term is negative. However, the measure of employment includes subsidized employment, but not labor-market training, so the results are difficult to interpret, although it is clear that they are not compatible with complete crowding out of regular employment. Cross-section estimates show a zero effect on the employment measure, which indicates a negative effect on regular employment (excluding subsidized employment).

References

Ackum Agell, S. 1996. Arbetslösas sökaktivitet, SOU 1996: 34, Aktiv Arbetsmarknadspolitik, Expertbilaga till Arbetsmarknadspolitiska kommitténs betänkande (Fritzes, Stockholm).

Agell, J., and H. Bennmarker. 2002. Wage policy and endogenous wage rigidity: a representative view from the inside. Working paper 2002: 12 (IFAU, Uppsala).

Agell, J., and P. Lundborg. 1995. Theories of pay and unemployment: survey evidence from Swedish manufacturing firms. *Scandinavian Journal of Economics* 97: 295–307.

Agell, J., and P. Lundborg. 2003. Survey evidence on wage rigidity and unemployment: Sweden in the 1990s. *Scandinavian Journal of Economics* 105: 15–29.

Ams. 1981. Erfarenheter av nyrekryteringsbidraget, Meddelanden från utredningsenheten 1981: 25 (National Labor Market Board, Solna).

Ams. 1983. Erfarenheter av den tillfälliga rekryteringsstimulansen, Meddelanden från utredningsenheten 1983: 11 (National Labor Market Board, Solna).

Ams. 1985. Erfarenheter av rekryteringsstödet, Meddelanden från utredningsenheten 1985: 18 (National Labor Market Board, Solna).

Ams. 1995. Rekryteringsstödets resultat, Uru 1995: 1 (National Labor Market Board, Solna).

Ams. 1997. Åtgärdernas undanträngningseffekter. En enkätstudie utifrån deltagarperspektivet, Ura 1997: 12 (National Labor Market Board, Solna).

Ams. 1998a. Åtgärdsundersökning 1998. En uppföljning av deltagare som avslutat konjunkturberoende åtgärd fjärde kvartalet 1996, Apra 1998: 3 (National Labor Market Board, Solna).

Ams. 1998b.Undanträngningseffekter av arbetsmarknadspolitiska åtgärder. En enkätundersökning ur både arbetssökande- och arbetsgivarperspektiv, Ura 1998: 8 (National Labor Market Board, Solna).

Anxo, D., and P. Dahlin. 1996. Utvärdering av det generella och det riktade anställningsstödet, EFA-rapport 45.

Axelsson, R., K. Brännäs, and K.-G. Löfgren. 1996. Arbetsmarknadspolitik, arbetslöshet och arbetslöshetstider under 1990-talets lågkonjunktur, Umeå Economic Studies 418, Umeå University.

Axelsson, R., and K.-G. Löfgren. 1992. Arbetsmarknadsutbildningens privat- och sam-hällsekonomiska effekter, EFA-rapport 25 (Ministry of Labor, Stockholm).

Behrenz, L. 2001. Who gets the job and why?—An explorative study of the recruitment behaviour of employers. *Journal of Applied Economics* 4: 255–278.

Björklund, A., and R. Moffit. 1987. The estimation of wage gains and welfare gains in self-selection. *Review of Economics and Statistics* 69: 42–49.

Blanchard, O., and J. Wolfers. 2000. The role of shocks and institutions in the rise of European unemployment: The aggregate evidence. *Economic Journal* 110: C1–C33.

Blomskog, S. 1997. The wage curve for different worker categories. The case of Sweden, Essays on the functioning of the Swedish labor market, Ph.D. thesis, Stockholm University.

Calmfors, L. 1993. Lessons from the macroeconomic experience of Sweden. *European Journal of Political Economy* 9: 25–72.

Calmfors, L. 1994. Active labor market policy and unemployment—a framework for the analysis of crucial design features. *OECD Economic Studies* 22: 7–47.

Calmfors, L. 1995. Labour market policy and unemployment. *European Economic Review* 39: 583–592.

Calmfors, L., and A. Forslund. 1990. Wage formation in Sweden, in: L. Calmfors (ed.), Wage formation and macroeconomic policy in the Nordic countries (Stockholm: SNS and Oxford University Press).

Calmfors, L., and A. Forslund. 1991. Real wage determination and labor market policies: The Swedish experience. *Economic Journal* 101: 1130–1148.

Calmfors, L., and H. Lang. 1995. Macroeconomic effects of active labor market programs in a union wage-setting model. *Economic Journal* 105: 601–619.

Calmfors, L., and R. Nymoen. 1990. Nordic employment. *Economic Policy* 5: 397–448.

Calmfors, L., and P. Skedinger. 1995. Does active labor market policy increase employ-ment? Theoretical considerations and some empirical evidence from Sweden. *Oxford Review of Economic Policy* 11: 91–109.

Carling, K., P.-A. Edin, A. Harkman, and B. Holmlund. 1996. Unemployment duration, unemployment benefits, and labor market programs in Sweden. *Journal of Public Econom-ics* 59: 313–334.

Carling, K., and L. Gustafson. 1999. Self-employment grants vs. subsidized employ-ment: Is there a difference in the re-unemployment risk? Working paper 1999: 6 (IFAU, Uppsala).

Carling K., and L. Larsson. 2000a. Att utvärdera arbetsmarknadsprogram i Sverige: Rätt svar är viktigt, men vilken var nu frågan? *Arbetsmarknad och Arbetsliv* 3: 185–192.

Carling, K., and L. Larsson. 2000b. Replik till Lars Behrenz och Anders Harkman. *Arbets-marknad och Arbetsliv* 4: 278–281.

Carling, K., and K. Richardson. 2001. The relative efficiency of labor market programs: Swedish experience from the 1990s. Working paper 2001: 2 (IFAU, Uppsala).

Dahlberg, M., and A. Forslund. 1999. Direct displacement effects of labor market programs: The case of Sweden. Working paper 1999: 7 (IFAU, Uppsala).

EC Commission. 1997. Guidelines for member states employment policies for 1998, http://europa.eu.int/comm/employment_social/elm/summit/en/papers/guide2.htm.

EC Commission. 2000. National action plans on employment 2001, http://europa.eu.int/comm/employment_social/news/2001/may/naps2001_en.html.

Edin, P.-A., A. Forslund, and B. Holmlund. 1999. The Swedish youth labor market in boom and depression, in: D. Blanchflower and R. Freeman (eds.), Youth employment and joblessness in advanced countries (University of Chicago Press).

Edin, P.-A., and B. Holmlund. 1991. Unemployment, vacancies and labor market programs: Swedish evidence, in: F. P. Schioppa (ed.), Mismatch and labor mobility (Cambridge University Press).

Edin, P.-A., B. Holmlund, and T. Östros. 1994. Wage behavior and labor market programs: Evidence from micro data, in: B. Holmlund (ed.), Pay, productivity, and policy (FIEF, Stockholm).

Elmeskov, J., J. Martin, and S. Scarpetta. 1998. Key lessons for labor market reforms: evidence from OECD countries' experiences. Swedish Economic Policy Review 5: 205–252.

European Commission. 2000. The EU economy—2000 review, European Economy.

Fackföreningsrörelsen och den fulla sysselsättningen. 1951. LO, Stockholm.

Fitoussi, J.-P., D. Jestaz, E. Phelps, and G. Zoega. 2000. Roots of recent recoveries: Labor reforms or private sector forces? Brookings Papers on Economic Activity 1: 237–291.

Forslund, A. 1992. Arbetslöshet och arbetsmarknadspolitik, Bilaga 7 till Långtidsutredningen 1992.

Forslund, A. 1995. Unemployment—is Sweden still different? Swedish Economic Policy Review 2: 15–58.

Forslund, A. 1996. Direkta undanträngningseffekter av arbetsmarknadspolitiska åtgärder, Rapport till Riksdagens revisorer.

Forslund, A., and A.-S. Kolm. 2000. Active labor market policies and real-wage determination—Swedish evidence. Working paper 2000: 7 (IFAU, Uppsala).

Forslund, A., and A. Krueger. 1997. An evaluation of the active Swedish labor market policy: New and received wisdom, in: R. Freeman, R. Topel and B. Swedenborg (eds.), The welfare state in transition (Chicago University Press).

Forslund, A., and O. Risager. 1994. Wages in Sweden. New and old results, Memo 1994: 22, Institute of economics, Aarhus University.

Fredriksson, P. 1997. Education, migration and active labor market policy, Economic Studies 28, Department of Economics, Uppsala University.

Fredriksson, P. 1999. The dynamics of regional labor markets and active labor market policy: Swedish evidence. Oxford Economic Papers 51: 623–648.

Fredriksson, P., and P. Johansson. 2002. Program evaluation and random program starts. Mimeo, IFAU, Uppsala.

Fukushima, Y. 1998. Active labor market programs and unemployment in a dual labor market, Department of Economics, Stockholm University.

Gramlich, E. M., and B.-C. Ysander. 1981. Relief work and grant displacement in Sweden, in: G. Eliasson, B. Holmlund and F. Stafford (eds.), Studies in Labor Market Behavior (IUI, Stockholm).

Hallgren, A. 1996. Job matching and labor market programs in Sweden, mimeo, Department of Economics, Uppsala University.

Hallström, N.-E. 1995. Genomförandet av ALU, arbetslivsutveckling. En studie i sex kommuner i tre län, EFA-rapport 36, Ministry of Labor, Stockholm.

Harkman, A. 1997. Den yrkesinriktade arbetsmarknadsutbildning 1994—effekter för individen, Ura 1997: 10 (National Labor Market Board, Solna).

Harkman, A., F. Jansson, and A. Tamás. 1996. Effects, defects and prospects—An evaluation of labor market training in Sweden. Working paper 1996: 5 (National Labor Market Board, Solna).

Harkman, A., A. Johansson, and S. Okeke. 1999. Åtgärdsundersökningen 1998—åtgärdernas effekter på deltagarnas sysselsättning och löner, Ura 1999: 1 (National Labor Market Board, Solna).

Heckman, J. J. 1979. Sample selection bias as a specification error. *Econometrica* 47: 153–161.

Heckman, J. J., R. J. LaLonde, and J. A. Smith. 1999. The economics and econometrics of active labor market programs, in: Ashenfelter O. C., and D. Card (eds.), Handbook of Labor Economics, Vol. 3A (Elsevier Science B.V., Amsterdam).

Heiborn, M. 1998. Essays on demographic factors and housing markets, Doctoral thesis, Economic Studies 40, Department of Economics, Uppsala University.

Heylen, F. 1993. Labour market structures, labor market policy and wage formation in the OECD. *Labour* 7: 25–55.

Holmlund, B. 1990. Svensk lönebildning—teori, empiri, politik, Bilaga 24 till Långtidsutredningen 90, Ministry of Finance, Stockholm.

Holmlund, B. 1995. Comment on Per Skedinger: Employment policies and displacement in the youth labor market. *Swedish Economic Policy Review* 2: 173–179.

Holmlund, B., and J. Lindén. 1993. Job matching, temporary public employment, and equilibrium unemployment. *Journal of Public Economics* 51: 329–343.

Jackman, R. 1994. What can active labor market policy do? *Swedish Economic Policy Review* 1: 221–257.

Jackman, R., R. Layard, and S. Nickell. 1996. Combating unemployment: Is flexibility enough? Discussion Paper 293, Centre for Economic Performance, London School of Economics.

Jackman, R., C. Pissarides, and S. Savouri. 1990. Labour market policies and unemployment in the OECD. *Economic Policy* 5: 449–490.

Johansson, K. 1999. Resursarbete—en uppföljning, Forskningsrapport 1999: 4 (IFAU, Uppsala).

Johansson, K. 2001. Do labor market programs affect labor force participation. *Swedish Economic Policy Review* 8: 215–234.

Johansson, K., and A. Markowski. 1995. Påverkar arbetsmarknadspolitik arbetskrafts-deltagandet?—en empirisk studie, Konjunkturläget maj 1995, Specialstudier, National Institute of Economic Research, Stockholm.

Johansson, P., and S. Martinsson 2000. Det nationella IT-programt—En slutrapport om Swit, Forskningsrapport 2000: 8 (IFAU, Uppsala).

Johansson, S., P. Lundborg, and J. Zetterberg. 1999. Massarbetslöshetens karaktär (FIEF, Stockholm).

Klingvall, M. 1998. Arbetsgivarnas attityder, Ura 1998: 9 (National Labor Market Board, Solna).

Korpi, T. 1994. "Employment stability following unemployment: evidence of the effect of manpower programs for youth" in Escaping unemployment—Studies in the individual consequences of unemployment and labor market policy, Ph.D. thesis, Stockholm University.

Korpi, T. 1997. Is utility related to employment status? Employment, unemployment, labor market policies and subjective well-being among Swedish youth. *Labour Economics* 4: 125–147.

Larsson, L. 2000. Evaluation of Swedish youth labor market programs. Working paper 2000: 1 (IFAU, Uppsala).

Larsson, L. 2001. Kommentarer till Okeke: Arbetsmarknadsutbildningen 1999—effekter för individen. Mimeo, IFAU, Uppsala.

Layard, R., S. Nickell, and R. Jackman. 1991. Unemployment: macroeconomic performance and the labor market (Oxford University Press).

Lindbeck, A. 1975. Svensk ekonomisk politik (Aldus, Stockholm).

LO. 1993a. Så här fungerar ALU i Sörmland, Undersökning av LO-distriktet hösten 1993 (LO, Stockholm).

LO. 1993b. Så här fungerar ALU i Värmland, Undersökning av LO-distriktet hösten 1993 (LO, Stockholm).

LO. 1994a. Så här fungerar ALU i Blekinge, Undersökning av LO-distriktet hösten 1994 (LO, Stockholm).

LO. 1994b. Så här fungerar ALU i Kalmar län, Undersökning av LO-distriktet hösten 1994 (LO, Stockholm).

Löfgren, K.-G., and M. Wikström. 1991. Lönebildning och arbetsmarknadspolitik, Ds 1991: 53, Bilaga till Arbetsmarknad och arbetsmarknadspolitik (Ministry of Labor, Stockholm).

Löfgren, K.-G., and M. Wikström. 1997. Undanträngningseffekter av arbetsmarknadspo-litik. Kommentarer till Forslund-Sjöstrandkontroversen. *Arbetsmarknad och Arbetsliv* 3: 207–223.

McCormick, B., and P. Skedinger. 1991. Why do regional unemployment differentials persist?, in: P. Skedinger, Essays on wage formation, employment, and unemployment, Doctoral thesis, Department of Economics, Uppsala University.

Meidner, R. 1969. Active manpower policy and the inflation-unemployment dilemma. *Swedish Journal of Economics* 71: 161–183.

Mortensen, D., and C. Pissarides. 1994. Job creation and job destruction in the theory of unemployment. *Review of Economic Studies* 61: 397–415.

Newell, A., and J. Symons. 1987. Corporatism, laissez-faire and the rise in unemployment. *European Economic Review* 31: 567–601.

Nickell, S., and R. Layard. 1999. Labor market institutions and economic performance, in: O. Ashenfelter and D. Card (eds.), Handbook of Labor Economics 3C (Elsevier).

Nilsson, C. 1995. Den interregionala omflyttningen i Sverige—konsekvenser av arbetsmarknadsläge, arbetsmarknadspolitik och regionala levnadsomkostnader, EFA-rapport 33.

NUTEK. 1994. Utvärdering av den arbetsmarknadspolitiska åtgärden Arbetslivsutveckling, ALU, R 1994: 66 (Nutek, Stockholm).

OECD. 1993. Employment outlook (OECD, Paris).

OECD. 1994. The OECD jobs study (OECD, Paris).

Ohlsson, H. 1993. Sysselsättningsskapande medel som stabiliseringspolitiskt medel, in: Politik mot arbetslöshet, SOU 1993: 43 (Fritzes, Stockholm).

Ohlsson, H. 1995. Labor market policy, unemployment and wages—A VAR model for Sweden 1969–1990, Department of Economics, Uppsala University.

Okeke, S. 1998. Lönekurvan i Sverige. En studie av sambandet mellan arbetslöshet och lönenivå 1991–1995. Working paper 1998: 5, Ams utredningsenhet (National Labor Market Board, Solna).

Okeke, S. 1999. Starta eget-bidragets effekter—utvärdering av företag tre år efter start, Ura 1999: 12 (National Labor Market Board, Stockholm).

Okeke, S. 2000. Sysselsättningseffekter av aktiv arbetsmarknadspolitik—en internationell jämförelse. Working paper 2000: 2 (National Labor Market Board, Stockholm).

Okeke, S. 2001. Arbetsmarknadsutbildningen 1999—effekter för individen, Ura 2001: 7 (National Labor Market Board, Stockholm).

Okeke, S., and A. Spånt Enbuske. 2001. Utvärdering av 1995 års nystartade företag, Ura 2001: 2 (National Labor Market Board, Stockholm).

Petersson, J., and V. Vlachos. 1978. En granskning av utbildningsbidraget för permitteringshotade (25/15-kronan), Department of Economics, Lund University and EFA.

Pissarides, C. 1990. *Equilibrium Unemployment Theory.* Blackwell.

Regnér, H. 1997. Training at the job and training for a new job: two Swedish studies, Doctoral thesis, Swedish Institute for Social Research, Stockholm University.

Regnér, H., and E. Wadensjö. 1999. Arbetsmarknadens funktionssätt I Sverige. En beskrivning baserad på nya intervjudata, Swedish Institute for Social Research, Stockholm.

Richardson, K., and G. van den Berg G. 2001. Swedish labor market training and the duration of unemployment. *Swedish Economic Policy Review* 8: 175–213.

Romer, D. 1996. Advanced macroeconomics. McGraw-Hill.

RRV. 1989. Rekryteringsstöd, Dnr 1988: 1848 (Riksrevisionsverheb, Stockholm).

Rødseth, A., and R. Nymoen. 1999. Nordic wage formation and unemployment seven years later, Memorandum 10/99, Sosialøkonomisk institutt, Oslo University.

Scarpetta, S. 1996. Assessing the role of labor market policies and institutional settings on unemployment: A cross-country study. OECD Economic Studies 26: 43–98.

Sehlstedt, K., and L. Schröder. 1989. Språngbräda till arbete? En utvärdering av bered-skapsarbete, rekryteringsstöd och ungdomsarbete, EFA-rapport 19 (Ministry of Labor, Stockholm).

Sianesi, B. 2001a. An evaluation of the active labor market programs in Sweden. Working paper 2001: 5 (IFAU, Uppsala).

Sianesi, B. 2001b. The Swedish active labor market programs in the 1990s: Overall effec-tiveness and differential performance. Swedish Economic Policy Review 8: 133–169.

Sjöstrand, K.-M. 1996a. Hastverk om arbetsmarknadspolitiska åtgärder. Ekonomisk Debatt 1: 39–51.

Sjöstrand, K.-M. 1996b. Arbetslösheten, inte sysselsättningen, är arbetsmarknadspoli-tikens målvariabel. Svar till Skedinger. Ekonomisk Debatt 3: 218–221.

Sjöstrand, K.-M. 1997. Några kommentarer till Anders Forslunds rapport Direkta undan-trängningseffekter av arbetsmarknadspolitiska åtgärder, Bilaga till riksdagsrevisorernas rapport (National Labor Market Board, Solna).

Skedinger, P. 1991. Real wages, unemployment, and labor market programs: A dis-aggregative analysis, in: Essays on wage formation, employment, and unemployment, Doctoral thesis, Department of Economics, Uppsala University.

Skedinger, P. 1995. Employment policies and displacement in the youth labor market. Swedish Economic Policy Review 2: 135–171.

Skedinger, P. 1996a. Sjöstrand vilseleder om forskningsresultat som tyder på stor undan-trängning. Ekonomisk Debatt 1: 52–59.

Skedinger, P. 1996b. Sjöstrands modell är felspecificerad. Ekonomisk Debatt 3: 221–224.

TEMO. 1993. Utvärdering av arbetslivsutvecklingsprojekt—ALU, september–oktober, Stockholm.

TEMO. 1994. Utvärdering av arbetslivsutvecklingsprojekt—ALU, Stockholm.

TEMO. 1995. Utvärdering av arbetslivsutvecklingsprojekt—ALU, Stockholm.

Thomas, A. 2000. The costs and benefits of various wage-bargaining structures: an empirical exploration (IMF, Washington).

Thoursie, R. 1990. Den offentliga arbetsförmedlingens utveckling under 1990-talet, in: SOU 1990: 31 (Fritzes, Stockholm).

Wadensjö, E. 1993. Arbetsmarknadspolitikens effekter på löner och priser, in: SOU 1993: 43, Politik mot arbetslöshet (Fritzes, Stockholm).

Westerlund, O. 1997. Employment opportunities, wages and interregional migration in Sweden 1970–1989. Journal of Regional Science 37: 55–73.

Westerlund, O. 1998. Internal migration in Sweden: The effects of mobility grants and regional labor market conditions. *Labour* 12: 363–388.

Widerstedt, B. 1998. Moving or staying? Job mobility as a sorting process, Doctoral thesis, Department of Economics, Umeå University.

Zetterberg, J. 1995. Unemployment, labor market policy and the wage bargaining system, in Labour market policy at the crossroads, EFA-rapport 34 (Ministry of Labor, Stockholm).

2

Benefit Entitlement and the
Labor Market: Evidence
from a Large-Scale Policy
Change

Rafael Lalive and Josef
Zweimüller

In the late 1980s, the Austrian government enacted a regional extended benefit program (REBP) granting entitlement to regular unemployment benefits for at most four years for job seekers aged 50 or older. The REBP was reformed in 1991 and abolished in 1993. These successive policy changes over time as well as the fact that entitlement depended strictly on region of residence and on age-created quasi-experimental variation in benefit duration. The aim of this paper is to study the impact of the REBP on various labor-market outcomes of the entitled individuals.

The REBP was enacted in response to the international steel crisis of the 1980s, which hit the traditional iron and steel regions in Austria particularly hard. The benefit extension was a policy response to the expectation of adverse labor-market conditions. Differences in the observed labor-market outcomes between treated and non-treated individuals are therefore a causal impact of the benefit extension on the labor-market behavior of individuals and firms as well as the result of a negative shock on the labor market. The present analysis will deal with this problem in an informal way, concentrating on meaningful comparisons of descriptive statistics.[1]

The generosity of the European unemployment insurance systems is viewed as a candidate explanation for the cross-Atlantic differences in labor-market performance (Katz and Meyer 1990). Hence, a first aim of this paper is to document the impact of the REBP on employment and unemployment levels.

We then discuss how the increase in unemployment can be split up into the unemployment inflow and the outflow. Unemployment inflow reflects to a large extent the incentives of the REBP on firms' employment decisions; unemployment outflow represents the effects of the REBP on the search behavior of workers. A possible impact of the unemployment insurance system not only works via its direct effect on the outflow from unemployment but may also significantly affect other dimensions of labor-supply behavior. This paper therefore aims to take a broader look at the problem by looking at non-employment, which represents to a large extent long-term sickness and early retirement. These latter states are of particular relevance because the increase in the benefit duration applied only to older workers and because the Austrian social security system handled access to disability and to early retirement benefits rather generously. With respect to possible effects of the REBP, the interesting question is whether this tremendous benefit extension was effectively a policy measure that led older workers to withdraw completely from the labor market.[2]

The REBP may not only have created a substantial disincentive to the supply of labor but may also have a potentially significant effect on employment decisions of firms. With seniority rules characterizing the wage policies covering older workers, the REBP may have provided an incentive for firms to get rid of older high-wage workers. As the REBP constituted an improvement in the workers' outside option, this may have made it easier for firms to defect on these long-term seniority contracts (Winter-Ebmer 2003). Hence, it is interesting to see how the REBP affected employment choices of the firms.

Our data are from two sources. The first source is the Austrian social security register, which contains detailed information on the workers' employment and earnings history. We use a 10 percent sample of male employees in the Austrian private sector in the age group 40–59 and follow these individuals over the period 1984–1998. The second source is the Austrian unemployment register. We use data covering the universe of males entering unemployment between 1986 and 1995, aged 45–54 when registering at the public employment service. This sample is observed until 1998.[3]

In section 1 we review the theoretical and empirical literature on the impact of unemployment insurance systems on the labor market. In section 2 we provide some information on the Austrian labor market, survey the Austrian unemployment insurance system, and give a detailed description of the Austrian REBP. Section 3 describes the data in more detail and gives an overview of the empirical approach we pursue. In section 4 we first present detailed evidence on effects of the REBP on the stocks of employment and unemployment and then discuss briefly the impact of the REBP on structural change in the concerned regions. Section 5 focuses on the dynamics of unemployment.

We look at the inflow and outflow from unemployment, not only considering transition rates to regular jobs but also putting particular emphasis on entry into early retirement. How the REBP affected the life-cycle labor force participation of various cohorts is analyzed in section 6. Section 7 studies the impact on the earnings structure.

1 Theory and Previous Empirical Evidence

Most of the previous literature that addresses the impact of the unemployment insurance system on the labor market has focused on its impact on the duration of unemployment. Important theoretical work in this area is based on job-search theory (Mortensen 1977; Burdett 1979; Van den Berg 1990). In these models, job seekers determine the optimal reservation wage and the job-search intensity given the current labor-market state and rational expectations concerning the future payoff to the relevant labor-market states. Theoretically, the effect of benefit generosity on unemployment duration is not clear. More generous unemployment insurance tends to decrease the unemployment exit rate at the start of the spell ("disincentive effect") but may increase the hazard rate at a later stage ("entitlement effect").

The empirical literature on the effects of unemployment insurance on unemployment has found that the disincentive effect tends to dominate the entitlement effect. Katz and Meyer (1990) estimate an increase in unemployment duration of 0.16–0.20 week per additional week of potential benefit duration, which is close to the findings of other US studies (Moffitt and Nicholson 1982; Moffitt 1985). Ham and Rea (1987) report a somewhat larger result for Canada. Hunt (1995) and Bratberg and Vaage (2000) find a similar effect, respectively, for Germany and for Norway, whereas Lalive and Zweimüller (2004) and Winter-Ebmer (1998) find a somewhat smaller impact for Austria.[4]

The theoretical literature that deals with the effects of the unemployment insurance system on the unemployment inflow can be distinguished between studies that concentrate on layoffs and studies that analyze voluntary quit behavior. The literature on layoffs has focused on imperfect experience rating (Feldstein 1976). Firms will choose to lay off workers who are covered by unemployment insurance rather than those who are not covered (Baily 1977; Jurajda 2000).[5] The theoretical prediction of unemployment insurance on quit decisions depends on the unemployment insurance system. In the United States, quits are not entitled to unemployment benefits; hence, higher generosity (e.g., due to longer benefits) should decrease the quit rate. In Austria, quits are entitled to unemployment benefits, but there is a waiting time of four weeks. The theoretical prediction is then less clear. More generous unemployment benefits in such a system tend to increase the likelihood of a quit as the value of unemployment increases. This has to be weighed against the negative effect mentioned above. The net effect essentially depends on the length of the waiting period.

The empirical literature on unemployment inflow has focused mainly on the US experience and is to a large extent concerned with the effects of imperfect experience rating. These effects are found to be large (Topel 1983, 1984, 1985; Card and Levine 1994). Topel (1985) uses a measure of the proportion of unemployment benefits subsidized by the government and shows that this measure affects unemployment inflow strongly. Andersen and Meyer (1994) find that, on the one hand, the benefit level strongly affects inflow into unemployment; on the other hand, the effect of entitlement to unemployment benefits on unemployment inflow is not significantly different from zero. In contrast, Jurajda (2001) finds that entitlement to unemployment insurance strongly affects layoffs whereas neither the benefit level nor the potential duration of benefits are significant (conditional on entitlement).[6] Anderson and Meyer (1997) show that the unemployment benefit take-up rate strongly increases in the expected level of unemployment benefits.

Baker and Rea (1998) and Christofides and McKenna (1996) analyze the effect of benefit eligibility on the hazard of ending an employment spell in Canada. They find that there is a positive spike in the week when individuals become entitled to unemployment benefits. Nickell (1982) analyzes time series of flows into unemployment in Britain and finds no effect of the level of unemployment benefits. Winter-Ebmer (2003) analyzes the Austrian REBP and finds that extended benefits increased the yearly inflow into unemployment by at least 3 percentage points per year.

The impact of unemployment insurance on labor-market dynamics and the level of wages can be studied in matching models (Pissarides 2000). The prediction is that unemployment insurance strengthens the bargaining position of workers thus leading to higher wages. However, wages do not increase one-for-one with unemployment benefits because higher wage pressure reduces profits leading to lower job creation (with fixed job productivity). This result holds with endogenous job destruction (Mortensen and Pissarides 1994) and match heterogeneity (Marimon and Zilibotti 1999). The bulk of the matching literature assumes risk neutrality of the workers. Acemoglu and Shimer (1999) analyze the optimal unemployment insurance in a model with risk-averse workers and investment on the part of firms in capital-intensive high-wage jobs. They show that the optimal unemployment insurance is characterized by high wages because generous unemployment insurance raises the incentives for firms to create capital-intensive jobs. While the theoretical literature on this issue is extensive (Mortensen and Pissarides 1999), the empirical literature on the effects of unemployment insurance on wages is sparse. Acemoglu (2001) finds a large effect of unemployment insurance on the capital intensity of jobs across states in the United States.[7] The literature concerned with structural estimation of job-search models established the positive effect of unemployment insurance on the reservation wage (Wolpin 1995).

There are two previous studies analyzing the impact of the Austrian REBP. In the first, Winter-Ebmer (1998) looks at the initial impact of the benefit extension on unemployment duration at the period of introduction of the REBP. He finds that the benefit extension decreased the job hazard rate by somewhat less than 20 percent. In the second, Winter-Ebmer (2003) studies the impact on the inflow into unemployment and finds substantial REBP effects also on unemployment entry. The conclusion is that the increase in unemployment entry probably was due to layoffs of high-tenured and older workers rather than voluntary quits.

The present paper goes beyond this study in at least five important respects. First, we consider not only the impact of the benefit extension after its introduction, but also the impact of the reform and of the abolishment of the REBP. Second, we use a more informative and much larger data set. This allows us to focus on a narrow age group and to avoid a possible bias resulting from a misspecification of the effect of age. Third, we put particular emphasis not only on the transitions between employment and unemployment, but we also look the problem of early retirement (including long-term sickness and disability pensions). This is of particular importance as access to early retirement was generous during the period under consideration. Fourth, we put particular emphasis on a distinction between steel workers and employees in other industries. This allows us to highlight in a rather informal way the relative importance of labor-market conditions (which were very severe for the former group) and causal effects of

Table 2.1
Unemployment in Austria, 1988 and 1993. Source: Arbeitsmarktservice Austria.

	1988	1993
Overall unemployment rate	5.3	6.8
Age 40–49	4.7	6.0
Age 50–54	5.1	9.9
Age 55–59	5.4	11.1

benefit entitlement rules (which may be a more dominant factor for labor-market behavior for workers in other industries). Finally, we also look at the question whether wage formation was affected by the change in the benefit system. As the program affected a large fraction of the male working population such effects could well show up. We will look both at median wages and the wage spread between high-wage and low-wage workers.

2   The Austrian Unemployment Insurance System

Austria had a low unemployment rate and a low average duration of unemployment, as measured by European standards. In 1994, the overall unemployment rate was 6.8 percent and the percentage of long-term unemployed (≥ 12 months) was less than 20, which is much closer to the US figures than to the European average.

Though Austria has been doing relatively well in terms of unemployment outcomes, the unemployment situation of workers above age 50 deteriorated dramatically over the period 1988–1993. The unemployment rate of the age group 50–59 was 5.1 percent in 1988, which was even below the 1988 overall unemployment rate of 5.3, but in 1993 it exceeded 10 percent (table 2.1). Figure 2.1 shows that there was a steady increase in the ratio of the unemployment rate of the age group 50–59, relative to the age group 40–49, a trend which did not stop until 1993, when the REBP was abolished. Figure 2.1 also shows that this increase in the relative unemployment rate was almost exactly matched by an increase in the relative incidence of long-term unemployment. The former ratio increased from 1.11 in 1988 to 1.67 in 1998 whereas the latter increased from 1.37 in 1988 to 2.09 in 1993.[8]

The Austrian system of unemployment insurance distinguishes two types of unemployment compensation: *Arbeitslosengeld* (regular unemployment benefits, UB) and *Notstandshilfe* (unemployment assistance,

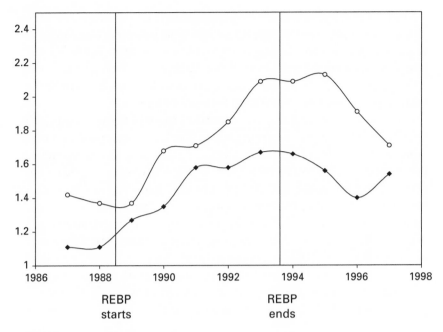

Figure 2.1
Relative unemployment rate (●) and relative incidence of long-term unemployment, ages
50–59/ages 40–49 (○). Figure refers to all regions.

UA). Until August 1989, the duration of UB benefits was 30 weeks
provided that the unemployed had paid unemployment insurance
contributions for at least 156 weeks within the last 5 years preceding
the current spell. These rules were changed in August 1989 and UB
duration became dependent not only on previous experience but also
on age. Benefit duration for the age group 40–49 was increased to 39
weeks if the job seeker has been employed 312 weeks within the last
10 years preceding the current spell. For the age group 50 and older,
UB duration was increased to 52 weeks if the unemployed has been
employed for at least 468 weeks within the last 15 years.

Quits and workers discharged for misconduct can claim benefits
not until a waiting period of 4 weeks has passed. Both UB and UA
recipients are expected to search actively for a new job which should
be within the scope of the claimant's qualifications, at least during the
first months of the unemployment spell. Noncompliance with the eligibility rules is subject to benefit sanctions that can lead to withdrawal
benefits for up to 4 weeks.

Once unemployment benefits have run out, the unemployed individual can apply for unemployment assistance. Austrian citizens and foreign workers with a long-term work permit are eligible to UA which is granted for successive periods of at most 39 weeks, after which entitlement can be renewed. There is no limit for the number of such renewals, so the UA duration is basically infinite.

Compared to other European countries, the replacement ratio (UB relative to gross monthly earnings) is rather low and depends on previous earnings. In 1990 the replacement ratio was 40.4 percent for the median income earner; 48.2 percent for a low-wage worker who earned half the median; and 29.6 percent for a high-wage worker earning twice the median income. On top of this, family allowances are paid. UB are not taxed and not means-tested. UA is means-tested and depends on the income and wealth situation of other family members and close relatives. UA payments are lower than UB and amount to at most 92 percent of UB. In 1990, UA was on average 78 percent of UB as a result of the means test. In 1990, the majority of the unemployed (59 percent) received UB and 26 percent received UA.

2.1   The Regional Extended Benefit Program (REBP)

In June 1988, the Austrian government enacted a law that extended UB entitlement to 209 weeks for a specific subgroup. This group consisted of individuals considered to suffer most heavily from the adverse labor-market consequences of the international steel crisis. The crisis hit certain regions of the Austrian economy, in particular regions where state-owned firms were located. Moreover, the measure intended to help also employees in other industries that were indirectly affected by the crisis and the restructuring process that was initiated in many nationalized firms thereafter (Hesoun 1988).

An unemployed worker became eligible to 209 weeks of UB if he or she satisfied each of the following criteria: (i) age 50 or older when registering at the public employment service, (ii) a continuous work history (780 employment weeks during the last 25 years preceding the current unemployment spell), (iii) location of residence in one of 28 selected labor-market districts since at least 6 months preceding the claim, (iv) new unemployment spell after June 1988 or spell in progress in June 1988.

The REBP was in effect until December 1991 when a reform of these rules took place which came into effect in January 1992. This 1991 reform left all claims in progress unaffected. Only new claims were subject to the new rules. The 1991 reform included two important changes. First, the reform abolished the benefit extension in six of the original 28 regions. The program ended in December 1991 in these districts because the respective labor markets were considered to have improved significantly so that the long UB entitlement was no longer justified. The second important change with the 1991 reform was a tightening of the eligibility criteria to extended benefits: new beneficiaries had to be not only residents, but also previously employed in one of the (now only 22) specified regions. The location of the previous employer as an additional eligibility requirement has a quantitatively important impact on the potential number of beneficiaries because a substantial number of residents in REBP regions were working in a labor-market district not covered by the benefit extension.

It is important to emphasize that all individuals in the sample that will be analyzed in section 5 are potentially eligible to unemployment assistance transfers. We cannot observe the level of UA since information on the income and wealth situation of family members and close relatives is not available in our data. A possible impact of extended benefits is therefore due to the more generous UB relative to UA; to reductions in UA due to the means test; and to the negative connotation of a "welfare recipient" associated with the UA status.[9]

3 Data and Method

Our data are from two sources. The first data source is the Austrian social security register, which contains detailed information on the workers' employment and earnings history. Our particular data set contains a 10 percent sample of male employees in the Austrian private sector, covers all workers in the age group 40–59, and follows these individuals over the period 1984–1998. There is a period of approximately $4\frac{1}{2}$ years (January 1984 to June 1988) before the REBP was introduced; a period of about 5 years (June 1988 to July 1993) when the benefit extension was in effect, and a further period of $5\frac{1}{2}$ years (August 1993 to December 1998) after this law was abolished. The second data source is the Austrian unemployment register. We consider the universe of male unemployment entrants in Austria in the age group 45–54 over the period 1986–1995 and follow these individuals up to end of the year 1998.

The main focus of our analysis will be on a comparison between the 45–49 age group and the 50–54 group. As we can assume that workers in this age group are close substitutes our estimates cannot be strongly affected by a direct effect of age. This is of particular importance since age is an eligibility criterion for the REBP. On the other hand, these two groups may be "too close" substitutes in the sense that, e.g., a strong reduction in employment for the age group 50–54 may feed back to the labor demand for age group 45–49 via general equilibrium effects. It will therefore be instructive to also consider age groups that are further away from the critical eligibility age 50. Moreover, a broader age window also allows us to look at life-cycle effects and look at possible persistence effects of the REBP on labor-market outcomes after the program has been abolished.

We present the results of our analysis in four steps. We first concentrate on the levels of employment, unemployment, and non-employment (predominantly some sort of early retirement); as one important motivation for the introduction of the REBP was to facilitate structural change (downsizing of the steel industry that came in severe troubles with the international steel crises in the mid 1980s), we will also look to which extent the structure of employment has changed in REBP regions relative to other regions.

The analysis clearly shows that unemployment levels are dramatically higher in those regions where the REBP was imposed. Higher levels of unemployment, of course, can either be the result of higher unemployment risk given the average duration of an unemployment spell; or a higher duration, given the risk of unemployment; or both. The second step of our analysis is therefore to look at the dynamics of unemployment and to see to which extent this higher unemployment levels have increased not only the average duration of an unemployment spell but also the inflow rate.

Partial equilibrium job-search theory holds that the variable that should be directly affected from an extension of unemployment benefits is the expected duration of job search. The question emphasized in partial equilibrium is thus how the outflow from unemployment has been different between unemployment entrants that were eligible to the REBP relative to those who were not. An important aspect in this evaluation is the question whether a longer duration of unemployment for REBP-eligible workers is due to a causal impact of extended benefits, and to which extent this is simply the result of worse labor-market conditions for these individuals, the latter fact being the reason why the REBP was introduced in the first place. This means the REBP was an endogenous policy response due to the expectation of worse labor-market conditions in those regions. A companion paper (Lalive and Zweimüller 2004) analyzes this question in detail. Here we will give some informal evidence about the possible size of the bias that arises when this endogenous policy adoption is not accounted for.

It is very likely that the REBP has had not only an important impact on the duration of unemployment but also on the risk of unemployment. The idea is that, by improving the workers' outside options, the REBP decreased the firing costs of firms and allowed firms to defect on long-term seniority contracts. Second, the aim of the REBP was not only to insure older workers against worse job chance in case they suffer an unemployment spell, but also to facilitate downsizing of structurally weak (in particular, iron and steel) industries that were concentrated in those regions. This means that the typical worker did face a higher risk of unemployment. It is therefore interesting to see whether the inflow into unemployment of older workers in these regions is significantly concentrated in those periods and regions where the REBP was in effect.

The third aspect we are interested in are life-cycle aspects. How did the introduction of the REBP affect labor-supply behavior of various cohorts? Since we are concerned with a program that helps older workers, the interesting question is how this program affected the transition process of these workers from labor force participation to retirement. We will contrast the experience of those workers who were never entitled to the REBP to cohorts that were partly and/or entirely eligible to the program.

The final variable which is analyzed in this study and which may have been potentially affected by the REBP is the structure of wages. We look at older workers' wages at the 3rd, 5th, and 7th deciles of the wage distribution and look at the differences between workers eligible to the REBP relative to the wages of those groups that were never eligible to that program. Also with respect to wages it is interesting to contrast wages of currently employed individuals (= the employment stock) and the relative wages of destroyed and new created jobs (= employment flows).

In addressing the causal impact of benefit entitlement on labor-market outcomes we rely primarily on comparisons across (treated and control) regions. Because the REBP was "large" in the sense that it applied to a substantial fraction of the unemployment entrants in the treated regions that were aged 50 or older one has to be careful in using control groups within the treated regions. It is quite likely that the outcomes of these groups are affected by general equilibrium effects. For instance, if the program leads to a reduction in job-search intensity for the treated (older) workers, firms will need to increase the hiring rate of the younger workers in order to meet their labor demand. Comparing outcomes within treated regions will produce a biased estimate of the effect of benefit entitlement on unemployment duration. Since cross region comparisons are subject to policy endogeneity bias, we report a series of different cross region comparisons that allow discussing the relevance of policy endogeneity. The primary sensitivity analysis entails discarding steel workers from the set of treated and control workers because REBP appeared to target primarily the problematic steel sector (Hesoun 1988).

4   The Impact of the REBP on the Levels of Employment and Unemployment

Figures 2.2 and 2.3 show how, for the age groups that were affected by REBP, the employment rate and the unemployment rate developed over the period 1984–1998. Note that the denominator of the ratio shown in these figures includes the whole population in that age group so the numbers in figure 2.2 are therefore comparable to the employment population ratio, whereas the numbers in figure 2.3 are the unemployment population ratio and not comparable to the unemployment rate, as it is usually measured (unemployed relative to employed plus unemployed). To avoid confusion we will refer to these measures as, respectively, the employment ratio and the unemployment ratio.

Figure 2.2 compares the employment ratios for elderly workers in REBP regions to those in non-eligible regions, separately for workers in the age group 50–54 and for workers in the age group 55–59. Consider first the age group 50–54. For this group there is almost no regional difference in employment performance before the REBP starts: about 90 percent of all workers observed in our sample are employed in 1984. In 1988, the period when the program started, the two indicators start to diverge and the employment ratio of workers in REBP regions falls behind the one of the non-eligible group. The difference increases and reaches its maximum in 1993, the year when the REBP was abolished. The regional difference in employment ratios in that period is very large and amounts to almost 10 percentage points. After the abolishment of the program, the employment ratio in REBP regions increases again and reaches the level of the non-treated regions in 1998. Note

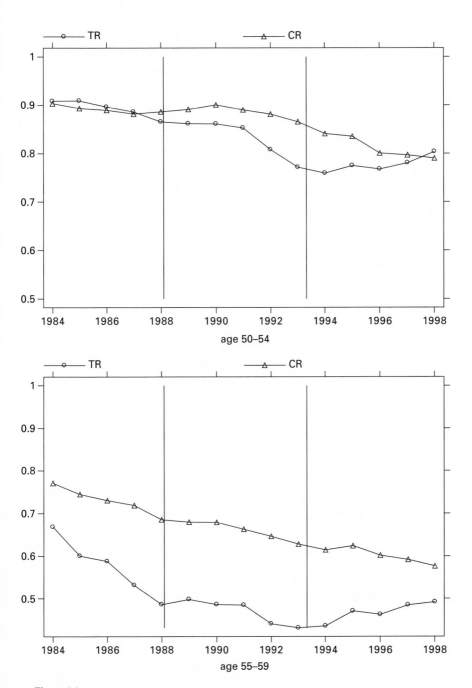

Figure 2.2
Effect of REBP on employment (percentage of population). TR: treated regions. CR: control regions.

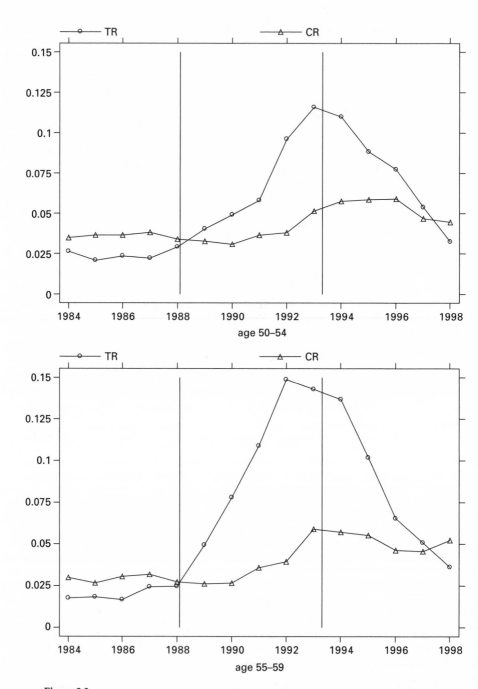

Figure 2.3
Effect of REBP on unemployment (percentage of population). TR: treated regions. CR:
control regions.

also the overall downward trend in the employment ratio over the whole period shown in the upper panel of figure 2.2: starting from a level of 90 percent in the mid 1980s, the employment ratio has come down to 80 percent by the end of the 1990s.

The employment situation is different for the age group 55–59. For these older workers there is a significant regional difference in the employment ratio already before 1988, when the REBP was introduced; moreover, in the treated regions this ratio decreases strongly until 1988, stays at a very low level during the REBP period and increases slightly thereafter. In contrast, the employment ratio follows a smooth downward trend in the control regions. Note that in the age group 55–59 the overall downward trend over the period under consideration is even stronger than for the age group 50–54. In the mid 1980s the employment ratio in control regions was almost 80 percent, and by the end of the 1990s this ratio has come down to less than 60 percent.

Figure 2.3 shows the corresponding picture for the unemployment ratios. For both age groups we see the same picture. Slightly lower unemployment ratios in the REBP regions before the program starts; an increase during the REBP period, and a decrease of the ratio after the program had been abolished. By the end of the 1990s the unemployment ratio in REBP regions has fallen below the one of control regions for both age groups. Note also that the differences in unemployment ratios are tremendous: for the age group 50–54, this difference becomes as large as 7 percentage points (in year 1992); for the age group 55–59 the difference becomes even higher (11 percentage points in 1993). (Note that differences in conventionally measured unemployment rates would be even higher.)

Two further points that emerge from figures 2.2 and 2.3 are worth mentioning. The first point concerns the long-term effects of the REBP on employment and unemployment. In both figures we see significant differences between treated and non-treated regions even after the program has been abolished. This is not surprising given the fact that unemployment entrants in REBP regions in 1993 (when the program ends) are still entitled to draw benefits until the year 1997. So we should actually see differences in our labor-market indicators until that period. Interestingly, exactly this picture shows up in figures 2.1 and 2.2 (the only exception being the employment ratio for the age group 55–59). The second interesting point refers to non-employment (= individuals neither employed nor unemployed). While for the age

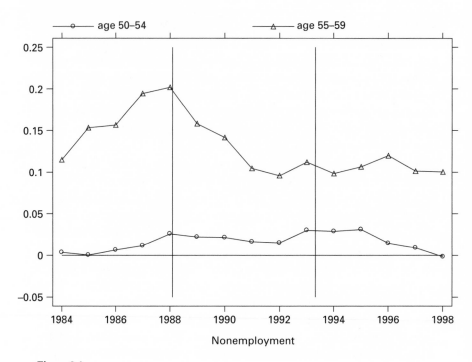

Figure 2.4
Difference TR – CR in non-employment ratio, ages 50–59.

group 50–54 there are no dramatic regional differences in the fraction of individuals that have completely withdrawn from the labor force throughout the considered period, these differences become large for the age group 55–59. Figure 2.3 shows that, in this age group, there are very strong regional differences in the fraction of individuals that have withdrawn from the labor market. But the highest difference already occurred at the date when the REBP was introduced and starts to decrease thereafter. Figure 2.3 suggests that a sizable fraction of those workers who otherwise would have been non-employed, became eligible to extended benefits. This increases unemployment and reduces non-employment. Nevertheless, it is obvious from figure 2.4 that non-employment remains much higher in REBP regions also during and after the program.

Figures 2.2–2.4 all refer to workers older than 50. A comparison of the regional difference in employment and unemployment ratios for workers under 50 is informative. If we would see the same picture as in figures 2.2 and 2.3 also for workers under 50, the obvious interpretation would be that adverse labor-market shocks, specific to the time period 1988–1993 and to the REBP regions—but not the increase in benefit entitlement in these regions—account for the empirical evidence. Only if there is a significant difference in labor-market performance between workers above and below age 50 we can causally link the large regional differences shown in figures 2.2 and 2.3 to the increase in benefit duration provided by the REBP.

Figure 2.5 clearly shows that, for workers below age 50, the regional differences between treated and non-treated regions are small in comparison to the regional differences for workers aged 50 and older. In fact, (un)employment performance of workers below 50 is even slightly better in REBP regions, both for the age group 40–44 and the age group 45–49. Differences in non-employment ratios are negligible. Figure 2.4 therefore clearly suggests that, in treated regions, workers above age 50 do not do worse because of worse labor-market conditions in these regions during the program. There appears to be a causal link between the benefit extension and the employment performance of the concerned individuals.

In sum, a very clear picture emerges: for eligible workers, both unemployment and employment ratios are rather equal between the two regions before the program starts; during the treatment period the employment ratio and the unemployment ratio strongly increase, reach a turning point around the year 1993, and decrease thereafter. The REBP effect is long-lasting: employment and unemployment levels in treated regions remain significantly higher even after 1993 and reach the corresponding levels of the non-treated regions not until the year 1998. No such pattern is observed for non-eligible workers. We are therefore led to conclude that there is a causal link from the entitlement to long benefits to employment performance.[10]

As mentioned above the REBP was introduced in reaction to the international steel crises in the mid 1980s. Regions covered by the program had typically a high percentage of workers employment in the iron and steel industry. The REBP did not only help older workers in case of unemployment but was also an indirect subsidy to employers as it allowed firms to get rid of older employees in overstaffed plants more easily. It is interesting to see to which extent this has changed the structure of employment in these regions relative to the rest of the economy.

Table 2.2 shows the fraction of steel workers in total employment at the period when the REBP started (1988), immediately before the

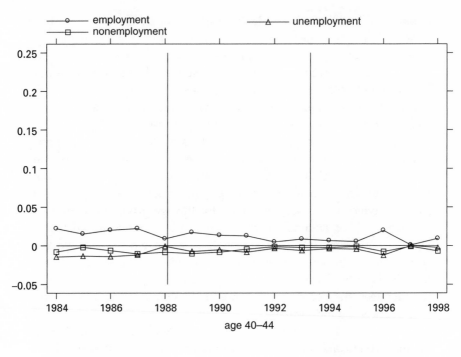

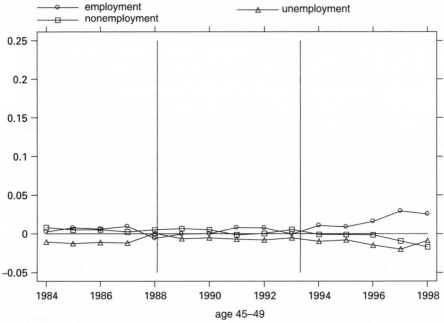

Figure 2.5
Difference TR − CR, ages 40–49.

Table 2.2
Steel workers (% of employment on May 10 of respective year, calculated on basis of Austrian social security data).

	1988	1991	1994	Average
Treated regions				
Age 55–59	6.90	7.82	6.84	7.19
Age 50–54	19.72	15.33	11.78	15.39
Age 45–49	18.51	16.42	14.57	16.64
Age 40–44	17.02	15.59	13.79	15.49
Control regions				
Age 55–59	3.89	3.66	3.90	3.82
Age 50–54	4.52	4.19	4.00	4.20
Age 45–49	4.14	4.04	4.13	4.10
Age 40–44	4.40	4.78	4.51	4.57
All regions	7.41	6.87	6.20	6.83

reform of the program (1991), and when it was abolished (1993). Among the age group above 55 the percentage of steel workers is already low, meaning that early retirement is prevalent for workers in these industries and it was so already before the program started. For the age group 50–54, however, the reduction is dramatic. During the REBP period, there is a continuous fall in employment in the steel industry, the fraction of workers aged 50–54 falls from almost 20 percent in 1988 to less than 12 percent in 1993. We see also a reduction in steel-industry employment shares for younger workers, but the fall for these groups is only half as large. It is clear from table 2.2 that there is no such trend in the non-treated regions. In these regions the employment share of iron and steel industries stays at around 4 percent, with no dramatic difference across age groups and time.

5   Unemployment Dynamics and the REBP

The higher level of unemployment during the REBP period may either be due to a longer average duration of unemployment for eligible workers; or it may be due to an increase in the unemployment inflow. As mentioned above, it is very likely that the REBP did not only lead to longer unemployment spells, but also to an increased inflow into unemployment, since the REBP provided a chance for firms to fire older workers at comparably low cost. We now proceed by looking at these two channels separately.

5.1 The REBP and the Increase in Unemployment Duration

Table 2.3 gives information about the unemployment spells in treated and non-treated regions. In total, 385,463 unemployment spells were started by males in the age group 45–54 during the period 1986–1995. The upper panel shows the survivor rates for these spells, separately for workers eligible to the REBP and for non-eligible workers. The message of table 2.3 is clear: unemployment spells suffered by individuals eligible to the REBP last longer. For these individuals, more than 30 percent of all spells are still in progress after one year, as opposed to only 9 percent for individuals that are not eligible.[11] On average, a treated spell lasts about 10 months and is about 2.5 times as long as a non-treated one. Note that this number refers to completed durations. The fraction of treated spells that is still in progress by the end of our observation period (December 1998) amounts to almost 8 percent.

Table 2.3

Unemployment spell characteristics. Sample covers all unemployment spells started between 1986 and 1995 of male individuals aged 45–54. Treated spells = age 50–54 at start of unemployment spell, location of residence in treated region (TR), spell in progress June 1988 or started between June 1988 and July 1993. Non-treated spell = age 45–49 and location of residence in TR OR age 45–54 and location of residence in CR, spell started between January 1986 and December 1995. Out of labor force = no information regarding labor market state in social security data. Source: calculations based on Austrian social security data.

	All spells		Treated spells		Non-treated spells	
	N	%	N	%	N	%
Duration						
≥3 months	79,241	39.53	12,251	51.72	140,116	38.73
≥6 months	21,684	18.98	9,162	38.68	63,998	17.69
≥9 months	10,998	13.35	8,236	34.77	43,232	11.95
≥12 months	16,790	10.50	7,497	31.65	32,958	9.11
≥24 months	23,671	6.14	5,493	23.19	18,161	5.02
Mean completed duration (days)		139.51		315.08		128.68
Exit status						
Employment	291,117	75.52	12,885	54.40	278,232	76.91
Long term sickness	29,272	7.59	3,391	14.32	25,881	7.15
Retirement	14,860	3.86	3,010	12.71	11,850	3.28
Out of labor force	40,302	10.46	2,535	10.70	37,767	10.44
Censored	9,912	2.57	1,866	7.88	8,046	2.22
Observations	385,463	100.00	23,687	100.00	361,776	100.00

Treated spells were started before August 1993, which means that the elapsed duration of a treated spell that is censored is at least $5\frac{1}{2}$ years.

Both for treated and non-treated spells, by far the most important exit status is employment. In total, three out of four unemployment spells end in a regular job, the remaining spells are followed by a spell of non-employment, predominantly long-term sickness[12] or some form of early retirement. The differences between spells eligible to the REBP and those that are not is large: among the former, only 54.4 percent among the eligible individuals return to a job; and about 27 percent of eligible spells (but only 10 percent of the non-eligible ones) end either in long-term sickness or early retirement. A sizable fraction of individuals exit to non-employment for reasons that cannot be observed in the data. There are no important differences between treated and non-treated spells along this dimension.

An open question is whether the extreme differences by eligibility to the REBP represents a causal relationship that goes from the extension in benefits to the duration of unemployment or whether this is a statistical artifact simply arising from adverse (regional and age-specific) labor-market shocks in the REBP regions. In order to investigate this question informally, we show two pieces of evidence.[13] The first is a separate analysis of the experience for steel and non-steel workers (table 2.4). Adverse labor-market conditions should predominantly be observed in the former group. Secondly, we report an analysis that distinguishes between REBP regions that had labor-market conditions

Table 2.4
Unemployment spell characteristics, steel workers vs. non-steel workers. Steel worker = previously employed in steel sector. See previous table for definition of treated and non-treated spells. Calculations based on Austrian social security data.

	All spells	Treated spells	Non-treated spells
Mean completed duration (days)			
Steel workers	234.07	504.49	172.68
Non-steel workers	128.46	220.52	124.30
Exit to employment (% of total)			
Steel workers	57.57	30.63	64.37
Non-steel workers	77.72	67.62	78.19
Observations			
Steel workers	42,010	8,468	33,542
Non-steel workers	343,453	15,219	328,234

Table 2.5
Unemployment spell characteristics, policy endogeneity bias. TR1 = 6 regions with REBP entitlement and no labor market problems. TR2 = 22 regions with REBP entitlement and severe labor market problems. TR1 treated = age 50–54, residence in TR1, inflow between June 1988 and December 1991. TR2 treated = age 50–54, residence in TR2, inflow between June 1988 and July 1993. Non-treated = age 45–49 and residence in TR (= TR1 + TR2) OR age 45–54 and residence in CR, inflow between January 1986 and December 1995. Source: Own calculations based on Austrian social security data.

	TR1 treated	TR2 treated	Non-treated
Mean completed duration (days)	178.45	332.13	128.68
Exit to employment (% of total)	75.22	51.96	76.91
Observations	2,482	21,205	361,776

which were comparable to the control regions and those which had particularly strong labor-market problems (table 2.5). A comparison of non-eligible spells with those treated spells in the former regions should entirely reflect a causal impact of the REBP.[14]

Table 2.4 shows that steel workers are unemployed longer and have a lower probability to return to employment than non-steel workers. This is shown by all comparisons presented in table 2.5, but among treated spells these differences are strongest. Only one third of REBP-eligible steel workers that enter an unemployment spell again find a regular job. Note that this number is not flawed by right-censoring. Right-censored, treated spells last at least $5\frac{1}{2}$ years, the likelihood that these workers will find a regular job is certainly close to zero. In sum, the evidence for steel workers shows that the worse unemployment experience for eligible workers must, to a non-negligible degree, be due to a bad labor market.

To see more closely possible causal effects of the benefit extension on unemployment duration, it is instructive to compare the experience of unemployed individuals that face similar labor-market conditions. The REBP provides an interesting natural experiment in this respect. The 1991 reform of the program, that came into effect in January 1992, excluded several districts that were eligible during the period 1988–1991. The reason was that labor-market conditions were found to have significantly improved, so REBP eligibility was no longer justified. In fact, it can be argued (see Lalive and Zweimüller 2004) that it turned out ex post that labor-market conditions in these regions were rather similar to control regions already during the pre-reform REBP period. A comparison of these regions to control regions should therefore not be biased by differences in regional labor-market performance. Hence, observed differences between treated and non-treated spells are due to differences in benefit duration rules.

Table 2.5 distinguishes unemployment duration outcomes of treated individuals in the set of regions that was excluded in the reform of January 1992 (treated, TR1), treated individuals in the remaining regions (treated, TR2), and job seekers who were not eligible to extended benefits. This group consists of individuals aged 45–49 in treated regions as well as all individuals aged 45–54 in control regions. The difference in mean completed duration between treated spells in TR1 and non-treated spells is about 7 weeks. Moreover, there is hardly any difference in labor force participation as indicated by the small difference in exits to a regular job. Benefit entitlement appears to prolong unemployment duration. Unemployment duration increases, roughly, by 0.04 $(= 7/179)$ week per week of benefit extension.

A comparison of treated spells in TR2 to non-treated spells allows discussing the magnitude of the policy endogeneity bias in estimating the effect of benefit entitlement on unemployment duration. The observed difference in mean completed duration between treated spells with location of residence in TR2 and non-treated spells is about 29 weeks. Moreover, the percentage of individuals who is ever observed to start a regular job is 25 percentage points lower for treated workers in TR2 than for non-treated workers. This comparison suggests that unemployment duration increases by 0.16 week per additional week of benefits. Thus, the bias due policy endogeneity is roughly 0.12 $(= 0.16 - 0.04)$ week of unemployment per additional week of benefits. This bias can thus even exceed the causal effect of changes in the maximum duration of benefits on unemployment duration.

5.2 Did the REBP Increase the Unemployment Risk of Older Workers?

The generous entitlement to regular unemployment benefits provided by the REBP may have represented a decrease in the reputational costs of firing older workers. Did this result in a higher risk of unemployment for the eligible group? Figure 2.6 gives an answer to this question. The numbers in figure 2.6 show quarterly unemployment inflow rates.[15] They refer to the age groups 50–54 (upper panel) and 55–59 (lower panel).

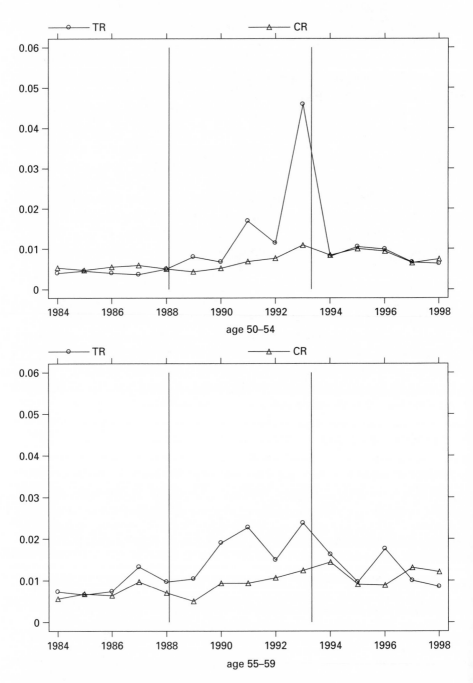

Figure 2.6
Effect of REBP on unemployment inflow (percentage of unemployment, per quarter).

For both age groups there are no particular regional differences in the inflow rates from employment to unemployment in the mid 1980s. For the age group 50–54 this picture changes in 1988 when the REBP was introduced; and already somewhat earlier for the age group 55–59. The observed regional differences are large: on average, the inflow rates of the treated group are about twice as large as the inflow rates of non-eligible workers.

Moreover, there is an interesting pattern as far as the timing of these inflows is concerned. For both age groups the inflow rate for workers eligible to the REBP reaches a peak in the years 1991 and 1993: a time pattern that is not visible for the non-entitled workers. The years 1991 and 1993 are, respectively, the periods immediately before the reform and the abolishment of the REBP. The reason why the inflow rates are higher during these periods can easily be rationalized by an "end-game" situation between firms and workers: firms who have to downsize their work force for structural reasons will find it easier to convince worker representatives to lay off workers in a period when the individual costs of unemployment are still comparably low. The expectation of a strong increase in these costs due to a shorter duration of unemployment benefits facilitates an agreement with high layoffs now and low layoffs later (when the extended benefits program has run out). The same pattern shows up not only for the year 1991 and the year 1993 but also for both age groups 50–54 and 55–59.

Figure 2.7 shows the regional differences in unemployment inflow rates for the younger age groups 40–44 and 45–49. It is evident from this figure that these differences are not particularly high and there are no time patterns comparable to those observed for the workers above age 50. However, it is interesting to see that, with only a few exceptions, inflow rates for younger workers are somewhat smaller in the treated regions over the entire period. This is consistent with the proposition that the REBP has improved the employment prospects of younger workers in treated regions via general equilibrium effects: The REBP increased the demand for workers below 50 relative to workers above 50 in these regions. Where employment reductions became necessary, and this has taken the form of firing the older workers but keeping the somewhat younger, closely substitutable employees.

The REBP was a reaction to a shock that did not only hit a particular region, but also one that hit a particular sector: the steel industry. It is therefore interesting to see whether the unemployment inflow rates were different by sectors. Figure 2.8 shows that there is very strong

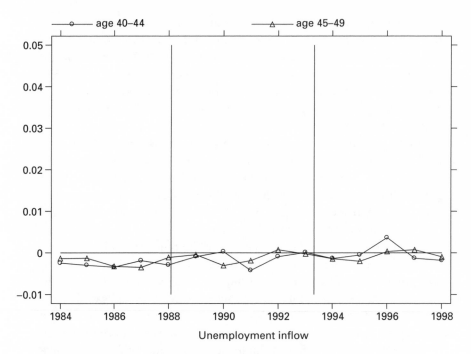

Figure 2.7
Difference TR – CR in unemployment inflow rate, ages 40–49.

difference between the unemployment risk of steel-workers (lower panel) and employees in other industries (upper panel). While also in the non-steel industry inflow rates for older workers in REBP regions are higher, the regional difference is comparably small. The difference is roughly 1 percentage point leading to an increase in the risk of unemployment by about 0.0055 ($= 1/179$) percentage point per additional week of unemployment benefits.

For the steel industry, the differences are tremendous: in 1993 the quarterly inflow rate amounts to as much as 15 percent for workers aged 50–54 and about 5 percent for workers aged 55–59. Interestingly, the above mentioned time pattern—peaks in the inflow rate in the years 1991 and 1993—are observed for all groups in figure 2.8.

REBP regions were regions that were hit particularly hard by the international steel crisis in the 1980s. The REBP transmitted this sectoral/regional shock into an age-specific shock. Firms who had to decrease their employment levels fired workers that had access to generous transfer payment from the government. What we see for steel

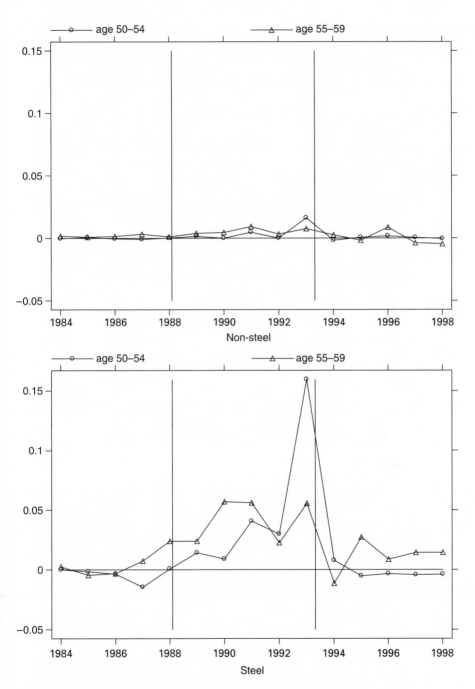

Figure 2.8
Difference TR – CR in unemployment inflow rate, steel workers vs. non-steel workers.

Birth cohort 1938

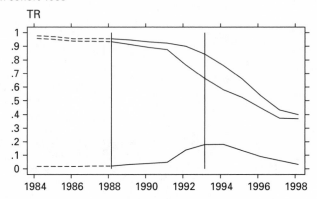

Birth cohort 1941

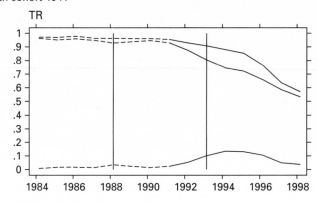

Birth cohort 1944

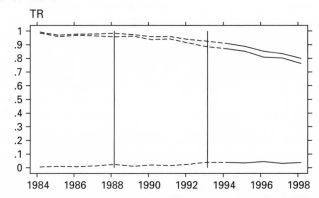

Figure 2.9
A life-cycle perspective. Top: labor-force participation. Middle: employment. Bottom: unemployment. Solid lines represent individuals aged 50 or older.

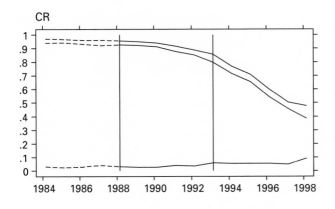

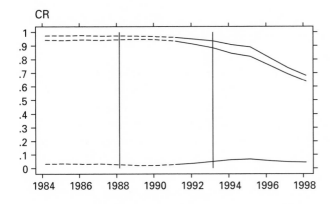

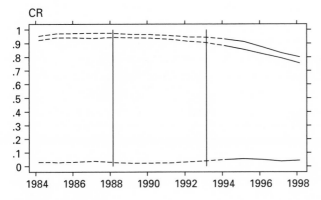

Figure 2.9 (continued)

workers in figure 2.8 can therefore not be interpreted as a causal impact of benefit duration on the unemployment inflow rate, but rather as the consequence of a very bad labor-market situation. The impact of the REBP was to concentrate the worse labor-market outcomes on the older steel workers. It is much more plausible to interpret the effect for employees in the non-steel sectors as an upper bound for a causal impact of benefit duration on the unemployment inflow. In REBP regions these sectors were in a shape similar to the rest of the economy but may have been hit by stronger indirect effects than the rest of the economy.

6   REBP Effects from a Life-Cycle Perspective

Was the REBP a program that mainly facilitated a smooth transition from work to retirement for elderly workers? In order to look at this question, we take a more long-term perspective and look at the dynamics of labor force participation of certain cohorts. Figure 2.9 shows, over the period 1984–1998, the unemployment ratio, the employment ratio, and the labor force participation ratio for the cohorts born, respectively, in 1938, 1941, and 1944. The graphs are drawn separately for treated and non-treated regions. The cohort 1938 (age 50 in 1988) was eligible to long benefits throughout the REBP period, the cohort 1944 was never eligible (age 50 in 1994), whereas the cohort 1941 (age 50 in 1991) was eligible only in the years 1991–1993. (A dotted line in figure 2.9 means that the cohort is below age 50).

First of all, figure 2.9 shows that unemployment ratio for the cohort 1938 increases during the REBP period, stays high also after the REBP has been abolished and falls to lower levels not until the period 1998. The labor force participation ratio starts to decrease strongly after the age 54 (in 1993). Only 76 percent of individuals of the cohort 1938 are still at work at that age. In comparison, the corresponding fraction in the control regions amounts to 85 percent. The difference is similar for the cohort 1941. At age 54 (year 1995, when the program was abolished, but the long-term effects of the REBP are still at work), in treated regions only 72 percent of the observed population aged 54 are still employed, whereas the corresponding number for the non-treated regions amounts to 82 percent.

No such difference is given for the cohort 1944. This cohort was never eligible to the REBP and neither the labor force participation ratio, the employment ratio, nor the unemployment ratio show any particular difference between treated and non-treated regions. Figure 2.9 therefore strongly supports the proposition that a main effect of the REBP was to open the door to retirement for workers that were dismissed from their jobs, even if they were still relatively young.

7   Did the REBP Affect the Wage Structure?

The final question concerns the level and distribution of wages and how this was changed by the REBP. One reason for the introduction of the REBP was to reduce the firing costs for overstaffed firms and allow these employers to lay off older workers that were expensive and were paid above their productivity. Did this actually happen in practice?

Table 2.6 gives a tentative answer to this question. We compare the previous earnings of unemployment entrants entitled to the REBP to the previous earnings of non-eligible entrants. We perform a difference-in-difference-in-difference (DiDiD) analysis that makes use of the fact that there are three criteria that determine eligibility to the extended benefit program: age, region, and time. From table 2.6 we see that previous wages of unemployment entrants aged 50–54 were

Table 2.6
REBP and wages of unemployment entrants (standard error in parentheses). Log of daily real wage in AS. Calculations based on Austrian social security data.

	Before policy	During policy	After policy	Time difference, before-during	Time difference, during-after
Workers aged 50–54					
Treated regions	6.566	6.839	6.821	0.273	−0.018
	821	1,611	1,019		
Control regions	6.603	6.734	6.849	0.131	0.115
	2,725	3,108	3,373		
Regional difference	−0.036	0.105	−0.029	0.141	−0.134
Workers aged 45–49					
Treated regions	6.598	6.709	6.759	0.111	0.050
	1,094	1,047	1,089		
Control regions	6.622	6.740	6.795	0.118	0.054
	3,159	3,569	3,798		
Regional difference	−0.024	−0.031	−0.036	−0.007	−0.005
DiDiD				0.149	−0.129
				(0.018)	(0.020)

rather similar between treated and control regions before the program came into effect. The median of the log daily wage distribution was 6.566 in treated and 6.603 in non-treated regions. This amounts to a wage-differential of −0.036. In the period during which the program was in force, previous wages of unemployment entrants were higher than before, the regional wage differential for the age group 50–54 amounted to +0.105. And this differential returned to −0.029, which is very close to the pre-program situation.

Did something similar happen in the age group 45–49? The answer is no. Throughout all three periods, unemployment entrants in treated regions had earned somewhat less than their colleagues in the control regions and the wage differential was surprisingly stable throughout the whole period. The differential amounted to −0.024, −0.031, and −0.036, respectively before, during, and after the REBP. The DiDiD estimate for the wage gap between eligible and non-eligible workers was +0.149 if one compares the pre-program with the during-program situation. And the gap was −0.129 if one compares the during-program with the post-program situation. This effect seems to be robust and estimated with a rather low standard error. The DiDiD estimator therefore suggests that unemployment entrants eligible to the REBP were older high-wage workers.

How did the REBP affect other dimensions of the wage structure? The first row in table 2.7 shows the DiDiD estimate for unemployment entrants when not only the median but also the spread (7th/3rd decile) of the log daily wage distribution is analyzed.[16] The result is that, just like for the median, the spread in the distribution of previous wages

Table 2.7
Effect of REBP on wages, DiDiD estimates (standard error in parentheses). Calculations based on Austrian social security data.

	Change in median		Change in difference, 7th decile-3rd decile	
	REBP starts	REBP ends	REBP starts	REBP ends
Unemployment entrants	0.149	−0.129	0.153	−0.107
	(0.018)	(0.020)	(0.026)	(0.028)
Exits from unemployment	0.029	−0.021	0.033	−0.061
	(0.020)	(0.023)	(0.028)	(0.032)
Employed	−0.011	−0.026	0.027	0.017
	(0.003)	(0.003)	(0.005)	(0.005)

is larger for eligible entrants and that this effect is of a comparable size as the effect on median log wages. The final row of table 2.7 addresses the question of whether extended benefits affected the distribution of accepted wages. There are two effects at work. Reservation wages will increase as benefits are extended for given duration; but, in a non-stationary environment, reservation wages will decrease with duration given benefit generosity.[17] We do not see any significant difference in accepted wages between treated and non-treated unemployed individuals. Thus, it may be that the two effects on accepted wages cancel exactly. Similarly, we do not see a clear picture on the spread of the distribution of accepted wages.

The final piece of evidence which we present here concerns the median log daily wage of all the employed individuals. Here we compare the distribution of log daily wages of the entire male labor force. The REBP seems to have lowered wages for the employed individuals in these regions by between 1 and 3 percentage points. The effect is originally small in the period during which the REBP was in effect, and becomes larger in the post-program period, and the effect is between 1 and 3 percentage points. The long-lasting effect of the REBP on wages may well reflect the wage pressure resulting from the long-lasting effects of the REBP on unemployment levels (see figure 2.3). While REBP had a negative effect on the wage level, it increased wage inequality. The 7th/3rd decile log wage differential increase both in the period when the program was introduced and in the post-REBP period.

Conclusions

This paper has analyzed the impact of benefit duration on various dimensions of the labor market. The basis of our empirical analysis was the quasi-experimental situation that was created by the introduction of the Austrian regional extended benefit program (REBP), which granted four years of regular unemployment benefits to workers above age 50 in certain regions. Our empirical analysis is based on two unique and very large data sets that cover, respectively, 10 percent of all male employees aged 40–59 over the period 1984–1998, and the universe of all male unemployment entrants in Austria aged 45–54 over the period 1986–1995.

A first message of our analysis is that the REBP has a profound impact on the labor markets of treated regions. This means that the dominant focus in the literature, namely the impact of the unemployment insurance system on the duration of unemployment is too narrow. Important effects may also come from transitions in and out of the labor force, in the case of older workers, the important transitions are exits from employment/unemployment to some form of early retirement.

The second message from our analysis is that a substantial increase in benefit entitlement rules may not have quantitatively strong causal effects. On the one hand, the unemployment as a percentage of the population of workers that was eligible for extended benefits increased dramatically when the program was in effect. Just before the program was abolished, this unemployment ratio was more than 3 times higher in treated regions than in control regions. On the other hand, the findings in this paper suggest that this drastic increase in unemployment may be due to a large proportion that the program was used to ease restructuring in the problematic, nationalized steel sector. When we compare non-steel workers across treated and control regions, we find that the prolonged benefit entitlement due to REBP led to an increase in unemployment duration by about 7 weeks. The corresponding effect on the quarterly risk of unemployment is at most 1 percentage point. These effects are not consistent with the large observed increase in the unemployment ratio. This suggests that policy endogeneity, the fact that policy design depends on the outcome of interest, may be an important confounding factor in the analysis of policy incidence.

The third message of our analysis is that benefit extension for older workers significantly affected the life-cycle pattern of labor force participation. The long benefit duration led to a situation where, in many cases, the start of an unemployment spell was the beginning of retirement. In other words, the benefit extension was a hidden form of early retirement. This was especially so for steel workers: one out of three unemployment spells suffered by steel workers ended in a new job. For the remaining spells of steel workers retirement had already begun. The final message of our analysis is that the wage effects of extended benefit programs should not be neglected. For the Austrian REBP we find that predominantly high-wage jobs were destroyed as a consequence of the REBP. Moreover, the high unemployment rates that the benefit extension created may have affected the process of wage formation. We find that REBP regions experienced lower wage increases than the rest of the economy, and that the spread in the wage distribution has increased.

Acknowledgments

We are indebted to two anonymous referees for helpful suggestions. Adrian Kienast, Andreas Kuhn, and Oliver Ruf provided superb research assistance, and Maria Hermann was very helpful in checking the manuscript.

Notes

1. In a companion paper (Lalive and Zweimüller 2004) we study in detail for the case of unemployment duration how the above-mentioned two effects can be separated.

2. The youngest eligible worker (one who starts his unemployment spell at age 50) can draw benefits until the age of 54. The likelihood to get some hidden form of early retirement benefits (long-term sickness, disability pension or pension due to reduced employability) is already significantly high in that age range.

3. Because females can start regular early retirement when they turn 55 it is difficult to separate effects on employment from effects on early retirement for this group. We focus on males because they are not allowed to enter early retirement until the age of 60.

4. Other recent studies that shed light on the importance of benefit eligibility compare between receivers and non-receivers of unemployment benefits (Carling et al. (1996) for Sweden and Bover et al. (2002) for Spain) or study major cuts in benefits (e.g., Carling et al. (2001) look at a major benefit cut in Sweden and Abbring et al. (1998) and Van den Berg et al. (2004) look at the impact of major benefit cuts due to sanctions in the Netherlands).

5. Burdett and Hool (1983) and Haltiwanger (1984) generalize the implicit contracts literature by introducing bargaining and by allowing for the interaction of stock adjustment and factor utilization decisions.

6. The two studies differ in terms of the statistical analysis. Whereas Jurajda estimates a multivariate mixed proportional hazard model to account for duration dependence and correlated unobserved heterogeneity, Anderson and Meyer (1994) focus on quarterly employment probabilities. For further differences, see Jurajda 2001.

7. Anderson and Meyer (2000) address the related but different question of how unemployment insurance taxes are shifted to workers when the system of unemployment insurance financing is changed from a fiat unemployment insurance tax to experience rating.

8. In 1988 the fraction of individuals in the unemployment stock who were unemployed for at least a year was 18.6 percent among in the age group 40–49 and 22.9 percent in the age group 50–59. In 1993 the corresponding figures were 17.8 percent and 37.2 percent.

9. The drop in unemployment benefits after exhaustion is smaller in the Austrian system than, for instance, in the United States. Thus, one would expect that the benefit duration effects found for Austria will be smaller than the disincentive effects reported for the United States.

10. It is not clear, however, how strong this causal link is due to policy endogeneity. The following section discusses this issue in detail for the unemployment ratio.

11. Note that these numbers are drawn from an inflow rather than a stock sample (to which official numbers on the percentage long-term unemployment usually refer). Clearly, the fraction of long-term unemployed at an arbitrary point of time is larger than 10 percent due to the well-known oversampling of long-term spells in stock samples.

12. In accordance with the literature, long-term sickness is defined as a sickness spell that lasts longer than 3 months. Unemployment spells that are interrupted by short-term sickness spells are lumped together. This is in line with UB-eligibility rules. During sickness the claim is interrupted, and can be used up after the sickness spell ends.

13. For a detailed econometric analysis of this problem, see Lalive and Zweimüller 2004.

14. For a paper that analyzes causal effects of extended benefits on exits to employment with a similar empirical strategy, see Card and Levine 2002.

15. The quarterly unemployment inflow rate is the number of workers that enter unemployment between May 10 and August 9 divided by the stock of the employed on May 10. We report the second quarter unemployment inflow because this quarter is the least affected by seasonality.

16. We focus on the 7th/3rd decile range of log wages because wages are top coded. Top coding affects the 8th decile in this sample of older workers earning considerably more than the average Austrian worker.

17. We are grateful to a referee for pointing out this fact.

References

Abbring, J., Van den Berg, G., and Van Ours, J. C. 1998. The Effect of Unemployment Insurance Sanctions on the Transition Rate from Unemployment to Employment. Working paper, Tinbergen Institute, Amsterdam.

Acemoglu, D. 2001. "Good Jobs versus Bad Jobs." *Journal of Labor Economics* 19: 1–22.

Acemoglu, D., and Shimer, R. 1999. "Efficient Unemployment Insurance." *Journal of Political Economy* 107: 893–928.

Anderson, P. M., and Meyer, B. D. 1994. The Effects of Unemployment Insurance Taxes and Benefits on Layoffs Using Firm and Individual Data. Working paper 4960, NBER.

Anderson, P. M., and Meyer, B. D. 1997. "Unemployment Insurance Benefits and Takeup Rates." *Quarterly Journal of Economics* 112: 913–938.

Anderson, P. M., and Meyer, B. D. 2000. "The Effects of the Unemployment Insurance Payroll Tax on Wages, Employment, Claims, and Denials." *Journal of Public Economics* 78: 81–106.

Atkinson, A. B., and Micklewright, J. 1991. "Unemployment Compensation and Labor Market Transitions: A Critical Review." *Journal of Economic Literature* 29: 1679–1727.

Baily, M. N. 1977. "On the Theory of Layoffs and Unemployment." *Econometrica* 45: 1043–1063.

Baker, M., and Rea, S. A. 1998. "Employment Spells and Unemployment Insurance Eligibility Requirements." *Review of Economics and Statistics* 80: 80–94.

Bratberg, E., and Vaage, K. 2000. "Spell Durations with Long Unemployment Insurance Periods." *Labour Economics* 7: 153–180.

Bover, O., Arellano, M., and Bentolila, S. 2002. "Unemployment Duration, Benefit Duration and the Business Cycle." *Economic Journal* 112: 223–265.

Burdett, K., and Hool, B. 1978. "Layoffs, Wages, and Unemployment Insurance." *Journal of Public Economics* 21: 325–327.

Burdett, K. 1979. "Unemployment Insurance as a Search Subsidy: A Theoretical Analysis." *Economic Inquiry* 17: 333–343.

Card, D., and Levine, P. B. 1994. "Unemployment Insurance Taxes and the Cyclical and Seasonal Properties of Unemployment." *Journal of Public Economics* 53: 1–29.

Card, D., and Levine, P. B. 2002. "Extended Benefits and the Duration of UI Spells: Evidence from the New Jersey Extended Benefit Program." *Journal of Public Economics* 78: 107–138.

Carling, K., Edin, P.-A., Harkman, A., and Holmlund, B. 1996. "Unemployment Duration, Unemployment Benefits, and Labor Market Programs in Sweden." *Journal of Public Economics* 59: 313–334.

Carling, K, Holmlund, B., and A. Vejsiu. 2001. "Do Benefit Cuts Boost Job Findings? Swedish Evidence from the 1990s." *Economic Journal* 111: 766–790.

Christofides, L. N., and McKenna, C. J. 1996. "Unemployment Insurance and Job Duration in Canada." *Journal of Labor Economics* 14: 286–312.

Devine, J., and Kiefer, N. 1991. *Empirical Labor Economics*. Oxford University Press.

Feldstein, M. S. 1976. "Temporary Layoffs in the Theory of Unemployment." *Journal of Political Economy* 84: 837–857.

Haltiwanger, J. 1984. "The Distinguishing Characteristics of Temporary and Permanent Layoffs." *Journal of Labor Economics* 2: 523–538.

Hesoun, J. 1988. Bericht des Ausschusses für soziale Verwaltung, Beilage zu den Stenographischen Protokollen Des Nationalrates 549, Vienna.

Ham, J., and Rea, S. 1987. "Unemployment Insurance and Male Unemployment Duration in Canada." *Journal of Labor Economics* 5: 325–353.

Hesoun, J. 1988. Bericht des Ausschusses für soziale Verwaltung, Beilage zu den Stenographischen Protokollen Des Nationalrates 549, Vienna.

Hunt, J. 1995. "The Effect of Unemployment Compensation on Unemployment Duration in Germany." *Journal of Labor Economics* 13: 88–120.

Jurajda, S. 2000. Unemployment Insurance and the Timing of Layoffs. CERGE-EI discussion paper 46, Charles University, Prague.

Jurajda, S. 2001. Estimating the Effects of Unemployment Insurance Compensation on the Labor Market Histories of Displaced Workers. IZA DP No. 294, IZA, Bonn.

Katz, L., and Meyer, B. 1990. "The Impact of the Potential Duration of Unemployment Benefits on the Duration of Unemployment." *Journal of Public Economics* 41: 45–72.

Lalive, R., and Zweimüller, J. 2004. "Benefit Entitlement and Unemployment Duration—The Role of Policy Endogeneity." *Journal of Public Economics*, forthcoming.

Marimon, R., and Zilibotti, F. 1999. "Unemployment vs. Mismatch of Talents: Reconsidering Unemployment Benefits." *Economic Journal* 109: 266–291.

Moffitt, R., and Nicholson, W. 1982. "The Effect of Unemployment Insurance on Unemployment: The Case of Federal Supplemental Benefits." *Review of Economics and Statistics* 64: 1–11.

Moffitt, R. 1985. "Unemployment Insurance and the Distribution of Unemployment Spells." *Journal of Econometrics* 28: 85–101.

Mortensen, D. T. 1977. "Unemployment Insurance and Job Search Decisions." *Industrial and Labor Relations Review* 30, no. 4: 505–517.

Mortensen, D. T., and Pissarides, C. A. 1994. "Job Creation and Job Destruction in the Theory of Unemployment." *Review of Economic Studies* 61: 397–415.

Mortensen, D. T., and Pissarides, C. A. 1999. "New Developments in Models of Search in the Labor Market." In *Handbook of Labor Economics*, volume 3B, ed. O. Ashenfelter and D. Card. North-Holland.

Nickell, S. 1982. "The Determinants of Equilibrium Unemployment in Britain." *Economic Journal* 92: 555–575.

Pissarides, C. A. 2000. *Equilibrium Unemployment Theory*. MIT Press.

Topel, R. 1983. "On Layoffs and Unemployment Insurance." *American Economic Review* 7, no. 4: 541–559.

Topel, R. 1984. "Equilibrium Earnings, Turnover, and Unemployment. New Evidence." *Journal of Labor Economics* 2, no. 4: 500–522.

Topel, R. 1985. "Unemployment and Unemployment Insurance." In *Research in Labor Economics*, volume 7, ed. R. Ehrenberg. JAI.

Van den Berg, G. 1990. "Nonstationarity in Job Search Theory." *Review of Economic Studies* 57: 255–277.

Van den Berg, G., Van der Klaauw, B., and van Ours, J. 2004. "Punishing Welfare Recipients for Noncompliance with Job Search Guidelines." *Journal of Labor Economics*, forthcoming.

Winter-Ebmer, R. 1998a. "Potential Unemployment Benefit Duration and Spell Length: Lessons from a Quasi-Experiment in Austria." *Oxford Bulletin of Economics and Statistics* 60: 33–45.

Winter-Ebmer, R. 2003. "Benefit Duration and Unemployment Entry: Quasi-Experimental Evidence for Austria." *European Economic Review* 47: 259–273.

Wolpin, K. I. 1995. *Empirical Methods for the Study of Labor Force Dynamics*. Harwood.

3 Flexibility vs. Rigidity: Does Spain Have the Worst of Both Worlds?

Gilles Saint-Paul

Among European countries characterized by rigid labor markets, Spain is notable for a certain number of specific characteristics. First, over the last 25 years its unemployment rate has virtually been the highest in Europe, oscillating between 15 percent and an appalling 25 percent. Second, at face value it has one of the most rigid sets of institutions, in particular concerning the structure of collective bargaining and employment-protection legislation.[1] It differs from other European countries, however, in having implemented a far-reaching liberalization of employment protection regulation. This liberalization occurred in 1984, when, rather than reducing dismissal costs across the board, which would have been politically unfeasible, the government eased the use of temporary labor contracts.[2] Following this reform an employment boom occurred, where temporary contracts accounted for almost 95 percent of new hires, and quickly reached a 30 percent employment share. However, in the subsequent recession of the mid 1990s, employment dropped very quickly as firms could easily get rid of their temporary workers. In the end, there is no strong evidence that such a reform reduced unemployment.

This does not mean, however, that the reform has not affected the structure of the labor market. It is reasonable to speculate that it has increased labor turnover, and even absent a positive effect on the aggregate stock of unemployment, this may be considered as beneficial as the duration of unemployment is reduced.

In order to learn more about the effect of the reform, or more generally the specifics of the Spanish labor market compared to other European countries, this paper compares unemployment levels and transition rates by education, sex, and age groups for Spain, France, and the United States. We take France as a similar European-style country, but where reform has been much more timid, while the United States is the benchmark case of a competitive labor market.

Cohen et al. (1997) compared the structure of unemployment in France and in the United States. Surprisingly, they found quite similar unemployment rates by cells, thus ascribing a great deal of the unemployment differential between France and the United States to a composition effect due to the higher proportion of Americans who go to college. They have also shown that despite these similar unemployment rates, the labor market in France functioned quite differently from the US one, since the exit from unemployment was much lower in France, and consequently the duration of unemployment was much longer. The similar unemployment rates came from the fact that the job loss rate was also much smaller in France than in the United States, presumably because of more stringent job protection legislation and/ or a cultural aversion to dismissals.

We look at the same variables as Cohen et al., using a decomposition of the population into three age groups, the two sexes, and three education groups. We also systematically report the numbers they find in order to ease the comparison. Finally, we look at some deeper characteristics of the Spanish labor market such as duration dependence and unemployment recurrence.

At each stage, we provide some tentative interpretations of the empirical facts in light of recent economic theories regarding transitions between unemployment and temporary and permanent jobs, as well as the arbitrage between hiring employed vs. unemployed job seekers. These interpretations are not direct tests of any model, nor do they rule out alternative explanations.

The main message of the paper, discussed at greater length in the conclusion, is that the greater unemployment rate observed in Spain throughout the 1980s and most of the 1990s is mostly due to a greater job loss rate rather than a smaller job finding rate. This suggests that Spain has the "worst of both worlds," i.e., a low job finding rate as in economies with rigid labor-market institutions, and a high job loss rate as in economies with flexible labor markets.

Other findings suggest that the young are disproportionately exposed to job loss (as compared to other groups) in Europe relative to the United States, while they are not specifically disadvantaged in terms of job finding. We also find evidence of duration dependence in exit rates from unemployment, which has been documented elsewhere, as well as unemployment recurrence, i.e., that unemployment spells reduce the stability of subsequent jobs. Finally, there is evidence of a lower job finding rate for the unemployed job seekers compared to employed ones, which is in accordance with Kugler and Saint-Paul's (2004) argument on discrimination against unemployed job seekers in economies with high employment protection.

1 Composition of the Labor Force

Following Cohen et al., we start by looking at the composition of the labor force across cells defined by age, sex, and education. We use the 1994 Spanish labor force survey (EPA) and compare it to the 1989–1990 data used for France and the United States by Cohen et al. Note that the three economies experience similar growth rates during these years. Here we report the composition of the labor force split into three educational categories, which correspond to primary (E1), secondary (E2), and tertiary education (E3), respectively. When we will deal with Spain alone, we will further distinguish between vocational training and general training, as far as secondary education is concerned. But for the sake of comparison with France and the United States it is better to use three categories.

Cohen et al. could explain a large fraction of the unemployment differential between France and the United States by a composition effect. For example, for the core age group of male workers (ages 25–49), all of the unemployment differential was explained by the fact that on average French workers are less educated. The same was true for women provided one looked at non-employment rates rather than employment rates. In Spain, where the unemployment rate is almost twice as high as in France, there is no way one can explain high unemployment by a simple composition effect. However, the composition effect is present, since the composition of the workforce is different.

As can be seen in table 3.1, Spain turns out to be the least educated of the three, as one would have expected. The data for the 16–24 age group are more difficult to interpret, as a substantial fraction of them have not completed their studies, and therefore left out.

2 Unemployment Rates

We now turn to a comparison of unemployment rates across groups and countries. Table 3.2 reports unemployment rates by categories for males; table 3.3 does the same for females.[3]

Table 3.1
Composition of workforce (percent).

	France	US	Spain
All			
E1	35.9	16.7	45.05
E2	48.1	60.1	45
E3	15.7	23	9.925
25–49			
E1	30.6	11.6	40.55
E2	51.0	60.6	45.2
E3	18.5	27.7	14.1
50–64			
E1	58.0	22.8	83.5
E2	31.6	55.4	11.7
E3	10.4	21.7	5.2

Table 3.2
Male unemployment rates, by categories.

	France	US	Spain
16–24			
E1	27.8	17.4	44.2
E2	14.3	8.45	36
E3	8.0	3.3	52.7
25–49			
E1	10.8	10.8	18.7
E2	5.25	5.03	15.4
E3	2.6	2.4	11.1
50–64			
E1	11.1	6.6	13.5
E2	6	3.2	9.1
E3	4.0	1.9	2.6

Table 3.3
Female unemployment by categories.

	France	US	Spain
16–24			
E1	39.6	16.4	53
E2	23.1	8.4	48.8
E3	7.5	2.4	60.5
25–49			
E1	16.7	10.4	30.8
E2	10	4.4	32.8
E3	4.6	2.2	20.4
50–64			
E1	14.3	4.0	14.9
E2	10.1	2.64	17.4
E3	2.9	1.1	2.2

The similarities between France and the United States regarding the core age group obviously breaks down when Spain enters into the picture, as Spain has an unemployment rate about twice as high as France. Nevertheless the property that the young are the most harmed is true of Spain as of France. But the composition effect certainly explains a lower fraction of Spanish unemployment than when one compares France and the United States. Note, however, that the unemployment differential between the most and least educated in the core age group is 7 percent for men and 10 percent for women. The rapid improvement in the quality of the Spanish workforce documented in the previous section will therefore reduce unemployment by a substantial amount. Although the net effect crucially depends on elasticities of substitution across groups as well as the curvature of the wage formation schedule, a reasonable estimate is probably in the range of 2–5 percentage points.

It is also true that women have a higher unemployment rate than men in both France and Spain, but not in the United States. A variety of hypotheses can be formulated to explain such a difference—from pure discrimination to statistical discrimination, to greater incentives for women to register as unemployed rather than as out of the labor force. The latter explanation may be especially relevant given that Cohen et al. have found quite similar employment rates between French and American women.

Table 3.4 reports the "age gradient" of unemployment—i.e., the relative unemployment rate of the young vs. the middle-aged—for each educational group. This gradient is remarkably constant across categories when computed as a ratio and is highest in France and lowest in the United States, with Spain in the middle.

Next we perform a similar exercise by looking at the relative unemployment rate of the least educated. Our benchmark is not the most educated but the next category, as some specific phenomena might be going on for the best educated.

The ratios are somewhat more stable than when one looks at differentials according to age, but the results are striking. The ratio between unskilled and skilled unemployment is about 2 in both France and the United States, and just 1.2–1.3 for Spain. Tables 3.4 and 3.5 imply that, while in Europe it is the young who are hit the hardest by unemployment relative to other groups, in the United States it is the least educated. This may be ascribed to two factors. First, technology is less biased in favor of the skilled in Europe, and being unskilled is less of a handicap when there are more unskilled people around. Second, the two-tier style of labor-market reforms in Europe has concentrated the burden of flexibility on new entrants, especially the young but also women. This is confirmed by the next tables that look at labor-market flows.

Table 3.4
Age gradient.

	Absolute difference			Ratio		
	France	US	Spain	France	US	Spain
E1	17	6.6	25.5	2.57	1.6	2.36
E2	9.05	3.42	20.6	2.72	1.68	2.33
E3	4.7	0.9	41.6	2.42	1.4	4.74

Table 3.5
Skill gradient.

	Absolute difference			Ratio		
	France	US	Spain	France	US	Spain
16–24	13.5	8.95	8.2	1.94	2.06	1.23
25–49	5.55	5.77	3.3	2.05	2.15	1.21
50–64	5.1	3.4	4.4	1.85	2.06	1.48

3 Flows

We now compare workers flows across the three countries. Cohen et al. report monthly flows while our data only allow us to catch quarterly flows. In order to make the figures comparable we report the monthly flows consistent with our data under the hypothesis that hirings and separations follow a Poisson process. This is done by computing the "cubic root" of our estimated three-state transition matrix. That is, if we call the latter P, Q such that[4] $Q^3 = P$.

We start by comparing hiring rates, i.e., transitions from unemployment to employment.

The aggregate job finding rates tell us that Spain is more comparable to France than to the United States. The labor market for men is more active than its French counterpart, while the reverse holds for women. In both countries men's job finding rate is higher than women's, while the pattern is inverted in the United States. A variety of explanations can be put forward for that pattern (see below).

We then compare more deeply by disaggregating across groups.

A few remarkable features should be noted.

First, monthly hiring rates in Spain are similar in magnitude to their French counter-part that is, far below the US number.

Second, while for the core age group job finding rates are roughly increasing with education in France, they are declining in both Spain and the United States. This may result from the fact that better-educated people are either more choosy or more specialized. On the other hand, the increasing pattern found in France may be the result of a "ranking," or "overqualification" effect by which the most skilled are preferred over the least skilled for any given job. This effect dominates in France, while the former effects dominate in Spain and the United States.

Third, in all three countries there is no evidence that the young have any more difficulty in finding a job than older workers, a point already commented on by Cohen et al. The only exception is the E1 category

Table 3.6
Aggregate job-finding rates (percent per month).

	France	Spain	US
Males	5.97	7.24	23.8
Females	4.77	4.06	29.4

Table 3.7
Monthly hiring rates, males.

	France	US	Spain
16–24			
E1	8.3	26.5	7.8
E2	10.85	31.1	8.3
E3	9.7	40.0	4.9
25–49			
E1	5.2	30.0	8.0
E2	7.5	30.7	7.05
E3	8.15	22.4	5.1
50–64			
E1	1.0	36.7	5.6
E2	1.4	28.5	3.4
E3	3.0	14.8	6.5

in the United States, and the difference is not very large. This confirms the above made point that the young's greater unemployment rate is explained by the fact that they bear the burden of flexibility rather than any reluctance of employers to hire them, as would be suggested by theories blaming youth unemployment on the minimum wage.

Fourth, older workers are at a slight disadvantage in Spain and the United States, while the French data suggest they are almost excluded from the workforce, with hiring rates as low as 1 percent for the least educated. This is consistent with the very large wage loss found for these workers by Cohen et al. (1997) for France and Rosolia and Saint-Paul (1998) for Spain. The interesting question is why is France so different in terms of the treatment of 50–64-year-old workers. One possible explanation is the prevalence of early retirement schemes and of other labor-market policies that exclude the "old" to "make room for the young," based on the widespread fallacy that total employment is fixed.

Table 3.8 reports female hiring rates.

The Spanish data suggest that Spanish society is more "traditional" than either French or US society.

For the 16–24-year-olds, the job finding rates are comparable between men and women in all three countries, indeed higher for women in the most educated groups (as much as twice higher in France), perhaps because men elect more specialized occupations. Yet

Table 3.8
Hiring rates, females.

	France	US	Spain
16–24			
E1	7.0	24.2	5.9
E2	10	29.4	4.96
E3	21.3	50.0	6.4
25–49			
E1	4.2	22.1	3.5
E2	6.82	25.1	2.95
E3	8.4	27.2	1.0
50–64			
E1	0.7	16.2	2.8
E2	2.05	25.05	2.1
E3	1.5		0.0

even for the young the Spanish flows are typically lower for women than for men (except for the most educated group), whereas they are basically the same for men and women in France and the United States, and higher for women in the most educated groups.

In the core age group, hiring rates are quite similar across sexes in both France and the United States, while they are dramatically lower for women in Spain. This may be due to the fact that in Spain they do not search as intensively as men because they are more likely to be secondary earners (and also because the primary earner is less likely to be unemployed, as many Spanish studies show a very low unemployment rate for household heads); or to the fact that employers prefer male applicants (discrimination). The two explanations are not mutually exclusive.

It would be interesting to know whether the difference of hiring rates between young and middle-aged women is a cohort effect or an age effect. Do young women find jobs more quickly in Spain than older ones because "times are changing" or because women's attachment to the workforce goes down after childbearing?

We now turn to the analysis of job loss. Table 3.9 shows aggregate rates, and table 3.10 decomposes across groups. It is not clear in the paper by Cohen et al. whether job loss represents transitions from employment to unemployment or from employment to either unemployment or out of the labor force. Furthermore the concepts

Table 3.9
Aggregate job loss.

| | | | Spain | |
| | | | Lower | Upper |
	France	US	Bound	Bound
Males	0.5	2.84	1.47	2.07
Females	0.83	3.18	1.79	2.93

Table 3.10
Job loss rate, males.

| | | | Spain | |
| | | | Lower | Upper |
	France	US	Bound	Bound
16–24				
E1	3.2	10.8	5	6.1
E2	2.6	6.6	3.6	5.5
E3	1.2	1.3	3	10.5
E1	0.69	5.4	1.8	2.1
25–49				
E2	0.48	2.05	1.33	1.53
E3	0.38	1.3	0.5	0.7
50–64				
E1	1.1	3.6	0.6	1.6
E2	0.7	2.6	0.32	1.0
E3	0.52	1.55	0.2	0.6

might not be that easy to compare across countries. For this reason, for Spain we report both a lower bound which is the employment to unemployment flow, and an upper bound which is the outflow from employment.

A few very interesting patterns emerge from this table.

First, Spain, just like France, has much smaller job loss rates than the United States. This is clearly due to the more stringent job security legislation in Europe compared to the United States.

Second, however, job loss is much more likely to occur in Spain than in France. In other words, the higher Spanish unemployment compared to France seems much more due to high job loss than to low job finding. An obvious suspect for explaining that is the wide use of temporary contracts by Spanish firms. It looks as if they increased job destruction but not job creation! However, if it were the only story it would not explain why unemployment was so high before the liberalization of temporary contracts. One possible explanation is that then job creation was much lower, and that temporary contracts increased job creation and job destruction by similar proportions, leaving the overall unemployment rate essentially unchanged. But then, that would imply that absent temporary contracts, job finding rates would be much lower than in France, a feature difficult to interpret given the then similar labor-market institutions and macroeconomic stance. More information could be obtained by looking at flows before the reform (i.e., before 1984), but this runs into the difficulty that the labor-force survey has a panel structure only since 1986, and the panel dimension is essential in order to compute flows.

Third, overall Spain reproduces the features of the other economies, namely a job loss rate that is falling with age and education (while the job finding rate is less sensitive to education). Note however that in both France and Spain, the job loss rate for young workers is 3–6 times greater than for the middle-aged, while in the United States it is 1–3 times greater. Thus in Europe the young's jobs are much more precarious relative to the middle-aged than in the United States, confirming our point that they bear the burden of flexibility.

Finally, women's job loss rate is higher than men's in all three countries, with the relative difference being perhaps highest in France.

4 Non-stationarity in Hazard Rates

Our data allow us to compute transition rates both on a quarterly basis and on a yearly basis. One can therefore compute the difference between yearly transition rates and their predicted values under the assumption that transition probabilities per unit of time are constant— i.e., under the assumption that the underlying process is Markov.

Discrepancies between the two may stem from several sources. Consider for example the exit from unemployment into employment ("job finding"). If we find that job finding over a horizon of one year is lower than predicted by the Markov model, this may be an indication that exit rates from unemployment are falling with the duration of the unemployment spell (*negative duration dependence*). But it may also mean that the jobs found by unemployed people are more precarious—i.e., have a higher death rate—than the average of the economy, so that a greater fraction of them will be back to unemployment after one year. We call that phenomenon *unemployment recurrence*.

For any two states A and B, we define as the *path dependence index* for the flow from A to B the following quantity:

$$PDI_{AB} = 1 - \frac{Y_{AB}}{Y_{AB}^{\text{Markov}}},$$

where Y_{AB} is the transition rate from A to B computed on a yearly basis and Y_{AB}^{Markov} is its predicted value on the basis of the quarterly transition matrix raised at the fourth power. A positive index implies that $Y_{AB} < Y_{AB}^{\text{Markov}}$. This means that conditional on what happens meanwhile, being in unemployment at t typically increases the probability of being unemployed one year from t. Path dependence reflects both the contribution of duration dependence and unemployment recurrence. These two phenomena may in turn be either "genuine"—i.e., a given person has lower chances to find a job if he or she has been unemployed longer—or reflect unobserved heterogeneity—i.e., long-term unemployed have a lower quality on average and therefore a lower exit rate.

4.1 Path Dependence in Spain

We first compute our path dependence index for the various categories of the Spanish economy. We now use a decomposition into four educational groups, splitting group E2 into general and vocational training.

Tables 3.11 and 3.12 summarize the path dependence index for men, for job loss and job finding respectively. Tables 3.13 and 3.14 give the same information for women; these figures are very unreliable for women older than 50 because there are only few people in each cell; we therefore do not report the results for that group.

The stylized facts are the following:

1. Transitions from employment to unemployment exhibit *positive* path dependence both for men and women. This means that job loss falls as tenure increases; or that people who just lost their jobs are back into the employment pool more quickly than the average of the unemployed, perhaps because of negative duration dependence of exit rates from unemployment.

Table 3.11
Path dependence in male job-loss rate.

	Yearly inflow	Yearly equivalent	P.D.I.
16–24			
E1	17.8	28.4	0.37
E2.1	11.3	17.7	0.36
E2.2	11.7	18.4	0.36
E3	10.8	18.5	0.41
25–49			
E1	6.6	12.1	0.45
E2.1	4.9	10.3	0.52
E2.2	3.7	8.7	0.57
E3	1.9	4.6	0.59
50–64			
E1	3.4	4.4	0.22
E2.1	1.7	3.1	0.45
E2.2	3.1	2.9	−0.06
E3	0.8	2.1	0.61

Table 3.12
Path dependence in job-finding rates, men.

	Yearly outflow	Yearly equivalent	P.D.I.
16–24			
E1	29.5	42.8	0.31
E2.1	32.9	39.5	0.17
E2.2	32.6	40.4	0.19
E3	20.8	21.2	0.02
25–49			
E1	35.4	54.9	0.35
E2.1	37	52.3	0.29
E2.2	35.4	54.6	0.35
E3	27.3	42.4	0.36
50–64			
E1	19.2	37.9	0.49
E2.1	17.9	24.6	0.27
E2.2	22.2	41.7	0.46
E3	25	53.5	0.53

Table 3.13
Path dependence in female job-loss rate.

	Yearly inflow	Yearly equivalent	P.D.I.
16–24			
E1	21.2	24.1	0.12
E2.1	14.9	22.2	0.32
E2.2	14.1	25.1	0.43
E3	13.1	40.1	0.67
25–49			
E1	5.9	12.1	0.51
E2.1	5.8	11.8	0.51
E2.2	5.8	15.5	0.62
E3	3.9	8.3	0.53

Table 3.14
Path dependence in job-finding rates, women.

	Yearly outflow	Yearly equivalent	P.D.I.
16–24			
E1	19.2	34.8	0.44
E2.1	22.1	25.3	0.126
E2.2	23.7	27.7	0.144
E3	28.8	27.5	−0.04
25–49			
E1	15.9	24.3	0.34
E2.1	14.1	24	0.41
E2.2	14.1	21.2	0.33
E3	24.6	29.8	0.17

2. Exits from unemployment also exhibit path dependence for both men and women.

3. For both men and women, path dependence is typically *increasing* with education as far as *job loss* is concerned. This suggests that accumulation of specific human capital on the job is more important for workers with higher education, implying a steeper negative effect of tenure on the job loss rate. The case of young women is particularly salient. For this group, job loss is increasing with education on a quarterly basis but falling on a yearly basis.

Table 3.15
Quarterly job-loss rate by tenure, men.

	Tenure	
	0	2
16–24		
E1	16.4	14.4
E2.1	12.9	11.2
E2.2	11.7	10.1
E3	8.6	7.3
25–49		
E1	10.1	8.7
E2.1	7.7	6.5
E2.2	6.8	5.7
E3	4.8	4.0
50–64		
E1	7.7	6.5
E2.1	5.7	4.7
E2.2	5.0	4.2
E3	3.5	2.8

4. For men, path dependence in job finding rates does not depend on education, except for the young where it is clearly decreasing with education. This suggests that unemployment recurrence and/or negative duration dependence is more pronounced at low education levels, for the young, while for older workers it seems to be evenly distributed across educational levels. For women, path dependence in job finding rates decreases with education for both the young and the middle-aged.

In order to measure the phenomenon of unemployment recurrence, i.e., to separate it from duration dependence as a source of path dependence, we have estimated a probit regression explaining the probability of losing one's job as a function of the worker's characteristics.[5] This is obviously a gross way of testing for recurrence, as ideally one would prefer to condition over the whole labor-market history of the worker. However, because of the limited panel dimension of the Spanish Labor Force Survey, we restrict ourselves to tenure in the current job. The results confirm a declining dependence of job loss with respect to tenure. Table 3.15 illustrates the effect. The effect is relatively modest.

Therefore, while there is evidence of unemployment recurrence in Spain, it does not seem to be a very important phenomenon quantitatively, even though fresh hires are more likely to hold a temporary contract. The bulk of path dependence is explained by duration dependence, a phenomenon widely documented elsewhere (see e.g. Bover and Gomez 1999). That is, while the long-term unemployed have trouble finding jobs, unemployment spells do not seem to result in a state of "precariousness," with frequent spells between employment and unemployment.

5   Discrimination between Employed and Unemployed Job Seekers

Another important aspect of the labor market that we have neglected up to now is the pattern of job-to-job mobility. In a rigid labor market we expect increased job to job mobility to partly make up for reduced mobility from unemployment to employment, because workers who want to change jobs are reluctant to go through a period of unemployment and prefer to search on the job instead. Furthermore, as Kugler and Saint-Paul (2004) argue, labor-market rigidities induce employers to prefer hiring employed job seekers over unemployed ones because employment protection regulation makes them more sensitive to unobserved worker quality—i.e., hiring an employed job seeker provides insurance against bad worker quality. The basic intuition is that low-ability workers are more likely to lose their jobs than high-ability ones, so that the pool of unemployed workers is of lower quality than the pool of employed job seekers. Absent employment-protection legislation hiring someone is a one way bet as one can always get rid of the worker if he or she turned out to be of low quality. The more stringent that legislation, the more employers are reluctant to take the risk of hiring an unemployed worker, and the lower the exit rate of the unemployed relative to the employed.

To what extent is that phenomenon present in the Spanish labor market? To measure it we just compute the ratio between the quarterly exit rate from unemployment and the job finding rate of employed job seekers, as defined by those employed workers who state that they are looking for another job in the EPA questionnaire. We call this ratio the *Unemployment Discrimination Indicator*. The lower that indicator, the greater the (statistical) discrimination against the unemployed. Table 3.16 reports the results, where again we only use three employment categories.

Table 3.16
Unemployment Discrimination Indicator.

	Men	Women
16–24		
E1	0.56	0.51
E2	0.62	0.43
E3	0.40	0.5
25–49		
E1	0.57	0.32
E2	0.54	0.26
E3	0.44	0.36
50–65		
E1	0.38	0.39
E2	0.17	0.14

Table 3.16 clearly confirms that the unemployed have a lower probability to find a job than employed job seekers, with a ratio of about 0.5. Another interesting aspect is that at least for men, discrimination against the unemployed increases with the worker's education. At face value, this may sound paradoxical because one might believe rigidities to be more binding for less educated workers. We suspect that our results indicate that unobserved ability is more of an issue at higher education levels. Interestingly, this does not seem to be so much true for women.

To further deepen our understanding of this phenomenon, we distinguish according to the type of contract of the new job. It is well known that the Spanish labor market has temporary and permanent workers, with the majority of new hires being on temporary contracts. A priori one might expect employers to be more reluctant to give a permanent contract to an unemployed job seeker, since the employer is more likely to regret such a decision due to the expected lower quality of the pool of applicants. Hence, we expect the proportion of temporary contracts in a new job to be higher for unemployed job seekers than for employed job seekers, or, equivalently, that the unemployment discrimination indicator is lower in permanent contracts than in temporary ones.

Tables 3.17 and 3.18 test that hypothesis by comparing the share of temporary contracts in new jobs for both employed and unemployed applicants. These tables confirm the earlier findings of the literature,

Table 3.17
Share of temporary contracts in new jobs according to job seekers' characteristics, men.

	Unemployed	Employed
16–24		
E1	91.11	97.0
E2	96.05	94.5
E3	86.9	94.6
25–49		
E1	91.6	93.8
E2	89.1	93.3
E3	79.5	84.7
50–65		
E1	91.4	93.1
E2	87.5	88.5
E3	66.7	71.4

Table 3.18
Share of temporary contracts in new jobs according to job seekers' characteristics, women.

	Unemployed	Employed
16–24		
E1	86.7	92.7
E2	90.9	93.7
E3	93.6	95.1
25–49		
E1	86.1	92.7
E2	89.6	92.0
E3	90.1	88.7
50–65		
E1	81.6	87.3
E2	55.6	80.9
E3	75.0	80

namely that temporary contracts account for the vast majority of new hires. More interestingly, with the exception of older women for whom there are too few observations to draw any confident conclusion, the results go strikingly against our prior belief. The fraction of new jobs that are temporary is systematically higher for employed job seekers than for unemployed job seekers. This may indicate that discrimination by the employer is not an important phenomenon, and that the lower job finding probability of the unemployed job seekers may be due to other factors, such as the disincentive effects of unemployment benefits. Another interpretation, however, is that workers differ across their (unobservable) preference for job duration, so that those who prefer long jobs will turn down offers more often and will represent a greater fraction of the unemployed. Because of this composition effect the unemployed are more likely to end up with a permanent contract than employed job seekers. Hence, in order to capture the pure effect of discrimination, it would be necessary to come up with a proxy for the unobservable taste for secure jobs.

Conclusion

We have highlighted a number of facts regarding the anatomy of the Spanish labor market at the beginning of the 1990s. We have discussed these facts in light of a number of possible interpretations. While these interpretations are speculative in that they are not directly tested and that alternative ones are not ruled out, the analysis yields a number of conclusions.

First, and most importantly, the large unemployment differential between France and Spain is mostly explained by a much larger job loss rate in Spain compared to France rather than a smaller job finding rate. Indeed, the job finding rate is also higher in Spain, but only marginally, while the job loss rate is substantially higher, putting Spain half-way between France and the United States.

This suggests that Spain has the "worst of both worlds," namely a job creation rate similar to that of a "rigid economy" and a job destruction rate comparable to that of a flexible one. Therefore, while employers do take advantage of the margin of flexibility allowed by temporary contracts at the time of firing, they do not consider that their availability reduces labor costs significantly. Following an argument developed by Bertola and Ichino (1996), one may speculate that this is due to the reform lacking credibility. That is, firms have been unsure about whether the reform would not be overturned, with some discretionary tightening of the conditions under which temporary contracts may be used. Consequently, they have been cautious when hiring people, fearing that firing restrictions might be increased between now and the time they might want to get rid of their workers. While lower firing costs increase dismissals right away, it is the *expectation* of lower firing costs in the future which increases hirings. The impact of the reduction in firing costs on hirings is lower, the less confident are firms that the reform will not be overturned. Hence, for a reduction in employment protection to increase hirings, it is fundamental for the reform to be *credible*. To be sure, a tightening of the conditions under which temporary contracts may be used need not affect existing temporary contracts at the time it takes place. However, some restrictions will, like limitations on the possibility to renew such contracts. Clearly, expectations of such restrictions in the future may lower the number of temporary jobs being currently created.

Second, the young suffer more from unemployment *relative* to the middle-aged in both Spain and France compared to the United States (where it is also true that they suffer more). It is often believed that this is due to rigidities such as the minimum wage which make it too costly for employers to hire youngsters. Our data on flows suggest that this interpretation is wrong. In fact, in all three countries a young unemployed person is *more likely* to find a job than a middle-aged. Their greater unemployment rate is explained by a greater *inflow* into unemployment, not a smaller outflow. We interpret that finding as evidence that in France and Spain the bulk of flexibility has been concentrated on young people.

Third, we find evidence of *path dependence* in labor-market transitions. This means that an unemployed worker is more likely to be in unemployment a year from now than his monthly exit rate would suggest. This feature may be due to either *duration dependence*, i.e., falling exit rates with the length of the unemployment spell, or *unemployment recurrence*, i.e. a higher job loss rate in one's next job than if the person had not gone through an unemployment spell. While duration dependence is documented by the existing literature, we find that unemployment recurrence is also present, although it does not appear to be a very strong phenomenon. This is somewhat surprising in the light of the presumption that a worker is very likely to exit unemployment with a temporary contract, and suggests that these contracts have not concentrated the burden of mobility on a subset of people who would move between employment and unemployment[6] (abstracting from the age dimension). Otherwise, one would probably have observed stronger unemployment recurrence.

Finally, there is evidence that the unemployed are twice less successful at finding jobs than employed job seekers. We interpret this as employers giving preference to employed applicants in their hiring decisions. According to Kugler and Saint-Paul (2004), this discrimination against the unemployed is due to employment-protection legislation; it explains why job-to-job moves account for a much greater fraction of worker reallocation in Europe compared to the United States; it also suggests that a reduction in employment-protection legislation would reduce employers' discrimination against the unemployed.

Acknowledgments

I thank Alfonso Rosolia for research assistance, as well as the Direction de la Prévision, ministère des finances, Paris, and fundacion BBV for financial support. Comments from Alfons Weichenrieder and an anonymous referee are gratefully acknowledged.

Notes

1. See Blanchard et al. 1995.

2. For accounts of this episode, see Bentolila et al. 1991; Bentolila and Saint-Paul 1992; Bentolila and Dolado 1994; Jimeno and Toharia 1992.

3. Sources for all tables: Cohen et al. 1997 for France and the US; our computations from the EPA survey for Spain. The years were 1989 for USA, 1990 for France, and 1994 for Spain, implying similar growth rates of about 2.5 percent.

4. In practice this is done by first diagonalizing $P : MFM^{-1}$, where F is diagonal, and computing Q as $Q = M\Phi M^{-1}$, where Φ is a diagonal matrix with coefficients equal to the cubic roots of the coefficients of F.

5. In order to increase the quality of the econometric results, the estimation was carried for years 1992, 1994, and 1996 pooled.

6. This is also the conclusion reached by Alba-Ramirez (1998).

References

Alba Ramirez, A. 1997. How Temporary Is Temporary Employment in Spain? Working paper 97-14, Universidad Carlos III, Madrid.

Bentolila, S., and J. Dolado. 1994. "Labor flexibility and wages: Lessons from Spain." *Economic Policy* 18: 53–99.

Bentolila, S., and G. Saint-Paul. 1992. "The macroeconomic impact of flexible labor contracts, with an application to Spain." *European Economic Review* 36, no. 5: 1013–1047.

Bertola, G., and A. Ichino. 1995. "Crossing the river." *Economic Policy* 21: 359–415.

Blanchard, O., J. Jimeno, J. Andres, C. Bean, E. Malinvaud, A. Revenga, G. Saint-Paul, D. Snower, R. Solow, D. Taguas, and L. Toharia. 1995. Spanish Unemployment: Is There a Solution? CEPR.

Bover, O., and R. Gomez. 1999. Nuevos resultados sobre la duracion del desempleo: El paro de larga duracion y la salida a un empleo fij. Documento de trabajo 99-03, Servicio de Estudios, Banco de España.

Cohen, D., A. Lefranc, and G. Saint-Paul. 1997. "French unemployment: A transatlantic perspective." *Economic Policy* 25: 265–285.

Garcia Perez, J. I. 1997. "Las tasas de salida del empleo y el desempleo en Espana." *Investigaciones Economicas* 21, no. 1: 29–53.

Jimeno, J., and L. Toharia. 1991. Productivity and Wage Effects of Temporary Employment Contracts. Mimeo, FEDEA.

Kugler, A., and G. Saint-Paul. 2004. "Hiring and Firing costs, adverse selection, and long-term unemployment." *Journal of Labor Economics*, forthcoming.

Rosolia, A., and G. Saint-Paul. 1998. The Effects of Unemployment Spells on Subsequent Wages in Spain. Working paper, Department of Economics, Universitat Pompeu Fabra.

Segura, J., F. Duran, L. Toharia, and S. Bentolila. 1991. *Analisis de la contratacion temporal en Espana*. Madrid: Ministerio de Trabajo.

4

Are Education Subsidies an Efficient Redistributive Device?

Robert Dur and Coen N. Teulings

Throughout the Western world, education is heavily subsidized. Public expenditures on education amount to some 6 percent of GDP on average in OECD countries and make up a considerable share of total public expenditures. Public policy regarding education typically has a broad character. Subsidies are not confined to primary education; secondary and higher education are also heavily subsidized. Moreover, governments do not only support schooling opportunities of the disadvantaged. In practice, government programs that encourage education also favor the rich. This chapter is concerned with the question of whether governments should subsidize education so heavily and comprehensively.

The economics literature offers two main arguments for subsidies to education. Neither of them can fully account for the wide prevalence of education subsidies. First, the endogenous growth literature has emphasized that investment in human capital may have positive spillover effects in production (Lucas 1988; Tamura 1991). As these externalities are not taken into account in individual schooling decisions, education subsidies are needed to prevent underinvestment in education and to promote economic growth. The externality argument calls for subsidies directed to all educational levels and all individuals in as far as externalities are present. However, the evidence for positive externalities is mixed (Acemoglu and Angrist 1999; Bils and Klenow 2000; Krueger and Lindahl 2000; Teulings and Van Rens 2002). Second, several studies have stressed the role of capital-market imperfections in limiting the educational opportunities of the disadvantaged (Saint-Paul and Verdier 1993; Perotti 1993; Benabou 2000, 2002). This argument is hard to reconcile with the comprehensiveness of government subsidies to education. If education subsidies only serve to attain equality of opportunity, subsidies targeted at the disadvantaged would be sufficient. Moreover, the empirical evidence for borrowing constraints in educational choices is limited (Cameron and Heckman 1998, 1999; Keane and Wolpin 2001; Shea 2000; Cameron and Taber 2000).

In this chapter, we discuss a new rationale for education subsidies. In the spirit of Tinbergen (1975), we argue that education subsidies may be a part of an optimal redistribution policy. Our argument hinges on general-equilibrium effects of an increase in the formation of human capital. When workers of different skill levels are imperfect substitutes in production, an increase in the mean level of human capital in the economy reduces the return to human capital. The supply of high-skilled workers goes up, reducing their relative wages, while the supply of low-skilled workers goes down, increasing their relative wages. Hence, the return to human capital (the difference between these two wage levels) and pre-tax wage inequality go down. The reduction in pre-tax income inequality implies that a given after-tax income distribution can be reached with less progressive income taxes. Hence, by promoting education, the distortionary cost of progressive taxation may be reduced. Optimal redistribution policy faces a trade-off between the distortions arising from education subsidies and the distortionary effect of income taxation.

Following Becker's (1983) efficient redistribution hypothesis, our analysis contributes to the understanding of observed institutions. Insofar as the political system has an incentive to consume Pareto-improving policy reforms, our model provides a positive theory of the tax structure: observed institutions should be constrained Pareto efficient. We present some empirical evidence that observed institutions fit our model reasonably well. Our theory predicts a correlation between the progressivity of the income tax and the level of education subsidies. We present data which give some support to this hypothesis. The level of this correlation and the average level of education subsidies, 6 percent of GDP, correspond surprisingly well with the predictions of the model for reasonable parameter values. Also, our model explains why cross-country differences in the dispersion of disposable income are primarily due to differences in the dispersion of gross income, not to differences in the progressivity of the tax system.

Our theoretical analysis stands in the tradition of Mirrlees's (1971) Nobel Prize winning paper on optimal income taxation. Mirrlees considers the case where worker types are perfect substitutes, so that relative wages for various ability types are independent of supply and demand. Imperfect substitution between worker types is crucial for our analysis. Feldstein (1973) analyzed this problem, and a whole 1982 issue of the *Journal of Public Economics* is devoted to the issue (Allen 1982; Stern 1982; Stiglitz 1982). The conclusion of these early contributions is that imperfect substitution between types of labor does not make a great deal of difference for realistic values of the elasticity of substitution. Our claim is that this conclusion is largely due to an unresolved technical problem. Where Mirrlees applied a continuous type distribution for the perfect substitution case, a continuous type production function with imperfect substitution was not available. Hence, a production function with a discrete number of types (in practice, two types; see Johnson 1984 for a model with three types) was applied. Teulings (2000) shows that using a production function with only two instead of a continuum of types yields a seriously downwardly biased estimate of the spill-over effects of minimum wages. Our claim is that the same problem applies for general-equilibrium effects of an increase in the mean level of human capital, since large shifts in relative wages within each of the types are ignored.

Our analysis calls for subsidies to all levels of education. This redistribution policy contrasts sharply with the usual idea of compressing the wage distribution via compression of the distribution of human capital, that is by putting special policy effort in raising the education of the least skilled. This latter policy relies on direct, partial equilibrium effects of investment in human capital. However, it is unclear why a subsidy to the human-capital acquisition of the poor would dominate generic income support. Standard economic theory suggests it does not. Moreover, subsidies to the human-capital acquisition of the poor might run into trouble due to adverse general-equilibrium effects. By a standard supply-and-demand argument, the additional human capital in the lower tail of the skill distribution is likely to reduce the wages for these skill types. Empirical evidence on the relation between the income distribution and the distribution of human capital in a panel of countries supports these ideas. There is a strong negative relation between the mean level of education and income inequality, supporting the general-equilibrium effect, but there seems to be no relation between the variance of education and income inequality, not supporting the direct effect. These findings suggest that the promotion of education at all levels contributes more to a progressive income policy than a policy focused at the low levels only.

However, there is a counterforce that limits the redistributive virtues of subsidies to education. The large literature on the ability bias in the return to education shows that education and innate ability are complementary (Angrist and Krueger 1991). Subsidies to all levels of education favor therefore predominantly the high-ability types, leading to a widening instead of a compression of the income distribution. We face the remarkable situation that the role of the direct effect on income (or utility) and the substitution effect in redistribution are reversed. Usually, redistribution is brought about by the direct effect of a policy on income (e.g., in the case of progressive income taxation), while the substitution effect (less productive effort) reduces its effectiveness. For education subsidies, it is the other way around. Substitution effects contribute to redistribution, while the direct effect on income works in the opposite direction. We derive the condition for education subsidies to be redistributive. Furthermore, we discuss some more elaborate schemes for education subsidies which reduce the adverse direct effect on income, while maintaining their favorable substitution effect.

Section 1 presents the main elements of our theoretical model, based on previous work, see Dur and Teulings 2001. Section 2 reviews the empirical evidence on three crucial elasticities in our model: elasticities of supply and demand for human capital and the degree of complementarity between education and innate ability. Section 3 analyzes the optimal redistribution policy. First, we discuss efficient redistribution policy in the absence of complementarity between ability and education. We present some crude empirical evidence regarding the relation between education subsidies and the progressivity of the tax system. Next, we examine how optimal policy is affected by the complementarity between ability and education. Section 4 discusses some further implications of our analysis. Four issues are at stake here. First, we discuss the proper level of centralization of education policy. As the effectiveness of education as a redistribution policy rests on an externality in schooling decisions, education policy should be sufficiently centralized for all externalities to be internalized. Second, we analyze the consequences of a lack of commitment on the side of the government regarding its income policy, which limits its capability to credibly internalize the externalities. Third, we discuss more elaborate schemes for education subsidies that help to reduce the adverse direct effect on the income distribution due to the complementarity between ability and education. Finally, we discuss the role of non-linearities in the income policy.

1   The Model of the Economy

Our theoretical analysis follows previous work, see Dur and Teulings 2001. The reader who wants to understand the formal details of the analysis should consult that reference. Here, we use a more intuitive presentation. In order to provide a clear-cut separation between our model and models based on imperfections in the capital market, we assume perfect capital and insurance markets. Individuals can borrow sufficient funds to finance their consumption during their years of education at the going interest rate. Also, they can insure perfectly the risk on their investment in human capital due to the uncertainty about their life expectancy. For the sake of simplicity, we ignore the direct cost of education and focus on the cost of forgone labor income. This fits the empirical observation that the direct cost of education are, relatively, of minor importance. Individuals choose their years of schooling as to maximize their lifetime utility. Hence, individuals invest in human capital up to the point where the marginal cost equals the market rate of return to human capital. For the transparency of the analysis, we abstract from imperfections in the labor market. We also abstract from production externalities in schooling decisions, like knowledge spill-overs. Workers therefore earn their marginal product of labor and there is no unemployment. Furthermore, these assumptions imply that the private return to education (i.e., the effect on wages) is equal to the social return (i.e., the effect on GDP). Finally, types of labor are the only factors of production.

Our economy consists of individuals who are born with different levels of innate ability, which we denote by a. They spend the first years h of their life at school. These two factors, innate ability and years of schooling, jointly determine the human capital or skill level s with which the worker enters the labor market. After the investment in human capital, individuals start their working career. The individual's log wage rate $w(s, \mu)$ per unit of effort depends on the individual's human capital s and on μ, the mean level of human capital among the workers in the economy. The partial derivative of log wages $\partial w / \partial s$ is the Mincerian rate of return to human capital. Gross income is the product of this wage rate and the effort the individual chooses to provide. Individuals set effort as to maximize their utility. We follow Diamond (1998) in simplifying the analysis by applying a utility function that is additive in the cost of effort and consumption. This additive specification rules out income effects on the supply of effort. The supply of effort of a worker is therefore increasing in her (net) wage rate.

Subsequently, we discuss the two most important building blocks of our model, the production function of human capital and relative wages, more extensively. For this discussion, it is useful to define a benchmark equilibrium of this economy. For this, we take the non-interventionist, redistribution free equilibrium, where the government does not implement any income policy, so that the income distribution is fully determined by market forces. Without loss of generality, we normalize our measure of human capital s such that in this redistribution free equilibrium, its Mincerian rate of return to human capital is unity, $\partial w / \partial s \equiv w_s = 1$, and its mean is equal to zero, $\mu = 0$. We shall apply one further normalization in this redistribution free equilibrium below.

1.1 Production of Human Capital

The human capital of a worker is a function of two inputs, the worker's innate ability, a, and the worker's years of education, h:

$$s(a, h) = a + (\beta h - \xi a) - \tfrac{1}{2} \psi (\beta h - \xi a)^2 \qquad (1)$$

where β, ξ, and ψ are (weakly) positive parameters. Without loss of generality, we normalize the ability measure a such that in this redistribution free equilibrium $\beta h - \xi a = 0$. The marginal return of an additional year of schooling is given by the partial derivative of $s(a, h)$ with respect to h:

$$s_h = \beta[1 - \psi(\beta h - \xi a)]. \qquad (2)$$

Since $\beta h - \xi a = 0$ in the redistribution free equilibrium, β measures the marginal return to a year of education, $s_h = \beta$. The term $-\psi(\beta h - \xi a)$ in equation (2) captures two essential features of the model, the decreasing returns to education, $s_{hh} \leq 0$, and complementarity of ability and education, $s_{ha} \geq 0$. Both features are discussed in some detail.

The decreasing returns to education provide an interpretation of the parameter ψ in the redistribution free equilibrium:

$$-\frac{d \ln s_h}{w_s s_h \, dh} = -\frac{s_{hh}}{w_s s_h^2} = \psi \qquad (3)$$

since $w_s = 1$ and $s_h = \beta$ in the redistribution free equilibrium. The numerator of the left-hand side is the relative change in the return to education, its denominator is the relative change in the value of the human capital of the worker, evaluated at market prices (since $w_s s_h \, dh$ measures the effect a change dh in the years of education on the log wage w). In the redistribution free equilibrium, workers set Mincerian rate of return to a year of education, $w_s s_h$, equal to its price. Hence, ψ^{-1} is the *price elasticity of the supply of human capital*: the percentage change in the value of human capital per percent change in its price.[2]

The parameter ξ captures the complementarity between ability and education. When $\xi = 0$, the marginal return to a year of education (keeping h fixed) does not depend on innate ability. Hence, optimal years of schooling is independent of innate ability. When $\xi > 0$, people with higher innate ability benefit more from schooling and, hence, they take up more years of schooling. We offer a simple interpretation of ξ. Consider equation (2). Workers choose their optimal years of education as to equate the marginal cost and revenue of a year of education. In the redistribution free equilibrium,

$$\frac{w_s s_h}{\lambda} = 1, \tag{4}$$

where λ is the sum of the interest rate and the rate of depreciation of the human. Most studies suggest that λ is around 10 percent. Let W be the wage level. The wage gain of an additional year of education is $W w_s s_h$. The lifetime revenue of an additional year of education is the net discounted value of this wage increase, using λ as the discount rate. The cost of an additional year is the forgone labor income W. Dividing both sides by W yields equation (4).[3] Workers set h such that $s_h = \lambda / w_s$, which is independent of h in the redistribution free equilibrium, since w_s is independent of h by assumption. Since s_h is independent of h, $\beta h - \xi a$ must be constant (see equation 2), or equivalently, years of education is a function of ability $h(a)$ with $dh(a)/da = \xi/\beta > 0$. By equation (1),

$$s(a, h) = a + \text{constant},$$

$$\frac{ds[a, h(a)]}{da} = s_a + s_h \frac{dh}{da} = s_a + \frac{\xi}{\beta} s_h = 1.$$

In this world, we would never be able to estimate the "true" return to education s_h, even if we had perfect information on the worker's ability. This is the case of a complete *ability bias in the return to education*. Ability and schooling are perfectly collinear in market equilibrium, since $h(a)$ is a function of a. Hence, we have no independent variation of h. Any variation in $s(a, h)$ can be equally well attributed to variation in year of education h as to variation in ability a.

Let us suppose that, from the point of view of the researcher, this is too gloomy a picture of the real world. Workers do not set their years of education exactly as predicted by the model, so that there is some random variation in h independent of a. Some workers have some kind of special preference for education, and choose therefore to take more education. Others simply make small optimization mistakes. This type of randomness in h would resolve the multicollinearity problem and allow us to identify s_a and s_h separately, with $s_a = 1 - \xi$.[4] This suggests a simple trick to estimate ξ. We can approximate s by log wages w. Consider the coefficients on ability in two log wage regressions, one with only ability as regressor, and another with both ability and years of education. The ratio of both regression coefficients should be equal to

$$\frac{s_a}{ds[a, h(a)]/da} = 1 - \xi.$$

We apply this methodology to obtain a rough estimate of ξ in subsection 2.3. However, this equation also provides an interpretation of ξ: it is the share of the return to ability that can only be realized by exploiting the complementarity of ability and education. Without education, a fraction ξ of the potential return to ability would be lost.

1.2 Production and Relative Wages
The wage rates for each skill type s depend on their supply and demand. Labor supply is determined by the distribution of innate ability and the production of human capital. Labor demand is determined by the aggregate production function, such that the wages for each skill type are equal to their marginal productivity in market equilibrium. We simplify the analysis by constructing the production function such that log wages $w(s, \mu)$ are linear in s:

$$w(s, \mu) = w_0(\mu) + \exp(-\gamma\mu)s, \tag{5}$$

where γ is a (weakly) positive parameter. This relation is derived from assignment or matching models in the tradition of Rosen (1974), Sattinger (1975), and Teulings (1995). In the appendix, we offer a formal derivation. The Mincerian rate of return to human capital is equal to the partial derivative of log wages:

$$w_s = \exp(-\gamma\mu).$$

The rate of return is a decreasing function of the mean level of human capital in the economy, μ. This captures the imperfect substitutability between workers with various degrees of human capital. Were workers perfect substitutes, γ would be equal to zero and relative wages would be independent of the supply of human capital in the economy.

This representation of imperfect substitution deviates from the commonly used CES production function with two broad types of labor: high-skilled and low-skilled (see, for example, Katz and Murphy 1992). In such a two-type framework, the full burden of imperfect substitution is put at the borderline between two broad types, since within each broad type workers are perfect substitutes. Hence, relative wages can only change between broad types, not within. Our interpretation allows for a continuum of worker types, each endowed with its own level of human capital s and with its own wage rate. In our economy these workers have to be assigned to jobs, which differ by their complexity, see Teulings 2002. The driving force of this model is the Ricardian concept of comparative advantage: high-skilled workers have a comparative advantage in complex jobs since skills have a greater effect on worker productivity in more complex jobs. In the Walrasian equilibrium, high-skilled workers will therefore be assigned to more complex jobs, where their skills yield the highest return. A general increase in the level of human capital reduces the return to human capital, since high-skilled workers have to do less complex jobs, where their human capital has a lower return. Alternatively, an increase in the mean of the skill distribution μ raises the supply of high-skilled workers, thereby reducing wages for the high-skilled, and reduces the supply of low-skilled workers, thereby raising wages for the low-skilled. Hence, the return to human capital, and thus wage dispersion, decrease when the mean level of human capital goes up. The size of this effect depends on the degree of substitutability between skill types. The smaller the degree of substitutability, as measured by γ, the more the return to human capital decreases for a given increase in the stock of human capital.

This model exhibits the Distance Dependent Elasticity of Substitution (DIDES) structure: the larger the "distance" of two types in terms of their level of human capital, the lower the substitutability between worker types. The situation is illustrated in figure 4.1. When an

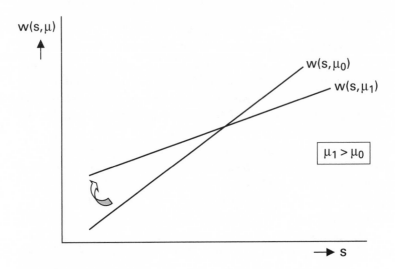

Figure 4.1
Twisting of the wage function.

individual worker raises her human capital from s to $s + d\mu$ while all
other workers keep their human capital constant, her wage goes up by
$w_s(\mu)\,d\mu$, which is a shift along the curve. However, when all workers
do the same, there is an additional, general-equilibrium effect, shown
as a twist of the curve to a flatter position. The mean μ goes up by $d\mu$.
Hence, the wage function twists and the return to human capital falls.
This "twisting" is due to substitution processes. Since substitution
effects sum to zero (under constant returns to scale), the workers with
an above average level of human capital will lose, while the workers in
the lower tier of the labor market gain. Somewhere in the middle, there
is a break-even point. These indirect effects of human-capital acquisition can be interpreted as a distributive externality of schooling decisions. An individual's decision to invest in human capital increases the
stock of human capital in the economy, and reduces, therefore, the
return on this capital.

   We can offer an interpretation of parameter γ in the redistribution
free equilibrium, similar to that of ψ:

$$-\frac{d\ln w_s}{w_s\,d\mu} = \frac{w_{s\mu}}{w_s^2} = \gamma, \tag{6}$$

since $w_s = 1$ in the redistribution free equilibrium. The parameter γ can
therefore be interpreted as the *compression elasticity*: the percentage

reduction in the return to human capital, $d \ln w_s$, per percent increase in the value of the stock of human capital, $w_s \, d\mu$, evaluated at market prices. Alternatively, its inverse γ^{-1} is the price elasticity of demand for human capital, the counterpart of ψ^{-1} for the demand side of the market.

2   Some Empirical Evidence

2.1   The Demand Elasticity for Human Capital: γ^{-1}
The crucial mechanism in our model is that an increase in the mean level of human capital causes its return to fall, due to imperfect substitution between types of labor. A lower return to education leads to a compression of the wage distribution. With perfect substitution between skill types, relative wages, and hence wage dispersion would be independent of the supply of human capital in the economy. Since this mechanism is crucial for our analysis, we review a number of studies documenting this relation.

There is substantial direct evidence for a negative relation between the stock of human capital in the economy and income dispersion. Tilak (1989) provides some early cross-country evidence. In addition, there are a number of case studies for various countries. Goldin and Margo (1992), Goldin and Katz (1999), and Goldin (1999) examine the returns to schooling and the dispersion of the wage structure in the United States between World Wars I and II. Educational returns clearly decreased during this period and the wage structure narrowed. Goldin and co-authors relate these developments to the enormous expansion of secondary schooling beginning in the 1910s. Only after 1980, following a period of low inflow into the university system, did the return to education and the dispersion of wages start to increase again (see Card and Lemieux 2000). In most other countries, the education revolution started later. Consequently, the fall in the return to education and the narrowing of the wage structure also lagged behind (see Hartog, Oosterbeek, and Teulings 1993 for the Netherlands in 1960–1985; Edin and Holmlund 1995 for Sweden; Kim and Topel 1995 for South Korea in 1960s and the 1970s). All these studies find that income dispersion is negatively related to the supply of human capital.

Katz and Murphy (1992) provide evidence for imperfect substitutability for the postwar period in the United States, using a two-type CES function. They estimate the elasticity of substitution between high-skilled and low-skilled workers from time-series data for the United

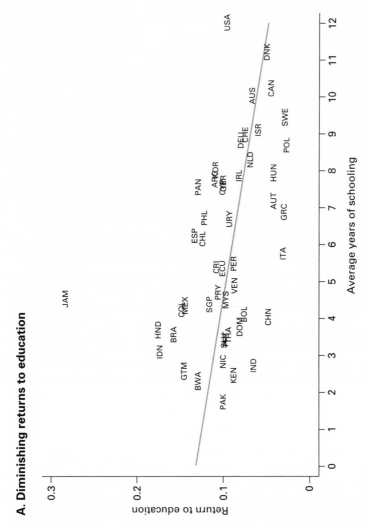

Figure 4.2

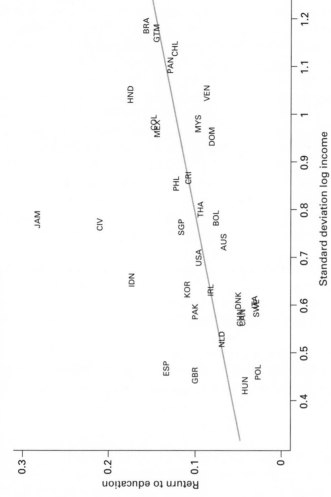

B. Returns to education and inequality

Figure 4.2 (continued)

States. They estimate the elasticity to be 1.4, supporting the idea of imperfect substitution between worker types. This elasticity drives the negative relation between the return to human capital and its supply in the postwar economic history of the United States. This elasticity of substitution between high-skilled and low-skilled workers translates into a compression elasticity of about 2.[5] Hence, an increase of the average education level by one year at an initial return to education of 10 percent leads to an increase in the value of the stock of human capital by 10 percent. That increase causes the return to human capital to fall by 2×10 percent $= 20$ percent, that is, from 10 percent to 8 percent.

Figure 4.2, taken from Teulings and Van Rens 2002, provides some direct evidence on the relation between the return to human capital for some 50 countries as measured directly from individual data on the one hand, and on the mean level of education and on income inequality on the other hand. There is a clear negative relation between the return to education and average years of schooling, suggesting that skill types are indeed imperfect substitutes in production, see panel A. Panel B relates the return to education to income inequality. There is a strong positive relationship. Taken together, the results suggest that by increasing average years of schooling, income inequality may be reduced. Some simple regressions based on the data presented in figure 4.2 reveal that the return to education is about 16 percent for countries with no education at all, and decreases by about 0.7 percent for every increase of one year in the average year of schooling.

Teulings and Van Rens (2002) analyze the evolution of logGDP per capita and the variance of log wages due to shifts in the stock of human capital in a panel of 100 countries over the period 1960–1990. In a perfect Walrasian world, the effect of the average years of education S on GDP should be equal to the Mincerian rate of return to human capital, since the Mincerian rate of return measures the effect of an additional year of education on wages, and since wages are equal to (marginal) productivity. If this return is negatively related to the mean level of education in the economy due to imperfect substitution, then the same should for the marginal effect of education on GDP:

$$\text{logGDP} = \beta_0 + \beta_1 S - \tfrac{1}{2}\beta_2 S^2,$$

$$\frac{d\,\text{logGDP}}{dS} = \frac{dw}{dh} = \beta_1 - \beta_2 S,$$

(7)

where S is the average number of years of education h in the economy. Hence, in a growth regression, we expect a positive effect of increases in the mean level of education, and a negative second-order effect of increases in the mean level of education.[6] For the variance of log wages, the following relation applies:

$$\text{Var}[w] = \left(\frac{dw}{dh}\right)^2 \text{Var}[h] = (\beta_1 - 2\beta_1\beta_2 S + \beta_2 S^2) \, \text{Var}[h]. \tag{8}$$

The variance is a negative function of the average years of education in the economy.

Tables 4.1 and 4.2 provide evidence from regressions on panel data for logGDP per capita and for the variance of log wages based on equations (7) and (8). Panel A presents a regression for logGDP on average years of schooling and years of schooling squared. The regression is run in first differences, using a 10-year time frame and controlling for the level of logGDP in the previous period. The effect of a year of education on GDP according to these regressions is much higher

Table 4.1
GDP, with robust t-statistics in parentheses. Controls for year effects, year x S, and all variables in levels lagged one year. Data source: Penn World, table 5.6a.

Variable	Equation in first differences
$S(\beta_1)$	0.24335
	(3.84)
$S^2(\frac{1}{2}\beta_2)$	−0.00848
	(2.16)

Table 4.2
Income inequality. Controls for year effects, year x S, and type of income data. Data sources: Deininger and Squire 1996; education data from Barro and Lee 1993, 1996. For more details, see Teulings and Van Rens 2002.

Variable	Equation in levels	Equation in first differences	
		(1)	(2)
$S^2(\beta_1\beta_2 \text{Var}[S])$	−0.08573	−0.09820	−0.05611
	(3.05)	(1.40)	(1.96)
$S^2(\beta_2^2 \text{Var}[S])$	0.00170	0.00320	
	(0.78)	(0.66)	
V_t	0.00105	0.00094	−0.00176
	(0.33)	(0.13)	(0.29)

than the Mincerian rate of human capital as usually measured, about 24 percent. However, due to the presence of the second-order effect, this return is measured at an average level of human capital of zero. The coefficient of the second-order term suggests $\beta_2 = 2 \times 0.8$ percent $= 1.6$ percent per year increase in the stock of human capital. The regressions presented in panel B on the variance of log income provide evidence for a negative effect of schooling on income inequality. We present three regressions, one in levels, one in first differences (to eliminate fixed country effects), and one where we allow only for a first-order effect in S, since the first and the second-order effect are highly collinear. Using the latter regression, a one-year increase in average years of education reduces the variance of log income by 0.05. The effect is somewhat larger in the equation measured in levels.[7]

One can use these numbers to calculate the value of the compression elasticity γ implied by the estimates. Starting from a return to human capital of 10 percent and using the 1.5 percent decline per year of additional human capital, the compression elasticity reads[8] $\gamma = 0.015/ 0.10^2 = 1.5$. Hence, Teulings and Van Rens's estimate of the size of the compression elasticity is broadly consistent with Katz and Murphy's (1992) estimate of the elasticity of substitution between low-skilled and high-skilled labor. We apply a value of γ of 2 in our subsequent calculations.

2.2   The Supply Elasticity of Human Capital: ψ^{-1}

The second important parameter in our analysis is the price elasticity of demand. This elasticity determines the effectiveness of subsidies in increasing the stock of human capital. The larger is the elasticity of schooling, the larger the effect of subsidies to education on the average level of human capital. Stanley (1999) analyzes the effects of the GI Bill education subsidies for veterans from World War II and the Korean War on their educational attainment. The GI Bill reduced the cost of education by 50 percent for Korea veterans and by 60 percent for World War II veterans. However, not all veterans of the Korean War were entitled to this subsidy, depending on a completely arbitrary rule regarding the date of enlistment. This "random" selection provides a natural experiment for testing the effect of financial incentives on educational attainment. The effects of these subsidies are necessarily limited to veterans with higher educational attainment, since they left the military at the age of 23. At that age, a substantial fraction has completed its investment in human capital. This fits the observation:

only 40 percent of the Korea veterans who were eligible took up any grants at all. Consistent with this observation, the veterans that took up grants descended predominantly from parents with a higher socio-economic status (SES). Among those eligible, educational attainment has increased on average by $\frac{1}{3}$ year. Were the subsidy effective for all education levels, the effect would have been $1/(3 \times 40\%) \cong 0.85$ year. Hence, the price elasticity of the supply of education equals $0.85/(10 \times 50\%) = 0.17$, or $\psi = 6$. For World War II veterans, the data allow a more refined disaggregation by SES. There, the upper quintile of the SES distribution achieves a gain in educational attainment of even 2 years. Hence, the semi-elasticity is $2/(10 \times 60\%) = 0.33$, or $\psi = 3$. One might suppose that for the group of veterans the cost of education has been higher than it would have been in case their educational career had not been interrupted by the war. We use a value of 4 for ψ in the subsequent calculations.

2.3   Complementarity of Education and Ability: ξ

In subsection 1.1 we discussed a simple trick to establish ξ: run two log wage regressions, one with only ability as explanatory variable, and another with both ability and years of education. The ratio of the regression coefficients on ability should be equal to $1 - \xi$. Table 4.3 presents the results of this type of regressions. Ability is measured by test scores. We use only males to avoid all the selectivity issues that arise due to women's labor-supply decisions. We have data for three countries, for each at two points in time: the UK (NCD data set and BCS data set), the Netherlands (1983 and 1993), and the United States (1974 and 1992).[9] For each data set, we present two regressions: one with ability as the only explanatory variable, the other with both ability and years of schooling as explanatory variables. For the UK, we have two variables for ability, one based on a math test the other on a reading test. Both are included in the regressions. This evidence suggest a value for ξ of about 0.3–0.6.

3   Efficient Redistribution Policy

3.1   Government's Policy Instruments

We can now analyze what would be the optimal policy rule for a government that wants to redistribute income, and wants to do so in the most efficient way. We take for granted that this government wants to redistribute progressively, from the rich to the poor, but our analysis

Table 4.3
Regressions of wages on individual's ability and years of schooling for males. T-statistics in parentheses.

Regressions	With schooling			Without schooling		ξ	
	Math ability	Reading ability	Schooling	Math ability	Reading ability	Math	Reading
UK[a]							
NCDS	0.0088	0.0079	0.0453	0.0121	0.0110	0.28	0.29
	(8.76)	(4.89)	(11.60)	(12.47)	(6.00)		
BCS	0.0082	0.0038	0.0410	0.0105	0.0052	0.22	0.28
	(7.90)	(3.77)	(11.09)	(10.15)	(5.17)		
Netherlands[b]							
1983	0.0041	—	0.0399	0.0092	—	0.56	—
	(2.92)		(8.67)	(6.96)			
1993	0.0090	—	0.0444	0.0150	—	0.40	—
	(5.11)		(8.15)	(8.84)			
United States[c]							
1974	0.0366	—	0.0496	0.0757	—	0.52	—
	(5.90)		(13.58)	(13.32)			
1992	0.0612	—	0.0920	0.1337	—	0.54	—
	(7.39)		(18.87)	(17.13)			

a. NCDS data: Ability measured at the age of 11; endogenous variable: log hourly wages at age 33; $N = 3202$; BCS Data: Ability measured at the age of 10; endogenous variable: log hourly wages at age 30; $N = 2661$.
b. Brabant Data: Ability measured at the age of 12 in 1952; endogenous variable: log wages; $N = 837$ for 1983, $N = 505$ for 1993.
c. Wisconsin Longitudinal Survey: Ability measured at the age of 16/7 in 1956; endogenous variable: log family income (selected data include only complete families); $N = 2742$ for both 1974 and 1992.

applies likewise for a degressive redistribution, from the poor to the rich. Let d be the worker's log disposable income made available by the government. The government is assumed not to provide grants to students still at school. Their net income is zero and they must finance their consumption by borrowing. At first sight, this seems to be an important limitation to our analysis. However, it is not. Due to the perfect nature of capital markets, the introduction of a grant financed from a reduction of education subsidies would be offset by a reduction of the take-up of credit by individuals during their years at school, leaving their lifetime consumption path, their years of education h, and their level of productive effort unaffected. Hence, the effect of grants for students is equivalent to subsidies for working individuals based on their educational attainment. We incorporate education subsidies in the income tax system only for analytical convenience. As in Mirrlees's (1971) seminal paper on optimal income taxation, the government can observe neither effort, nor innate ability, nor the skill level that is obtained by taking up education. It can only observe the years of schooling taken by an individual, h, and her gross log labor income, y. The latter is equal to the wage rate per unit of effort times effort, in logs $y = w + e$, where e is log effort. The income policy can therefore be contingent on h and y only. We simplify our analysis at this point by considering log linear income policies only:

$$d = d_0 + d_y y + d_h h = d_0 + d_y(w + e) + d_h h.$$

Here d_0, d_y, and d_h are the policy instruments of the government. In a non-interventionist, redistribution free equilibrium, we have $d_0 = 0$, $d_y = 1$, and $d_h = 0$, so that $d = y$. The parameter d_y is Musgrave and Musgrave's coefficient of residual income progression and measures the progressivity of the income tax. The special case $d_y = 1$ yields a proportional tax system. Progressive income taxation implies $d_y < 1$. The log linear specification implies a constant elasticity of net with respect to gross income. This constant elasticity specification implies that the marginal tax rate is increasing for $d_y < 1$, a feature which turns out to be important for the subsequent discussion. The parameter d_h measures the subsidy for taking up an additional year of education relative to the net discounted value of disposable income; $d_h < 0$ implies a tax on education. Analogous to equation (4) for the redistribution free equilibrium, the first-order condition for the optimal years of education in this new, redistributive equilibrium reads[10]

$$\frac{d_y w_s s_h}{\lambda} = 1 - \frac{d_h}{\lambda}.$$

Setting the policy parameters equal to the redistribution free case, $d_y = 1$, $d_h = 0$, yields condition (4). The left-hand side measures the return to an additional year of education. A progressive tax, $d_y < 1$, reduces the private return to education. Hence, workers' privately optimal choice is to take up less education. The right-hand side measures the cost of education. The education subsidy raises yearly disposable income by a fraction d_h. This benefit is discounted at a value λ. Where the first term on the right-hand side measure total social cost of education (the forgone labor income), d_h/λ measures the subsidies to education as a share of total cost, or alternatively the marginal subsidy rate. A subsidy to education d_h raises the level of educational attainment.

As in Mirrlees 1971, redistributive income taxes distort the choice of effort, as marginal revenue of effort from the point of view of the individual is below that for the society as a whole. Similarly, a subsidy or a tax to education distorts the take-up of education. Therefore, policy makers face the trade-off between efficiency and redistribution. The question of interest is what combination of education subsidies (or: taxes) and income taxation yields the lowest distortion for a given amount of redistribution. The government's choice of feasible income policies, characterized by d_0, d_y, and d_h, is obviously constrained by a budget constraint, which tells that the sum of labor income for all ability types, $\exp(w + e)$, must be equal to the sum of the disposable income for all types, $\exp(y)$. This budget constraint is used to eliminate d_0 from the set of available policy instruments. Intuitively, the policy maker first chooses d_y and d_h to realize his goals with respect to the income distribution, and he then adjusts d_0 to balance the budget. It turns out that, given the convenient, log linear structure of all our equations, the lifetime utility of worker of type a is also linear in a:

$$u(a; d_y, d_h) = u_0(d_y, d_h) + u_a(d_y, d_h)a, \tag{9}$$

where $u(a; d_y, d_h)$ is the lifetime utility of worker type a conditional on the policy variables d_y and d_h. The function $u_0(\cdot)$ is the utility level of a worker with innate ability zero. The function $u_a(\cdot)$ describes how a worker's utility depends on his innate ability. It should be stressed that (9) is not a social-welfare function. However, we can think of the parameters $u_0(\cdot)$ and $u_a(\cdot)$ as the goals of the policy maker, where $u_a(\cdot)$ measures income (better: utility) inequality and $u_0(\cdot)$ measures the efficiency of the economy. A more egalitarian income policy reduces $u_a(\cdot)$ at the cost of a lower $u_0(\cdot)$. An efficient redistribution policy sets d_y and d_h to maximize $u_0(\cdot)$, taking as given the value of $u_a(\cdot)$ (i.e., the distributional preference of the policy maker). In the following subsections, we characterize for any feasible level of inequality $u_a(\cdot)$, the mix of policy instruments d_y and d_h that minimizes efficiency losses, i.e. maximizes $u_0(\cdot)$. We refer to these combinations d_y and d_h as constrained Pareto efficient. The adjective "constrained" refers to information constraints on effort, ability, and skill, which limit the policy options that are available to the government. We analyze these efficient redistribution policies first ignoring the complementarity between ability and education and second allowing for this complementarity.

3.2 Efficient Redistribution without Complementarity: $\xi = 0$

Without complementarity of ability and education, all individuals choose the same years of schooling and education subsidies have no direct effect on the income distribution. The only way in which education subsidies affect the income distribution is through general-equilibrium effects on the labor market. If the compression elasticity is positive (i.e., skill types are imperfect substitutes), education subsidies contribute to redistribution. The optimal level of education subsidies depends on the political demand for redistribution as well as the distortionary effects of the policy instruments. The following equation describes, for any level of distributional preference $u_a(\cdot)$, the constrained Pareto-efficient ratio of tax progressivity $1 - d_y$ and education subsidies d_h / λ:

$$\frac{d_h}{\lambda} = \left[1 + \frac{\eta}{(1+\eta)^2} \gamma \right] (1 - d_y), \tag{10}$$

where η is the wage elasticity of effort supply. In the absence of striving for redistribution, $d_y = 1$, optimal education subsidies are equal to zero. Hence, the redistribution free equilibrium, $d_y = 1$, $d_h = 0$, is constrained Pareto efficient. This mirrors the first theorem of welfare economics: with perfect markets, investment in human capital is Pareto efficient. If there is no demand for redistribution, the best a policy maker can do is not intervene in the market mechanism.

When the government wants to redistribute income from rich to poor, both progressive taxes and education subsidies should be used, since in (10), if $d_y < 1$, then $d_h > 0$. Education subsidies are optimal in our model for two reasons, corresponding to the two terms within square brackets. The first term captures the effect that education subsidies offset the disincentive effects of increasing marginal tax rates on schooling. Progressive income taxation implies that the benefits of education (higher future earnings) are taxed at a higher rate than forgone earnings. Therefore, individuals underinvest in human capital, which should be corrected by providing education subsidies, see Bovenberg and Jacobs 2001. The relevance of this effect depends on the functional form of the tax scheme. Our log linear system does indeed imply increasing marginal rates. However, a linear scheme would not yield this effect, since then marginal rates were constant. Hence, we do not want to stress this effect here. It just shows up due to the convenient log linear specification of income policy.

The second term refers to the general-equilibrium effects of education, which are relevant when types of labor are less than perfect substitutes, $\gamma > 0$. Then, a constrained Pareto-efficient income policy requires a subsidy to education above the subsidy required to offset the distortions of the income tax. By encouraging schooling, wages are compressed, implying smaller pre-tax income inequality. Hence, a given after-tax income distribution can be reached with less progressive income taxes, and hence less distortionary cost of progressive taxation. Just like progressive income taxes, education subsidies entail distortions. The optimal subsidy to education induces individuals to overinvest in education. The distortion in the schooling decision due to the education subsidy is traded off against the distortion in the effort decision due to marginal tax rates. The optimal redistribution policy mixes both distortions, in line with the principles of tax smoothing. The higher the compression elasticity, γ, the stronger the compression of relative wages by additional investment in human capital, and hence the higher is the optimal value of education subsidies. For the relevant range of $\eta < 1$, the optimal subsidy is increasing in η. The more elastic the supply of effort η, the higher the distortion caused by marginal tax rates, and hence the higher is the optimal subsidy to education. Note that the price elasticity of the demand for schooling does not show up in this equation. Since the schooling decision is distorted by both progressive taxation and subsidies to education, the elasticity (measuring the size of the welfare loss) does not affect the ratio between income taxes and subsidies to education.

The subsidy to education can be interpreted as a Pigouvian subsidy to offset an externality in individual schooling decisions. When deciding to take up an additional year of education, the individual raises the mean level of human capital in the economy and therefore compresses wage differentials. This generates both positive and negative income effects for other workers. The value weighted sum of these effects is exactly zero (as applies always for substitution effects in a constant returns to scale economy). However, this compression effect is a positive externality from the point of view of the policy maker, who wants to redistribute income from the rich to the poor and who can do so only at an efficiency cost when using other instruments. We refer to this effect as a distributional externality.

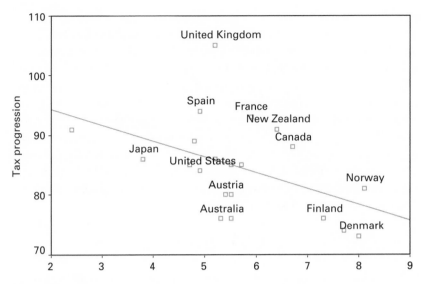

Figure 4.3
Education subsidies and progressivity of the income tax in OECD countries. Vertical axis represents change in after-tax wage as percentage of change in before-tax wage; horizontal axis represents public expenditure on education as percentage of gross domestic product in 1994. Sources: Life Long Learning for All (OECD, 1996), table 1.12; Education at a Glance—OECD indicators (OECD, 1997); Implementing the jobs study: Member countries experience (OECD, 1997) (for Belgium, p. 91, table 28). This figure has been taken from Van Ewijk and Tang 2000.

3.3   Some Empirical Evidence on Efficient Redistribution

When we follow Becker (1983) and interpret our model as a positive theory of the policy mix used for redistribution, the model predicts that countries with a stronger preference for redistribution and hence, a stronger progressivity of the tax system, have higher public spending on education. Figure 4.3 provides some crude evidence on these issues, just to give an idea of the orders of magnitude implied by the model. The horizontal axis plots education subsidies as a percentage of GDP; the vertical axis plots d_y, the percentage change in after-tax income when the before-tax wage increases by 1 percent.[11] There is a clear relation between the progressivity of the income tax and the level of education subsidies: countries with a more progressive income tax (a lower value of d_y) tend to have higher education subsidies.

Remarkably, the actual level of subsidies to education and its relation to the progressivity of income taxes is close to what our model predicts. Clearly, when taxes are proportional ($d_y = 1$), subsidies to education should be zero. This is consistent with the data in figure 4.3. The model allows a crude calculation of the optimal level of subsidies to education as a share of GDP, ignoring the effect of the increasing marginal tax rate (the first term between square brackets in equation (10)). The efficient level of education subsidies for redistributive purposes depends on the values of η and γ. As was discussed above, an empirically plausible value for γ is 2. Similar to Diamond (1998), we assume the supply elasticity of effort η to be equal to $\frac{1}{2}$. The coefficient of residual income progression (d_y) is on average 0.85 in OECD countries (see also figure 4.3). Hence, for the average OECD country, imperfect substitution justifies a subsidy to education of approximately 7 percent of the cost of forgone labor income:

$$\frac{d_h}{\lambda} = \frac{\eta\gamma}{(1+\eta)^2}(1 - d_y) \cong 0.44 \times (1 - 0.85) \cong 7\%.$$

Suppose that the average worker takes up 10 years of education, which is a reasonable value for OECD countries, and suppose that labor accounts for $\frac{2}{3}$ of GDP. Then, subsidies to education as a percentage of GDP should be

$$\tfrac{2}{3} \times 10 \times 0.44 \times 0.10 \times (1 - 0.85) = 4.4\%.$$

For the mean level of progressivity of income taxes in OECD countries, subsidies to education for the purpose of redistribution should account for approximately 4.4 percent of GDP. This is close to the actual value of 5.5 percent. Our argument for education subsidies thus goes a long way towards explaining the actual pattern and level of education subsidies in OECD countries.

3.4 Allowing for Complementarity of Ability and Education

When we allow for complementarity between education and innate ability, it is no longer clear whether education subsidies contribute to redistribution of income from rich to poor. On the one hand, by stimulating human-capital formation, education subsidies reduce wage dispersion because skill types are imperfect substitutes in production. On the other hand, the complementarity between education and ability implies that individuals with high ability go to school longer. Since the amount of education subsidies is increasing in the years of education an individual takes up, education subsidies disproportionately favor the people with high ability. Hence, the complementarity of education and ability may cause education subsidies to increase income dispersion.

The constrained Pareto-efficient level of education subsidies allowing for complementarity between ability and education is described by

$$\frac{dh}{\lambda} = \left[1 + \frac{\eta}{(1+\eta)^2} \frac{(1-\xi)\gamma - \psi\xi}{1-\xi}\right](1 - d_y). \tag{11}$$

The first term between square brackets in equation (11) is again the subsidy to education needed to correct for the distortionary effect of progressive taxation on the schooling decisions. As in the preceding subsection, we ignore this effect in the subsequent discussion. The second term consists of two opposing forces: the progressive general-equilibrium effect of education subsidies and the degressive direct effect on income due to the higher take-up of education by high-ability high-income types. The condition for the former effect to dominate the latter reads

$$\psi\xi < (1-\xi)\gamma.$$

The condition has a simple economic interpretation. The parameter ξ is the share of wage dispersion that is attributable to the cost of human-capital acquisition, while ψ^{-1} is the price elasticity of the supply of education. Hence, the left-hand side is the adverse direct effect of the subsidy: the increase in inequality due to a subsidization of the cost of human-capital acquisition per value unit increase in the average human capital. The right-hand side measures the reduction in inequality: $1 - \xi$ is the share of wage dispersion that is directly attributable to ability differentials, while γ^{-1} is the price elasticity of the demand for education. Whether this condition is satisfied is sensitive to the exact empirical values of the relevant parameters. For the values discussed before, both sides of the inequality are just equal, which implies that the direct income effect of education subsidies is as large as the indirect substitution effect. Hence, education subsidies do not contribute to redistribution. Much depends, however, on what one believes about the price elasticity of the demand for education. The higher the elasticity, the more education should be subsidized. The intuition is straightforward: the higher the elasticity, the lower education subsidies need to be for a given compression of wages, the smaller is the direct income effect. Moreover, a clever policy design may mitigate the direct income effects while maintaining the indirect substitution effect on income inequality. Examples of this will be discussed in sub-sections 4.3 and 4.4.

4   Further Implications

4.1   The Adequate Level of Centralization

As discussed before, our argument for subsidizing education rests on an externality in individual schooling decisions. Individuals do not take into account the effect of their schooling on pre-tax wage inequality and, thus, on the distortions arising from progressive income taxation. Decision making must be sufficiently centralized to internalize externalities.

Consider the case of a small district in a large country. Assume that labor is mobile, or there is free trade of products between districts, or both. Hence, by the Heckscher-Ohlin factor-price-equalization theorem, relative wages are then determined by the nationwide skill distribution, not that in the own district. Evaluated at the decentralized level, education subsidies increase the dispersion of utility when ability and education are complementary. Since the district is too small to have an effect on relative wages in the economy, the only distributive effect stems from the complementarity between ability and education in skill formation. Without complementarity, education subsidies are only used to offset the distortionary effect of increasing marginal tax rates on schooling decisions. With complementarity, progressive taxation is combined with a subsidy to education which is lower than the subsidy needed to offset tax distortions. When there is strong complementarity, even a tax on education may become constrained Pareto efficient at the decentral level. Clearly, taxing education contributes to redistribution as high-ability types take up more education than low-ability types. The (local) distortionary effect on schooling decisions is traded off against the disincentive effect of the other redistributive instrument, progressive taxation. Since the general-equilibrium effect of education subsidies on relative wages is not taken into account at the decentralized level, subsidies are inefficiently low. Hence, decentralization yields underinvestment in human capital.

The case discussed above matches closely the US institutional structure, where decisions on education are made at the level of school districts. The main difference is that the tax policy is decided predominantly at a federal level. This feature of the US system may strengthen our result that decentralized bodies provide too low subsidies to education. The reason is that central decision making on taxes introduces an additional externality in decentralized decision making, discouraging investment in human capital. While in the analysis above the direct consequences of underinvestment in human capital for the government budget are fully taken into account, this is no longer the case if local income is subject to federal taxes. Studying these issue more fully would require the introduction of separate budget constraints for the school district and the federal government.

4.2 Time Consistency of the Policy

So far, we have studied optimal income policy from the perspective of an individual at the beginning of his life. Moreover, we have assumed that the optimal income policy is set once and for all. In this subsection, we relax both assumptions to gain insight into the political viability of education subsidies in a world where the decisive voter has already started his working career and cannot commit to future policies.

Consider a dynamic economy where old generations die and new generations enter the labor force. Inhabitants differ along two dimensions. First, they are either at school or working. Second, they differ according to their ability level. For simplicity, we assume that while at school, inhabitants vote as if they are working. In this way we ignore slight differences between the interest of those at school and those working. The main interest is within generations: the low-ability people have an interest in past accumulation of human capital (because of general-equilibrium effects on relative wages) and today expropriation of the fruits of human capital (for redistribution).

The temptation to expropriate the fruits of past human-capital formation conflicts with the desire to stimulate current human-capital formation by young generations. In particular, consider the median voter at a particular point in time. He is tempted to ignore the effect of income policy on schooling decisions. Since years of schooling are assumed to be observable, this implies that he can fully expropriate the high-ability types who have taken up more education (since innate ability and education are complements). However, in that case, future generations of new entrants will no longer invest in education. This will gradually depress the mean education level among the workforce, thereby raising gross wage differentials, at the expense of the median voter. Since the median voter expects to live beyond today, he is also negatively affected by this long run negative effect on his gross wage rate.

Interestingly, one can prove that when voters cannot commit on their future voting behavior, the political process brings the economy exactly half way between complete internalization of redistributive externalities of schooling decisions and complete decentralization, where externalities are fully ignored, see Dur and Teulings 2001. At that point, the temptation to expropriate past investments in human capital is exactly offset by the fear of adverse general-equilibrium effects by lower future investments. The lack of ability to commit to future voting behavior works to the detriment of the lower half of the income distribution, which gets less redistribution than with commitment. It is therefore in their interest to seek ways to commit not to tax investments in human capital in the future. For that reason, it may be important not to allow years of education to be a variable in the tax system. As soon as that variable enters the system, it opens the door for debate on heavier taxation of human capital in the future. The debate alone may be enough to undermine the credibility of the incentives for investment in human capital, and thereby their effectiveness. Therefore, it may be much better to frame subsidies to the education system in the form of irreversible grants during the years at school or of direct subsidization of the schools themselves, since this type of subsidies are much more credible.

4.3   Subsidies to Schools versus Grants for Students
The conclusion of subsection 3.3 that the direct and the indirect general-equilibrium effects tend to cancel in the simple log linear setup, does not imply that we should forget about raising the level of education as an efficient redistribution instrument. Education subsidies make most sense if one can find policies that limit the direct effect on income while at the same time maximize the substitution effect on the mean level of human capital. Such more sophisticated policies are observed in practice. For instance, in the present model, the only cost of education is forgone earnings, keeping the quality of the education system fixed. One could extend the analysis to the trade-off between the quality and the direct cost of the education system. Then, a typical policy parameter might be the quality of education in general, and of primary education in particular. Leuven, Oosterbeek, and Van Ophem (2002) show that there are considerable differences in the quality of education across countries. An eyeball test suggests that these differences are related to the amount of government subsidy to the education system. The big advantage of raising the quality of primary

education is that it has no adverse direct effect on income and is likely to raise the average skill level in the economy. However, depending on the exact specification of the education production function $s(a, h)$, the greater quality of primary education might be just offset as people reduce their years of schooling such that marginal cost and revenues remain equal. A general increase in the quality of education might be a more attractive alternative, as it opens quality of education as a second dimension for substitution next to years of education. The greater the total elasticity of educational attainment to incentives, the cheaper it is for the government to increase the average level of education by subsidies, and in particular, the less subsidies need to be paid to high-ability types who take up a lot of education.

4.4 Subsidies Based on Parental Income
Another option for improving the effect of a given amount of subsidy on the average education level in the economy is to include intergenerational information in the subsidization scheme. The socio-economic status of the previous generation is a good indicator of the expected educational attainment of the next generation, partly by nature effects, partly by nurture, see Plug and Vijverberg 2003. On average, kids of low education families drop out of the education system at a younger age and with a lower skill level. An optimal subsidy to education operates at the margin, to invoke people to stay at school longer. The problem is that the margin is located at a different point for each skill group, so that high-skilled workers benefit along the whole range. By using the educational attainment of the previous generation, subsidies can be tailored more precisely to the margin, improving the ratio of beneficial incentive effects versus adverse direct effect on income. In practice, this boils down to subsidies that are conditional on parental income, an institution that is widely applied.

4.5 Direct Compression of the Human Capital Distribution?
Many policies are geared towards direct compression of the human capital distribution. The recent Luxembourg and Lisbon summits of the European Union have again focused the efforts for investment in human capital on raising the level of education of the least skilled. From a distribution point of view, this seems to be an obvious idea as it raises the human capital of the most disadvantaged group. However, a second thought reveals a number of complications. First, relative to the free-market outcome, it is much simpler to raise everybody's skill level

by a bit than to raise a particular group's skill level by a lot, since the dead-weight loss increases quadratically with the deviation from the market outcome. Second, the general-equilibrium effect of stimulating human-capital accumulation in the lowest strata of the distribution work perverse: they raise supply in the lower part of the distribution, thereby reducing relative wages of the least skilled, see Teulings 2002 for a detailed analysis. Table 4.2 provides some, though far from conclusive empirical evidence on this issue. The regressions include the variance of education as explanatory variable (V_t). The effect of this variable on the variance of log wages is close to zero. Hence, the direct effect of a compression of the variance of education on the variance of earnings is fully offset by adverse general-equilibrium effects.

The argument is very much comparable to the discussion on minimum wages. An increase in minimum wages reduces labor supply at the bottom of the labor market, thereby increasing the relative wages of their best substitutes, slightly better-skilled workers. The argument is illustrated in figure 4.4. Suppose that we introduce a minimum wage, that eliminates the left tail of the human-capital distribution, reducing the effective supply of low-skilled workers. Firms will shift their demand for these low-skilled workers to the closest available substitute, slightly better-skilled workers, type s_+. Hence, the introduc-

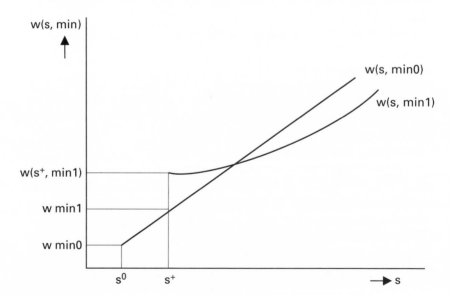

Figure 4.4
The wage function before and after an increase in the minimum wage.

tion of the minimum wage will increase the wages of type s_+ workers substantially. Firms that used these type s_+ workers before the introduction of the minimum wage will find their cost having been increased. They will substitute to the closest substitute, type s_{++} workers, s_{++} being slightly higher than s_+. Hence, their wages go up, but by slightly less than the wages of type s_+. This yields the type of pattern shown in figure 4.4, with large spill-over effects of an increase in the minimum wage to workers earning wages just above the minimum. This type of pattern has been documented for the United States by Lee (1999) and Teulings (2000, 2003). A decrease of the minimum wage by 10 percent causes the wages of workers earning slightly more than the minimum to go down by 8 percent (Teulings 2003). Basically, all of the increase in inequality in the lower half of the labor market in the United States during the eighties can be explained by the fall in minimum wages.

Similarly, programs like the EITC and New Deal can be victim of their own success. The large subsidies to the employment of the least skilled raise their supply, and thereby invoke adverse general-equilibrium effects, which might undo the gains of the initial subsidies. The only net effect would be an increase in the marginal tax rates for the better-skilled workers to finance the subsidies to the least skilled.

Conclusion

The general-equilibrium effect of investment in human capital provides a forceful argument for the subsidization of education for a government that wants to redistribute income. Previous studies on optimal taxation have always downplayed the importance of general-equilibrium effects. The reason that these effects show up much more prominently in this study is that we use a more realistic production technology, based on comparative advantage of high-skilled workers in complex job types. Contrary to a two-type CES technology, this production technology implies that the whole wage schedule becomes flatter as a result of an increase in the average stock of human capital. An efficient redistribution policy should therefore combine progressive income taxation and subsidies to the formation of human capital. Crude calculations suggest that this model provides a rationale for subsidies to the education system of about the level that we observe empirically. Moreover, the model suggests positive cross-country relation between the progressivity of income taxes and the rate of subsidization of the education system: the more redistributive a country's

income policy, the higher will be both the progressivity of the tax system and the subsidy to education system. This relation is also borne
out by the data, with a slope that fits the theoretical predictions closely.

However, there is an effect working in the opposite direction. Since
the take-up of schooling is complementary to innate ability, the direct
effect of a subsidy to education tends to favor high-ability types. Our
overview of some empirical studies suggests that both effects cancel.
Much depends on what one believes about the price elasticity of the
demand for education. The higher the elasticity, the more education
should be subsidized. Moreover, the result that the direct and the indirect effect more or less cancel does not imply that we should forget
about the argument. The simple log-linear income policy analyzed in
this paper is applied merely for reasons of tractability. One can think of
more elaborate schemes that increase the substitution effects of education subsidies, while at the same time reduce the adverse direct effect
on income, in particular policies aimed at raising the quality of education and grants for students which depend on parental income.

The log linearity of the income policy imposes another strong
restriction. It implies increasing marginal tax rates (for $d_y < 1$), offend-
ing the logic of Sadka's (1976) argument for low marginal rates at both
ends of the income distribution. Interestingly, this argument can be
extended towards education subsidies, but then reversed. Where in the
case of income taxation, the direct effect on income are desired for the
purpose of redistribution while the substitution effects only cause efficiency losses, here the substitution effects contribute to the redistribution while the direct effect on income works in the opposite direction.
Hence, the marginal rate of education subsidies should be high at
the bottom and at the top, where they do not cause substantial direct
effects on income since there are no people earning less than the lowest
or more than the highest income. The previous argument regarding the
quality of primary education exploits this idea at the lower end of the
distribution. Where this idea fits the layman's intuition, its counterpart
is more surprising. A subsidy for top education programs has little
adverse direct effect on income (since there are not many people taking
up more years of education), while it raises the average level of education. The production function applied in this paper implies that all
lower ability types will benefit from the general-equilibrium effects of
this policy, see Teulings 2002.

The analysis of the optimal functional form of taxes and education
subsidies has strong policy implication for programs like the Earned

Income Tax Credit and the New Deal, along the lines suggested by Heckman, Lochner, and Taber (1999). These programs aim at a reduction of marginal tax rates for the lowest ability types in order to combat low-skilled unemployment. The government budget constraint then dictates that marginal rates should be increased for higher ability types. The logic of the argument in this paper suggests that this policy can be victim of its own success. To the extent that the subsidies induce low-ability types to go to work, the relative increase in low-skilled labor supply will reduce their wages, thereby partially undoing the initial effect of the subsidy. Stated more crudely: there is limit to the demand for hamburger flippers. At the same time, the increase in marginal rates for somewhat higher skill types, which is necessary to satisfy the government budget constraint, reduces the incentive for investment in human capital, which further aggravates the problem. This points to the need of a more formal analysis of the functional form of the optimal policy.

Appendix: Production Technology and Wages

Consider an economy where the production of one unit of output requires the input of an infinite number of tasks, indexed by their level of complexity, c. The price of a unit of output is taken as the numeraire and is therefore normalized to unity. Both the skill level s and the complexity level c vary continuously and can take any real number. The transformation of tasks into output takes place by a Leontief technology: tasks are required in fixed proportions.[12] The skill distribution is normal, $s \sim N(\mu, \sigma^2)$. The size of the workforce is normalized to unity. The input requirements of c-type tasks per unit of output are described by a normal distribution, with the same variance as the skill distribution, $c \sim N(0, \sigma^2)$. A c-type task can be produced by any s-type worker. However, the relative productivities of various worker types differ according to the complexity of the task:

$$g(s, c) = -\frac{1}{\gamma} e^{\gamma(c-s)},$$

where $g(s, c)$ is the log productivity of skill type s in a task of complexity c. This specification implies comparative advantage of high-skilled workers in complex jobs, since $g_{sc} > 0$: the productivity ratio of type s_1 and s_2, $s_2 < s_1$, is increasing in c. Teulings (1995) shows that this set-up implies that every task type c is uniquely assigned to a single worker type $s(c)$, and vice versa. Furthermore, better-skilled workers are assigned to more complex jobs, $s'(c) > 0$, due to comparative advantage. The equilibrium of supply and demand for each task type c requires, in logs,

$$-\left(\frac{s(c) - \mu}{\sigma}\right)^2 + g[s(c), c] + \ln s'(c) = -(c/\sigma)^2 + Y, \tag{12}$$

where Y is log output per unit of the workforce. The left-hand side is the log supply of labor of type $s(c)$ (the log of the normal density function) plus its log productivity in task type c plus the log Jacobian $ds/dc = s'(c)$. The two terms on the right-hand side measure the log demand for task type c: the Leontief coefficient (again the log of the normal density) plus log output. Equation (12) is a differential equation in $s(c)$. The special case, where the variances of the skill distribution and the complexity demand distribution are equal, is the only for which this differential equation has an analytical solution:

$$s(c) = c + \mu,$$
$$\tag{13}$$
$$Y = L - \frac{1}{\gamma} e^{-\gamma\mu}.$$

For the derivation of the (unique) wage equation that is consistent with this assignment, we define $x(s, c)$ to be the log production cost of c-type tasks by a s-type worker:

$$x(s, c) = w(s, \mu) - g(s, c) \tag{14}$$

(that is, log production cost in log wages per worker minus log productivity per worker). In a market equilibrium, workers are assigned to tasks such that production cost for task c is minimized. The first-order condition reads

$$x_s[s(c), c] = w_s[s(c), \mu] - g_s[s(c), c] = 0 \Rightarrow w_s(\mu) = g_s[c - \mu, c] = e^{-\gamma\mu}. \tag{15}$$

The intercept $w_0(\mu)$ remains to be determined. This is derived from the numeraire. Production cost per task weighted by their Leontief coefficient add up to unity:

$$1 = \int_{-\infty}^{\infty} \frac{1}{\sigma} \phi\left(\frac{c}{\sigma}\right) e^{x[s(c), c]} \, dc$$
$$= \int_{-\infty}^{\infty} \frac{1}{\sigma} \phi\left(\frac{c - \sigma^2 e^{-\gamma\mu}}{\sigma}\right) e^{w_0 + (\mu + \gamma^{-1})e^{-\gamma\mu} + \frac{1}{2}\sigma^2 e^{-2\gamma\mu}} \, dc,$$

where the second line follows from the substitution of equations (13), (14), and (15), and some rearrangement. Hence,

$$w_0(\mu) = -(\mu + \gamma^{-1})e^{-\gamma\mu} - \mu e^{-\gamma\mu} - \tfrac{1}{2}e^{-2\gamma\mu}\sigma^2.$$

Notes

1. A referee suggested that this might seriously bias our conclusions. If students' hours and other inputs are fully complementary in the production of human capital, the direct cost of education can be modeled as a simple surcharge on the Mincerian rate of return. If not, new and interesting questions arise, which are discussed tentatively in section 4.

2. Usually, the price elasticity of the supply of human capital θ is defined not with respect to the value of human capital, but with respect to the years of education:

$$\theta \equiv -\frac{d \ln h}{d \ln s_h} = -\frac{s_h}{s_{hh}h} = \frac{1}{w_s s_h h}\psi^{-1}.$$

However, since the average years of education $E[h] \cong 10$ and since the Mincerian rate of return $w_s s_h \cong 10\%$ in developed economies, both concepts happen to be numerically the same.

3. Equation (4) ignores some terms that appear to be irrelevant in the full model, like difference in the level of effort when working and when at school. We omit these here for the sake of transparency. See Dur and Teulings 2001.

4. We apply a first-order Taylor expansion of h around its equilibrium value $h(a)$. Since $\beta h(a) - \xi a$ is a constant, the second-order term $-\tfrac{1}{2}\psi[\beta h(a) - \xi a]^2$ in equation (1) can be ignored. Rewriting the remaining terms yields $s(a, h) = (1 - \xi)a + \beta h + \text{constant}$.

5. Teulings (2002) derives a relation between the compression elasticity and the elasticity of substitution between high-skilled and low-skilled workers:

$$\gamma = \frac{1}{\text{Var}[w] \times \eta_{\text{low-high}}} \cong \frac{1}{0.60^2 \times 1.4} \cong 2,$$

where $\text{Var}[w]$ is the variance of log wages and $\eta_{\text{low-high}}$ is the substitution elasticity between low-skilled and high-skilled labor.

6. This interpretation of the role of human capital in the evolution of GDP contrasts sharply with the endogenous growth literature, where the relation between schooling and growth is driven by externalities. For instance, in Barro and Sala-i-Martin 1999 a higher level of education makes the labor force more able to deal with technological innovations. This yields a relation between the level of education and growth, not the level of GDP; see Krueger and Lindahl 2000 for a discussion.

7. We can back out an estimate for β_2 from these regressions. Since $\text{Var}[h] \cong 12.6$, and using $\beta_1 = 0.24$, the coefficient of the first-order term suggests $\beta_2 = 0.09/(2 \times 12.6 \times 0.24) = 1.5\%$ per year.

8. Recall that, by (6), $\gamma = -d \ln w_s/w_s \, d\mu$. Hence,

$$\gamma = \frac{\dfrac{d(\log(dw/dh))}{dS}}{\dfrac{d \log\text{GDP}}{dS}} = \frac{\beta_2}{(\beta_1 - \beta_2 S)^2} = \frac{0.015}{0.10^2} = 1.5.$$

9. We thank Peter Dolton for the regressions on UK data, Hessel Oosterbeek for those on Dutch data, and Erik Plug for those on US data.

10. As in equation (4), some slight complications that arise in the full model are ignored here.

11. Clearly, this is only a crude measure of tax progressivity. For instance, figure 4.3 does not take into account differences in tax progressivity between countries as a result of differences in VAT.

12. Contrary to suggestion by some commentators, the assumption of a Leontief technology is not crucial for our results. Teulings (2000) shows that replacing the Leontief technology by a Cobb-Douglas technology is (almost) observationally equivalent to halving the value of γ. As long as there is a slight imperfection in the substitutability between c types in the production of output, the distribution of c does not fully adjust to shifts in the distribution of s, and hence relative wages have to change. The advantage of using the Leontief technology is that the differential equation (12) can be solved analytically.

References

Acemoglu, Daron, and Joshua Angrist. 1999. How Large Are Social Returns to Education? Evidence from Compulsory Schooling Laws. Working paper MP/W7444, National Bureau of Economic Research.

Allen, Franklin. 1982. Optimal Linear Income Taxation with General Equilibrium Effects on Wages. *Journal of Public Economics* 17, no. 2: 135–143.

Angrist, Joshua D., and Alan B. Krueger. 1991. Does Compulsory School Attendance Affect Schooling and Earnings? *Quarterly Journal of Economics* 106, no. 4: 979–1014.

Barro, Robert J., and Jong Wha Lee. 1993. International Comparisons of Educational Attainment. *Journal of Monetary Economics* 32, no. 3: 363–394.

Barro, Robert J., and Jong Wha Lee. 1996. International Measures of Schooling Years and Schooling Quality. *American Economic Review* 86, no. 2: 218–223.

Barro, Robert J., and Xavier Sala-i-Martin. 1999. *Economic Growth*. MIT Press.

Becker, Gary S. 1983. A Theory of Competition among Pressure Groups for Political Influence. *Quarterly Journal of Economics* 98, no. 3: 371–400.

Benabou, Roland. 2000. Unequal Societies: Income Distribution and the Social Contract. *American Economic Review* 90, March: 96–129.

Benabou, Roland. 2002. Tax and Education Policy in a Heterogeneous Agent Economy: What Levels of Redistribution Maximize Growth and Efficiency? *Econometrica* 70, no. 2: 481–517.

Bils, Mark, and Peter J. Klenow. 2000. Does Schooling Cause Growth? *American Economic Review* 90, no. 5: 1160–1183.

Bovenberg, A. Lans, and Bas Jacobs. 2001. Redistribution and Education Subsidies. Mimeo, University of Amsterdam.

Cameron, Stephen V., and James J. Heckman. 1998. Life Cycle Schooling and Dynamic Selection Bias: Models and Evidence for Five Cohorts of American Males. *Journal of Political Economy* 106, no. 2: 262–333.

Cameron, Stephen V., and James J. Heckman. 1999. The Dynamics of Educational Attainment for Blacks, Hispanics, and Whites. Working paper W7249, National Bureau of Economic Research.

Cameron, Stephen V., and Christopher Taber. 2000. Borrowing Constraints and the Returns to Schooling. Working paper W7761, National Bureau of Economic Research.

Card, David. 1999. The Causal Effect of Education on Earnings. In *Handbook of Labor Economics*, volume 3, ed. O. Ashenfelter and D. Card. Elsevier.

Card, David, and Thomas Lemieux. 2000. Can Falling Supply Explain the Rising Return to College for Younger Men? A Cohort-Based Analysis. Working paper W7655, National Bureau of Economic Research.

Deininger, Klaus, and Lyn Squire. 1996. A New Data Set Measuring Income Inequality. *World Bank Economic Review* 10, no. 3: 565–591.

Diamond, Peter A. 1998. Optimal Income Taxation: An Example with a U-Shaped Pattern of Optimal Marginal Tax Rates. *American Economic Review* 88, no. 1: 83–95.

Dur, Robert A. J., and Coen N. Teulings. 2001. Education and Efficient Redistribution. Discussion paper 01-090/3, Tinbergen Institute.

Edin, Per-Anders, and Bertil Holmlund. 1995. The Swedish Wage Structure: The Rise and Fall of Solidarity Wage Policy? In *Differences and Changes in Wage Structures*, ed. R. Freeman and L. Katz. University of Chicago Press.

Feldstein, Martin S. 1973. On the Optimal Progressivity of the Income Tax. *Journal of Public Economics* 2, no. 4: 357–376.

Fernandez, Raquel, and Richard Rogerson. 1996. Income Distribution, Communities, and the Quality of Public Education. *Quarterly Journal of Economics* 111, no. 1: 135–164.

Goldin, Claudia. 1999. Egalitarianism and the Returns to Education during the Great Transformation of American Education. *Journal of Political Economy* 107, no. 6: S65–S94.

Goldin, Claudia, and Lawrence F. Katz. 1999. The Returns to Skill in the United States across the Twentieth Century. Working paper 7126, National Bureau of Economic Research.

Goldin, Claudia, and Robert A. Margo. 1992. The Great Compression: The Wage Structure in the United States at Mid-Century. *Quarterly Journal of Economics* 107, no. 1: 1–34.

Hartog, Joop, Hessel Oosterbeek, and Coen Teulings. 1993. Age, Wages and Education in the Netherlands. In *Labour Markets in an Ageing Europe*, ed. P. Johnson and K. Zimmermann. Cambridge University Press.

Heckman, J. J., L. Lochner, and C. Taber. 1999. Explaining Rising Wage Inequality: Explorations with a Dynamic General Equilibrium Model of Labor Earnings with Heterogeneous Agents. Working paper 6384, National Bureau of Economic Research.

Johnson, George E. 1984. Subsidies for Higher Education. *Journal of Labor Economics* 2, no. 3: 303–318.

Katz, Lawrence F., and Kevin M. Murphy. 1992. Changes in Relative Wages, 1963–1987: Supply and Demand Factors, *Quarterly Journal of Economics* 107, no. 1: 35–78.

Keane, Michael P., and Kenneth I. Wolpin. 2001. The Effect of Parental Transfers and Borrowing Constraints on Educational Attainment. Working paper 01-018, Penn Institute for Economic Research.

Kim, Dae-Il, and Robert H. Topel. 1995. Labor Markets and Economic Growth: Lessons from Korea's Industrialization, 1970–1990. In *Differences and Changes in Wage Structures*, ed. R. Freeman and L. Katz. University of Chicago Press.

Krueger, Alan B., and Mikael Lindahl. 2000. Education for Growth: Why and For Whom? Working paper W7591, National Bureau of Economic Research.

Lee, David S. 1999. Wage Inequality in the U.S. during the 1980s: Rising Dispersion or Falling Minimum Wage? *Quarterly Journal of Economics* 114, no. 3: 941–1023.

Leuven, Edwin, Hessel Oosterbeek, and Hans van Ophem. 2002. Explaining International Differences in Male Wage Inequality by Differences in Demand and Supply of Skill. Mimeo, Tinbergen Institute.

Lucas, Robert E., Jr. 1988. On the Mechanics of Economic Development. *Journal of Monetary Economics* 22, no. 1: 3–42.

Mirrlees, James A. 1971. An Exploration in the Theory of Optimum Income Taxation. *Review of Economic Studies* 38, no. 114: 175–208.

Perotti, Roberto. 1993. Political Equilibrium, Income Distribution, and Growth. *Review of Economic Studies* 60, no. 4: 755–776.

Plug, Erik, and Wim Vijverberg. 2003. Schooling, Family Background, and Adoption: Is It Nature or Is It Nurture? *Journal of Political Economy* 111, no. 3: 611–641.

Rosen, S. 1974. Hedonic Prices and Implicit Markets: Product Differentiation in Pure Competition. *Journal of Political Economy* 82, no. 1: 34–55.

Sadka, Efraim. 1976. On Income Distribution, Incentive Effects and Optimal Income Taxation. *Review of Economic Studies* 43, no. 2: 261–267.

Saint-Paul, Gilles, and Thierry Verdier. 1993. Education, Democracy and Growth. *Journal of Development Economics* 42, no. 2: 399–407.

Sattinger, M. 1975. Comparative Advantage and the Distribution of Earnings and Abilities. *Econometrica* 43, no. 3: 455–468.

Shea, John. 2000. Does Parents' Money Matter? *Journal of Public Economics* 77, no. 2: 155–184.

Stanley, Marcus. 1999. College Education and the Mid-century GI Bills. Mimeo, Harvard University.

Stern, Nicolas. 1982. Optimum Income Taxation with Errors in Administration. *Journal of Public Economics* 17, no. 2: 181–211.

Stiglitz, Joseph E. 1982. Self-Selection and Pareto Efficient Taxation. *Journal of Public Economics* 17, no. 2: 213–240.

Tamura, Robert. 1991. Income Convergence in an Endogenous Growth Model. *Journal of Political Economy* 99, no. 3: 522–540.

Teulings, Coen N. 1995. The Wage Distribution in a Model of the Assignment of Skills to Jobs. *Journal of Political Economy* 103, no. 2: 280–315.

Teulings, Coen N. 2000. Aggregation Bias in Elasticities of Substitution and the Minimum Wage Paradox. *International Economic Review* 41, no. 2: 359–398.

Teulings, Coen N. 2003. The Contribution of Minimum Wages to Increasing Wage Inequality. *Economic Journal* 113: 801–833.

Teulings, Coen N. 2002. Comparative Advantage, Relative Wages, and the Accumulation of Human Capital. Discussion paper TI 02-081/3, Tinbergen Institute.

Teulings, C. N., and T. van Rens. 2002. Education, Growth and Income Inequality. Discussion paper 02-001/3, Tinbergen Institute and Princeton University.

Tilak, Jandhyala B. G. 1989. Education and Its Relation to Economic Growth, Poverty and Income Distribution. Report, World Bank.

Tinbergen, Jan. 1975. *Income Distribution: Analysis and Policies*. North-Holland.

Van Ewijk, C., and P. J. G. Tang. 2000. Efficient progressive taxes and education subsidies. Research memorandum 170, Centraal Plan Bureau.

5 Mandated Severance Pay in an Efficiency-Wage Economy

Laszlo Goerke

Employment-protection legislation (EPL) is frequently claimed to be a major cause for the employment problem in many European countries. Empirically, however, this assertion has not fared well.[1] This conflict between empirical evidence, on the one hand, and theoretical argument, on the other, has brought about at least three types of responses: first, the theoretical literature has paid greater attention to the institutional details of EPL, based on the hypothesis that the effects of its various components—such as pure firing costs, procedural restrictions or severance pay—may differ. Second, the idea has been put forward that the consequences of EPL result primarily from interactions of such restrictions with other features of the labor market. Third, to perform more thorough empirical analyses of the relation between EPL and labor market outcomes, more refined indicators of EPL have been called for.[2]

The present study belongs to the first group of investigations, taking as its starting point the observation that EPL is generally more extensive for collective redundancies than for individual dismissals. This, the paper argues, is because payments in the event of a collective redundancy can raise the payoff of firms, workers, and the government, while such a Pareto improvement is less likely for payments for individual dismissals. This argument is developed by incorporating payments in the event of an individual dismissal (labeled *dismissal* pay) and in the event of collective redundancies (denoted *redundancy* pay) into a shirking model of efficiency wages. More specifically, it is shown that:

• Dismissal payments in the event of an individual job loss make shirking more attractive. Accordingly, the efficiency wage has to rise. Higher wages and greater dismissal costs reduce profits, but can raise the payoff of employed workers. While workers may, thus, support an introduction or expansion of dismissal pay, this will not be feasible by consensus since firms would lose more than workers gain.

• In contrast, redundancy pay for collective dismissals mitigates the incentives to shirk and allows for a reduction in wages. Overall labor costs can fall and profits rise. Moreover, at least those workers who experience a mass redundancy will gain, while an employed worker's payoff is unaffected. Accordingly, payments in the case of collective redundancies may be Pareto improving.

Section 1 describes EPL and, in particular, regulations pertaining to dismissal and redundancy pay in OECD countries. Section 2 characterizes previous analyses of EPL, predominantly for efficiency-wage economies. Section 3 describes the shirking model of efficiency wages which is used to investigate the consequences of dismissal and redundancy pay, relying on the set-up by Shapiro and Stiglitz (1984). Section 4 analyzes the consequences of these payments on the agents' payoffs. Section 5 discusses the robustness of findings. Formal details are mostly relegated to an appendix.

1 Some Facts about Dismissal and Redundancy Pay

In most OECD countries, there is an extensive set of laws or stipulations governing dismissals. These restrictions may be procedural, in that they require worker representatives or government authorities to be informed in advance for a dismissal to take effect. Alternatively, they may involve direct payments due to notification periods or severance pay.[3] A comprehensive analysis by the OECD (1999) indicates that EPL rises with tenure, depends on personal characteristics, can be conditioned on thresholds with respect to firm size, differ for individual and collective redundancies, and be related to previous income, inter alia.

Table 5.1 summarizes some features, whether legislated or the result of collective bargaining. Columns I and II illustrate the extent of dismissal payments in the case of no-fault individual dismissals. The unweighted average of dismissal pay in the sample of 27 countries amounts to 1.42 (2.98) monthly wages, after a tenure of 4 (20) years. A no-fault dismissal will be legally justified, for example, if the firm faces a decline in demand and needs to adjust its workforce. Such dismissals, often referred to as fair dismissals, can be distinguished from unfair dismissals which are regarded as a violation of the obligations of the employment contract.[4] Column III indicates how restrictive the characterization of an unfair dismissal is; a greater number signaling the definition to be more extensive. For example, a score of 0 implies that adequate reasons for a dismissal are insufficient worker capability or redundancy of the job, while a 1 was awarded by the OECD if social considerations, age or job tenure influence the choice of who can be dismissed. A score of 2 implies that a transfer to another job within the firm or retraining must be attempted for a dismissal not be regarded as unfair. A score of 3 resulted if worker capability cannot justify a fair dismissal.

An unfair dismissal may entitle workers to reinstatement in their job, as it is, for example, fairly often in the Czech Republic, Greece, Hungary, Italy, Japan, Korea, Norway, Poland, and Portugal. Alternatively, a finding of an unfair dismissal may lead to an award of a dismissal payment since reinstatement is either conditional on the employer's consent (Finland, France, Spain) or rarely made use of (Austria, Canada, Denmark, Germany, Mexico).[5] Column IV illustrates that payments in the event of an unfair dismissal are substantially higher than for fair dismissals, where these payments have been calculated as multiple of monthly wages for workers with a tenure of 20 years and are, thus, comparable to those in column II.

A dismissal for (gross) misconduct is feasible in most OECD countries without the employer being obliged to make dismissal payments. Therefore, firms have an incentive to fire workers for (gross) misconduct, although the allegation may not be true. Accordingly, in a number of OECD countries inadequate work performance does not constitute a sufficient reason for firms to escape obligations for dismissal payments.[6] Moreover, given sizable dismissal payments, workers who have grossly violated their contractual obligations have an incentive to claim the allegation of misconduct to be unjustified. Since dismissals can be disputed in (labor) courts or arbitration institutions in many countries (Bertola et al. 1999), there is a positive probability that workers will succeed with their claim. To avoid such costly procedures, firms may be willing to offer a worker dismissal pay in exchange for a voluntary termination of a contract. This is a common practice in Germany (Franz and Rüthers 1999). In the United States, "23% of employers reported the 'use of severance agreements with terminated employees for release of any claims against the organization.'"[7] In Germany, moreover, if a dismissal is disputed, courts will often attempt to

Table 5.1
Employment-protection regulation in the OECD in the late 1990s. Sources: OECD 1999, pp. 55–56, 65–66; author's calculations.

	Individual dismissals				Collective redundancies		
	Dismissal pay after tenure of 4 years I	Dismissal pay after tenure of 20 years II	Ease of unfair dismissal III	Unfair dismissal pay IV	Notification requirements V	Notification Period VI	Additional cost VII
Australia	0.7	1.2	0	NA[a]	2	0	0
Austria	1.2	2.5	1	15	1	21	1
Belgium	2.8	9	0	15	2	44	1
Canada	0.5	0.5	0	NA	2	111	0
Czech Republic	2.5	2.5	2	8	2	83	0
Denmark	3	4.3	0	12	2	29	0
Finland	2	6	1.5	12	1	32	0
France	2	2	1.5	15	0	22	1
Germany	1	7	2	24	1	28	1
Greece	1.5	8	0.5	15.8	1	19	1
Hungary	1.2	3	0	10	2	47	0
Ireland	0.5	2	0	24	1	18	0
Italy	1.1	2.2	0	32.5	1.5	44	1
Japan	1	1	2	26	1	0	0
Korea	1	1	2	NA	1	0	0
Mexico	0	0	3	16	2	0	1
Netherlands	1	3	1.5	18	1	30	1
New Zealand	0.5	0.5	0	NA	0.5	0	0
Norway	1	5	2.5	15	1.5	28	0

Poland	3	3	0	3	1	32	2
Portugal	2	2	2	20	0.5	65	1
Spain	1	1	2	22	1	29	1
Sweden	3	6	2	32	2	113	0
Switzerland	2	3	0	6	2	29	1
Turkey	2	2	0	26	1	29	0
United Kingdom	0.9	2.8	0	8	1.5	57	0
United States	0	0	0	NA	2	59	0
Unweighted average	1.42	2.98	0.94	17.06	1.35	35.9	0.48

a. Data not available. See text for explanations.

provide workers with payments by suggesting according amicable settlements between firm and employee, even if the latter exhibited misconduct (Willemsen 2000). Similarly in Spain, dismissals on disciplinary grounds frequently lead to agreements about dismissal payments (Toharia and Ojeda 1999). Taken in conjunction with the fact that payments for unfair dismissals are by and large substantially higher than in the event of a fair dismissal, firms have a strong incentive to grant a worker who is dismissed for insufficient work effort the same payment as a worker who loses the job, for example, owing to an economic reason.

Nevertheless, firms may not always treat workers fired for shirking in the same manner as those who are dismissed individually for economic causes. This can be the case, for example, to establish a reputation for being tough on shirkers or because firms see a chance for a summary dismissal. This uncertainty about the payment in the event of being dismissed for shirking is explicitly taken into account in the formal analysis below. Accordingly, for the purpose of this study, the regulations for individual dismissals may be summarized as follows:

Fact 1 In many OECD countries, payments in the event of an individual no-fault dismissal are substantial, particularly for workers with long tenure. Payments for unfair dismissals can be considerably higher. In a number of countries, even workers who do not provide the required level of effort cannot be dismissed without restrictions. To circumvent these constraints, firms de facto often make dismissal payments in the case of misconduct.

Table 5.1 also provides information on collective redundancies. Columns V and VI indicate additional notification requirements and periods (measured in days) for collective redundancies beyond those for individual dismissals. The score for no additional notification requirements is 0. The score is 1 if either worker representatives or a government agency have to be informed. It is 2 if both or more institutions are to be notified. Additional notification requirements exist in all but one of the 27 countries while further delays are found in 22 of them. Column VII indicates whether a collective dismissal is more costly per person than an individual dismissal. This is the case in 12 of the 27 countries. A score of 0 indicates no additional cost, a score of 1 implies that either redundancy pay in excess of dismissal payments has to be made or social compensation plans have to be financed, while, finally, a score of 2 indicates the existence of both requirements. Columns V–VII yield the following:

Fact 2 EPL pertaining to collective redundancies is more extensive than for individual dismissals. In particular, notification periods virtually always exceed those for individual dismissals while redundancy payments are higher than dismissal pay in about half of the OECD countries.

While encompassing and systematic data on the frequency of dismissal and redundancy payments are hard to obtain, the information for some countries may indicate the prevalence of such transfers. In the United Kingdom during the first half of the 1990s, 1%–2% of all employees lost their job in any year and were entitled to severance pay, representing about 45% of all separations (Deakin and Wilkinson 1991, pp. 46–47). In the Netherlands, dismissals are subject to prior authorization. During the period 1990–1997, according applications for collective redundancies (respectively, individual dismissals) exceeded 7,000 (67,000) annually (Delsen and Jacobs 1999, pp. 129–133), given about 7 million employed people. Since a collective redundancy involves at least 20 dismissals in the Netherlands, the number of workers involved in mass redundancies is substantial. In Spain, collective redundancies represent roughly 20 percent of all dismissals, amounting to about 275,000 on average per year (Toharia and Ojeda 1999, p. 245), given somewhat more than 12 million employed. For the United States, Pencavel (1991, p. 63) reports that "some 39 percent of unionized workers represented by major US collective bargaining contracts in 1980 are covered by clauses relating to severance pay." Moreover, there is evidence that the share of firms in which formal severance policies exist, ranges from less than 20 percent in small companies to 64 percent in those with more than 1,500 employees (By the Numbers 1996). Accordingly, dismissal and redundancy payments seem to be widespread.

2 Employment-Protection Legislation and Efficiency Wages

Severance payments are cost to firms but income for former employees. Applying the Coase theorem to the case of mandated payments, Lazear (1988, 1990) has shown that severance pay may affect neither marginal nor absolute payoffs in a competitive market and, thus, has no employment consequences. This irrelevance result will occur if wages in a bad state of nature, which entails a reduction of the workforce, rise by the extent of severance payments, while they decline in the equally likely good state, in which employment expands, by the same amount. The increase of wages in the bad state by the full amount of severance pay ensures that marginal cost of a dismissal rise to the same extent as marginal cost of continued employment. Thus, the number of dismissals is unaffected. Moreover, a reduction in wages in the good state by the amount of severance pay guarantees that overall expected labor costs, i.e., the sum of wages and expected severance payments, remain constant. If expected labor costs are the same, so will be the expected income of workers. Given risk neutrality, labor demand and supply are unaffected by mandated severance payments.

Lazear's (1988, 1990) irrelevance result has proved to be an important benchmark. First, the prediction can be replicated in various settings, including approaches which explicitly allow for unemployment.[8] Second, the irrelevance result indicates that in the absence of differential risk attitudes or time preferences, severance payments will only affect payoffs in the presence of some externality, for example, due to differential taxes on wages and severance pay, additional firing costs, or imperfections in the capital market.

The analysis of EPL in efficiency-wage models has been based mainly on the shirking model by Shapiro and Stiglitz (1984), in which workers trade off the gain from delivering a required effort level, that is a reduced probability of a job loss, against the cost of such behavior due to the disutility of labor. This trade-off arises because firms are unable to perfectly monitor the worker's behavior. A job loss will be costly if a dismissed worker cannot immediately find a new job at the previous wage. An equilibrium will only exist if the efficiency wage exceeds the market clearing level, so that unemployment results. Hence, the informational asymmetry requires unemployment in equilibrium and causes a welfare loss.

In such a context, EPL can be modeled in various ways: if EPL reduces the probability that a worker is unfairly dismissed because he or she has been falsely blamed to have delivered insufficient effort, then EPL will have positive employment and welfare effects since it mitigates the consequences of the informational asymmetry between workers and firms. If, however, more restrictive EPL entails that workers who have shirked can only be dismissed with greater difficulties, the reverse findings will be obtained.[9]

Table 5.1 indicates that procedural restrictions represent but one element of EPL. Another important component is severance pay on which this investigation concentrates. Severance pay in shirking models has been looked at under alternative assumptions. Fella (2000), for example, presumes that workers who lose their job for insufficient effort never obtain dismissal pay, thereby focusing on the first part of fact 1. In such a setting, dismissal pay raises employment since the incentives to shirk decline. In contrast, Staffolani (2002) presumes that all dismissed workers receive dismissal payments, irrespective of the cause of the job loss, thus taking into account the second part of fact 1. Incorporating all macroeconomic repercussions, he shows in a simulation exercise that dismissal pay can raise employment. Staffolani's (2002) approach is in line with that by Galdón-Sánchez and Güell (2003), who presume that although dismissed shirkers are not entitled to dismissal pay, they can take the respective case to court and will be awarded dismissal pay if the court decides the dismissal to have been unfair. Accordingly, dismissed shirkers obtain dismissal pay with a positive probability. Moreover, Galdón-Sánchez and Güell (2003) hypothesize that workers who are dismissed for economic reasons may be denied dismissal payments, although they are legally entitled to them. In such a setting, the employment consequences of dismissal payments are ambiguous, because their impact on the relative payoff of a shirker is uncertain. Goerke (2002b) investigates the consequences of payments solely for collective redundancies, i.e. taking into account fact 2 but not fact 1. He focuses, inter alia, on the interaction of unemployment benefits and redundancy pay and the impact of wage-related transfers. Finally, Goerke (2002a) analyzes the incentives for an introduction of severance payments cooperatively at the firm level or for mandating such transfers in the entire economy. He shows that mandatory redundancy pay may be Pareto improving since changes in the unemployeds' payoff are not taken into consideration at the firm level.

The previous literature, hence, has considered only some of the empirically observable features of mandated severance pay. In particular, the co-existence of differential regulations for individual and collective dismissals, as summarized in fact 2, has been neglected. Accordingly, the subsequent analysis is based both on facts 1 and 2 in that job losses for economic reasons always entitle to dismissal pay in the event of individual dismissals or redundancy pay for collective redundancies of a possibly different amount, while a job loss for disciplinary reasons yields dismissal pay with a positive probability.

3 A Shirking Model with Dismissal and Redundancy Pay

3.1 Framework

Firms, it is assumed, cannot perfectly monitor the work effort of their employees but only observe an insufficient level with a positive probability. The asymmetric information about true effort creates incentives to shirk, that is to provide less effort than is required by the firm. To prevent this, a firm must make a job loss costly for someone who has been detected shirking and fired. An individual firm can do so by paying a wage in excess of the competitive, market-clearing level. If all firms behave in this manner, the equilibrium wage will exceed the market clearing level and unemployment will result. Accordingly, the probability of finding a new job subsequent to a dismissal is less than unity and a job loss becomes costly. Thus, the efficiency-wage model based on the assumption of asymmetric information about work effort generates unemployment in equilibrium as a result of individually rational behavior. The use of this analytical tool does not imply that other labor market features, such as collective bargaining or search frictions, are unimportant. Nevertheless, insofar as imperfect information about work effort is an important element of industrial relations, the results continue to apply to markets also characterized by other features.

Workers, it is assumed, can lose their job for three distinct reasons. They might shirk and will be caught doing so with the exogenous probability q per unit of time. There might be a 'small' exogenous shock which induces a firm to dismiss individual workers. In this case, dismissal payments have to be made. The probability that a worker is dismissed owing to such a small shock is given by b. Finally, there might be a 'large' exogenous shock which requires a firm to fire a substantial fraction of its workforce and to make redundancy payments. The probability that a worker loses the job owing to such a mass redundancy is given by h. The probabilities b, h, and q are small, to ensure that firms never dismiss a worker for two reasons simultaneously (implying $bq \approx bh \approx qb \approx 0$).

The simplifying assumption that shocks are either small or large does not affect subsequent results, since the decisive distinction is that workers may lose their job either due to a mass redundancy or not. Moreover, the difference between collective redundancy and other dismissals is well defined in many countries.[10] Accordingly, the starting point for the analysis is that firms face a firm-specific adverse shock that requires a reduction in the labor force. If the number of job losses is sufficiently high to constitute a mass redundancy, the shock will be large; otherwise it will be defined as small.

3.2 Workers

Workers are risk neutral, infinitely lived, discount future payments at the rate r $(r > 0)$, and cannot borrow or save. They are characterized by an instantaneous utility $w - e$, where w is the wage and e their effort, respectively the disutility from exerting effort. For simplicity, workers can only choose two effort levels: either effort is high $(e = \bar{e})$, conforming to the level required by the firm, or it is low $(e = 0)$.

Presume, first, that a worker chooses the low level of effort and shirks $(e = 0)$. If the worker retains the job, he will get an expected utility stream $V(0)$. An individual dismissal and a mass redundancy result in unemployment and in payoffs of $U(0, i)$ and $U(0, m)$, respectively. The expected utility of a dismissed shirker $EU(0, s)$ consists of the payoff of an individually dismissed worker $U(0, i)$, weighted by the probability that shirkers and individually dismissed workers obtain the same payments, plus the payoff of a worker who is dismissed as a shirker $U(0, s)$, multiplied by the respective probability that a shirker receives no dismissal pay. Assume, second, that the worker exerts the required effort level $(e = \bar{e})$ and, therefore, will not be fired for shirking. The resulting expected utility streams in the case of unemployment due to an individual dismissal or a mass redundancy are denoted $U(\bar{e}, i)$ and $U(\bar{e}, m)$. Finally, employment yields $V(\bar{e})$.

The actions of workers, the potential states of nature which these actions entail, and the various payoffs are depicted in figure 5.1. Given the worker's choice of effort, the player 'Nature' decides whether a shirker is detected (for $e = 0$)—with probability q—or whether a shock occurs. In all these cases, a worker loses the job and obtains the respective payoffs from unemployment. The probabilities of a job loss due to economic reasons are presumed to be the same for a shirker and a non-shirker. The probability that a worker remains employed is, thus, given by $1 - h - b$ for a non-shirker and $1 - h - q - b$ for a shirker.

To focus on severance pay, it is presumed that unemployment benefits $\bar{w}$ are paid to every unemployed worker, irrespective of the cause of the job loss. Unemployment insurance systems in OECD countries often condition payments on a person being capable and willing to take up a new job and/or on not being responsible for the job loss.[11] A voluntary quit or gross misconduct are sometimes regarded as

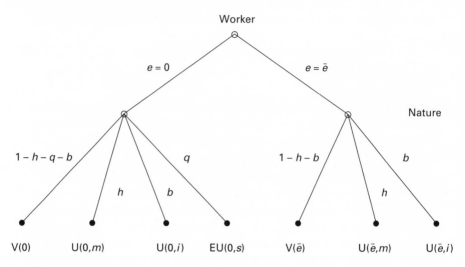

Figure 5.1
Worker's payoffs.

sufficient conditions for an unemployed worker to have caused the job loss. Restricting unemployment compensation for shirkers can, accordingly, mitigate the adverse employment and welfare consequences arising in an efficiency-wage economy.[12] However, the comparative effects of dismissal and redundancy pay remain the same because only unemployment benefits but neither dismissal nor redundancy payments are conditioned on the cause of the job loss.

The instantaneous utility stream $rV(\bar{e})$ from being employed and providing the required effort $\bar{e}$ consists of the wage w less the disutility from effort and the utility loss when fired. Such a utility loss may either arise due to a small shock, in which case it amounts to $V(\bar{e}) - U(\bar{e}, i)$, or it may be caused by a large shock, in which case it is $V(\bar{e}) - U(\bar{e}, m)$. Therefore, an employed non-shirker can be described by the asset equation

$$rV(\bar{e}) = w - \bar{e} + b[U(\bar{e}, i) - V(\bar{e})] + h[U(\bar{e}, m) - V(\bar{e})]. \tag{1}$$

Suppose that a dismissed shirker is denied dismissal pay with the probability $(1 - \alpha)$, where $0 \leq \alpha \leq 1$. The expected utility stream in the case of a job loss due to shirking is then

$$EU(0, s) = \alpha U(0, i) + (1 - \alpha)U(0, s).$$

For $\alpha = 1$ (0), shirkers always (never) obtain dismissal payments. Fact 1 suggests a substantially positive value for α as an adequate assumption for many OECD countries. An employed shirker can accordingly be described by

$$rV(0) = w + b[U(0,i) - V(0)] + q[EU(0,s) - V(0)] + h[U(0,m) - V(0)].$$
(2)

Given the existence of negative shocks, a steady state of the labor market—that is, a situation in which the number of workers who lose their jobs equals the number of unemployed who find a new job—requires that firms can be exposed to positive shocks as well. Therefore, the instantaneous expected utility stream $rU(\bar{e},i)$ of a non-shirker who has been dismissed individually is defined by unemployment benefits $\bar{w}$ and dismissal payments D per period of unemployment, plus the expected utility gain from finding a new job. Dismissal and redundancy payments are made in every period of unemployment.[13] An unemployed worker finds a new job with probability a per period, the job-acquisition rate. Irrespective of whether an unemployed has shirked or not, he has the same probability of obtaining a new job. Thus, past effort choices are private information of a worker and do not affect future job opportunities.[14] Re-employment yields a utility gain $V(\bar{e}) - U(\bar{e},i)$. The instantaneous expected utility stream of a non-shirker who is dismissed individually is then

$$rU(\bar{e},i) = \bar{w} + D + a[V(\bar{e}) - U(\bar{e},i)].$$
(3)

The expected utility streams of the other unemployed, namely those who have lost their job because of insufficient effort or due to a mass redundancy, can be defined accordingly. For example, a worker who loses the job because he has been caught shirking and is denied dismissal payments, is characterized by a utility stream $U(0,s)$ which differs from the utility stream $U(\bar{e},i)$ of a non-shirker who is dismissed individually by dismissal payments D, implying

$$rU(0,s) = \bar{w} + a[V(0) - U(0,s)].$$

A worker who is dismissed in the context of a collective redundancy does not receive dismissal but redundancy payments R instead. In line with fact 2, it is presumed that dismissal payments D are not less than redundancy payments R, and that D and R can be altered separately.

A worker will not shirk if $V(\bar{e}) \geq V(0)$ holds. Having set out the main ingredients of the model which allow to calculate the wage which warrants this inequality, further details are relegated to the appendix. From equations (1)–(3), the efficiency wage w^e, which ensures that workers provide the effort level $\bar{e}$, is found to be (see appendix)

$$w^e = \frac{\bar{e}}{q}(r + b + h + a + q) + \bar{w} - h\frac{R}{r+a} - \frac{D}{r+a}\{b - \alpha(r + b + h + a)\}.$$

(4)

More generous unemployment benefits $\bar{w}$ increase the payoff of a shirker. In order to induce workers to exert effort, the efficiency wage has to rise. Moreover, payments to workers who have lost their job due to a large shock increase the utility from selecting the required amount of effort $\bar{e}$. The existence of redundancy pay R allows for a reduction of the wage: effectively, payments for collective dismissals enable a partial distinction between job losses for exogenous reasons and due to insufficient effort. This distinction is not perfect as workers who have lost their jobs owing to small shocks have not shirked either. But raising R makes only those workers better off who have not been caught shirking.

The impact of payments D to individually dismissed workers on the efficiency wage depends on the extent to which shirkers can be denied dismissal pay (cf. Galdón-Sánchez and Güell 2003). If this is not feasible at all ($\alpha = 1$), the term in curly brackets in equation (4) will collapse to $-(r + h + a)$ and dismissal pay will raise the efficiency wage since shirking becomes more attractive. This is because such payments increase the payoff of non-shirkers with the probability b and of shirkers with the probability $b + q$. However, if shirkers can be denied dismissal payments completely ($\alpha = 0$), dismissal and redundancy pay will be equivalent and lower the efficiency wage because shirking becomes less desirable (Fella 2000). As was argued in section 1, the relevant empirical case is the one in which an exclusion of shirkers from the impact of dismissal pay is incomplete, if not impossible.

Substituting in equation (1) for, first, the efficiency wage w^e and, second, the expected utility streams of unemployed, the instantaneous expected utility stream of an employed non-shirker can be derived explicitly:

$$rV(\bar{e}) = \frac{\bar{e}}{q}(r + a) + \bar{w} + \alpha D.$$

(5)

Equation (5) has a straightforward interpretation: the instantaneous expected utility of an employed non-shirker $rV(\bar{e})$ equals the sum of the expected monetary payoff of a shirker and a measure of the disutility of effort. A shirker's monetary payoff per period consists of unemployment benefits $\bar{w}$ and dismissal pay D with probability α. The utility of an employed non-shirker decreases with the probability q of being detected shirking. The higher this probability is, the lower the efficiency wage will be (cf. equation (4)). A lower wage, in turn, reduces the expected utility of a non-shirker. Moreover, the utility of an employed non-shirker rises with the probability a of finding a new job since a job loss entails a lower expected duration of unemployment.

3.3 Firms

There is a fixed number μ of ex-ante identical firms. Consistency with the specification of the workers' maximization problem requires that firms choose a level of employment prior to the revelation of the firm-specific shock which will be too high if the shock is negative and too low if positive. Such a situation will arise, for example, if firms can vary employment at no cost before the type of shock is revealed, while they incur adjustment costs subsequent to its disclosure. To capture this adjustment behavior, a simplified approach is pursued. Before the beginning of a period, each of the μ firms sets an efficiency wage and chooses employment n. Thus, the wage is not contingent on the economic situation (cf. equation (4)). A firm will employ more (less) than n people if a positive (negative) shock occurs. Employment levels in the various states of nature are predetermined. This assumption, which is relaxed in subsection 4.2, guarantees that severance pay has negative employment effects in the absence of wage adjustments.[15] Shocks last one period and are not correlated over time. For simplicity, and as the relative impact of the two types of severance pay under consideration is not affected, the costless adjustment of employment prior to a period takes place by reallocating workers from firms with excessive employment to those with an insufficient number of workers. Hence, dismissal probabilities and the job-acquisition rate are unaffected by the adjustments. Given these assumptions, expected profits are invariant over time.

Dismissals can involve cost in addition to transfer payments, such as for legal proceedings or the adherence to procedural regulations (see table 5.1). These are represented by a firing-cost mark-up $\xi \geq 0$ on severance payments. While empirical evidence is scarce, data for Italy and the United Kingdom suggest that the non-transfer component of dismissal costs may be less than 15 percent.[16] Total cost per worker in the case of an individual dismissal amount to $D(1 + \xi)/(r + a)$. This is the case since, first, firms are assumed to also use the discount factor r and, second, a worker finds a new job with probability a, severance pay being discontinued in this case, such that the effective discount rate for severance payments is $r + a$.

The firm's production function f is strictly concave in effective employment ($f(en) > f''\, 0$), while the capital stock is fixed and its costs are normalized to zero. Firms pay taxes $\tau \geq 0$, defined as a fraction of wage payments. Since the incidence of a tax on the worker's income is identical to that on the firm's payroll in the present model, given that unemployment benefits $\bar{w}$ are not taxed,[17] the rate τ includes all taxes levied on wages. The effective tax rate on labor income in many countries is in the range 30%–40%.[18] A plausible assumption, hence, is that the tax rate τ exceeds the firing-cost mark-up ξ.

Denoting aggregate employment by N, and normalizing labor supply to unity, a steady state on the labor market, in which flows into and out of unemployment are equal implies $(b + h)N = a(1 - N)$ because shirking does not occur in equilibrium. Using this steady-state condition in the expression for expected profits and maximization with respect to employment yields the firm's first-order condition (see the appendix for a derivation):

$$\pi_n = \hat{f}'\bar{e} - w^e(1 + \tau) - \frac{hR + bD}{r + a}(1 + \xi) = 0. \tag{6}$$

Equation (6) shows that the firm chooses employment to balance the value of the expected additional output of a worker $\hat{f}'\bar{e}$ with the cost of an additional worker which consist of the efficiency wage w^e, taxes τw^e and expected severance pay. Individual dismissal payments D arise with the probability b, while redundancy payments R for collective redundancies are incurred with probability h. Both are subject to the firing-cost mark-up ξ.

4   Who Benefits from Dismissal and Redundancy Payments?

As a first step, the effects of introducing or raising dismissal and redundancy pay on expected profits $E(\Pi)$ and the expected utility stream of an employed non-shirker $V(\bar{e})$ are investigated. When looking for an explanation for the empirical observation that entitlements to payments in the case of mass redundancies are more extensive than those for individual dismissals, the payoffs of all economic actors need to be considered. Accordingly, as a second step, unemployed workers and the government are included in the investigation. The analysis is initially based on the assumption that the job-acquisition rate is fixed. Subsection 4.2 incorporates general equilibrium repercussions by endogenizing the job-acquisition rate. Moreover, it is assumed that shirkers cannot be excluded from dismissal pay, implying $\alpha = 1$, and that the probabilities b and h are constant.

4.1   Fixed Job-Acquisition Rate

Severance payments decrease profits for a given wage. Since dismissal pay D for individual dismissals drives up wages, profits unambiguously decline with D. However, redundancy pay lowers the wage because only those workers benefit who have not been caught shirking. Profits will be unaffected by a variation in redundancy pay if the tax rate and the firing-cost mark-up are the same ($\tau = \xi$; see appendix). This is because the fall in wages has to exactly compensate the rise in expected redundancy pay to induce workers to supply the same effort. If the fall in wages is amplified by taxes to the same extent as the increase in redundancy pay is magnified by the firing-cost mark-up, marginal employment cost, profits and employment will remain constant. This finding replicates Lazear's (1988, 1990) irrelevance result. However, given the empirical evidence mentioned above, a tax rate which exceeds the firing-cost mark-up ($\tau > \xi$) is a plausible assumption. In this case, the decrease in marginal employment costs is amplified as firms save not only on wages but also tax payments. Employment becomes cheaper and profits rise.[19]

The change in the expected utility stream $V(\bar{e})$ of an employed worker due to severance payments can be derived from equation (5) and is positive for dismissal payments and zero for redundancy pay. Dismissal payments increase the utility stream of an employed worker for two reasons: first, firms raise the wage since the incentives to shirk become greater. Higher wages raise the payoff of an employed worker directly but also via the utility stream in the event of a dismissal. Second, a currently employed worker obtains a utility increase due to higher dismissal pay as the payoff rises should he be dismissed individually. Both effects work in the same direction.

Redundancy payments, in contrast, leave the utility stream of an employed worker unaffected. This is the case because both redundancy pay and wages reduce the incentives to shirk. Given risk neutrality, the decision to provide the required level of effort only depends on expected income. Therefore, any rise in redundancy pay induces firms to lower the wage. Wage and redundancy pay effects cancel out such that the utility stream from non-shirking is independent of the magnitude of redundancy pay (cf. equation (5)). Such a complete adjustment cannot occur for dismissal pay because this type of transfer raises the incentives to shirk, so that higher wages are needed to counteract the impact on the choice of effort.

Turning to unemployed workers, it is convenient to assume that variations in severance pay have no retroactive consequences but only alter their future payoff. Thus, the expected utility stream of a currently unemployed non-shirker consists of unemployment benefits $\bar{w}$ and the utility gain if employed again $[\bar{w} + aV(\bar{e})]/(r + a)$ (cf. equation (3)). This shows that unemployed workers will solely benefit from severance payments if employed workers are also better off. This is because both the direct wage effect and the indirect impact via a variation in the payoff if dismissed will only be enjoyed if an unemployed worker finds a new job.

Finally, consider the government. Generally, there are two effects at work. First, a change in wages entails an alteration of employment of the opposite direction (cf. equation (6)), so that the payroll and also tax receipts $w^e N \tau$ vary in an uncertain manner. Second, more employment implies less expenditure on unemployment compensation. If additional employment raises tax receipts, the government, like firms, will benefit from redundancy payments for $\tau > \xi$, while dismissal payments cause a budget deficit.[20] Accordingly, taking into account the budgetary repercussions tends to strengthen the positive welfare impact of payments in the event of collective redundancies, relative to dismissal pay for individual dismissals.

The intuition for the possibility of redundancy pay generating a Pareto improvement may be summarized as follows: redundancy payments are only obtained by workers who have not been caught shirking. Accordingly, they mitigate the incentives to shirk and the efficiency wage declines. Risk-neutral workers are indifferent to this change in the composition of their expected remuneration. If wages are taxed at a higher rate than redundancy payments are burdened by a firing-cost mark-up, employment and profits will rise. The increase in profits due to lower tax payments reduces government revenues by the same amount. However, the increase in employment, which has no first-order profit effect, reduces expenditure for unemployment benefits and raises output. Thus, the overall payoff of workers, firms and the government rises. This virtuous chain cannot arise in the case of dismissal payments for individual dismissals, since dismissal pay tends to accentuate the shirking problem, unless shirkers can be excluded from its receipt.

4.2 Variable Job-Acquisition Rate

It has been assumed thus far that, first, the probabilities of finding and losing a job are constant and, second, a steady state on the labor market prevails. However, the two presumptions are not consistent. This is because a change in employment N requires at least one of the probabilities b, h, a to vary, given the steady-state condition

$$(b + h)N = a(1 - N).$$

Suppose, therefore, that the inflow rates into unemployment b and h remain unaffected by variations in employment, while the outflow rate a adjusts. Employment increases the job-acquisition rate a, so that a declines with dismissal pay and rises with redundancy pay for $\tau > \xi$ (see appendix).

Focusing, first, on dismissal pay, the decrease in the probability of finding a new job reduces the utility from being unemployed and raises the incentives to provide effort. This implies a fall in the efficiency wage and higher employment. Lower wages raise profits and reduce an employed worker's payoff. Whether this impact is sufficient to reverse the initially positive consequences on a worker's payoff for a given job-acquisition rate cannot be ascertained analytically. Moreover, unemployed workers suffer from a lower job-acquisition rate directly as their chances of finding a new job decline. Finally, if the government's payoff equals its tax receipts $Nw^e t$, less the expenditure for unemployment compensation $(1 - N)\bar{w}$, this payoff will change in a potentially ambiguous manner as any wage variation entails an employment alteration of the opposite direction, but of uncertain magnitude. Therefore, all results on agent-specific payoffs due to higher dismissal pay, computed above for a given job-acquisition rate a, may be overturned if the adjustment in the probability of finding a new job is taken into account.

However, if the variation in the aggregate payoff is computed, it can be shown that this uncertainty disappears. First, if wages fall due to the lower job-acquisition rate, firms will benefit from this effect to the same extent as workers lose. Thus, the overall payoff is unaffected by additional wage adjustments. Second, tax alterations cancel out since less (or more) tax payments by firms imply a variation in tax receipts by the government of exactly the same magnitude. Accordingly, the only additional effect which has to be taken into account arises from the direct impact of a lower job-acquisition rate on the payoffs of workers, firms, and the government. The fall in the job-acquisition rate reduces the payoff both of employed and unemployed workers, relative to a situation in which the job-acquisition rate is constant, because a lower acquisition rate reduces the utility from being unemployed.[21] It can, therefore, be concluded that the overall incentives for introducing dismissal payments for individual dismissals will be negative if, first, such payments have adverse employment effects in the absence of wage adjustments and, second, shirkers cannot be excluded from such payments. This finding can rationalize the empirical feature that entitlements to dismissal payments in many OECD countries are low unless workers are characterized by a long job tenure (see fact 1).

Turning, second, to redundancy payments, it is helpful to remember that they will raise the job-acquisition rate a if the tax rate τ exceeds the firing-cost mark-up ξ. Accordingly, wages rise and employment falls, relative to the case of a given job-acquisition rate. Thus, the increase in profits due to redundancy payments occurring for a constant job-acquisition rate is reduced and may even become negative. By the same argument as for dismissal pay above, the additional wage and tax effects of redundancy payments do not alter the combined payoff of firms, workers, and the government. However, a higher job-acquisition rate a makes workers better off, since those who currently are or in future will be unemployed obtain a new job with a higher probability. Furthermore, the increase in the job-acquisition rate raises the number of redundancies, for given dismissal probabilities. Accordingly, payments to workers but also the non-transfer component due to the firing-cost mark-up rise. It can be shown that if this effect is not too strong, redundancy pay will make firms, workers, and government together better off. This result will unambiguously hold if there is no firing-cost mark-up and redundancy pay has negative employment effects in the absence of wage adjustments.

5 Extensions

It has been shown above that payments in the event of individual dismissals will reduce the society's payoff if shirkers are entitled to these benefits ($\alpha = 1$). Subsection 5.1 relaxes this assumption and investigates the consequences of (partially) excluding shirkers from dismissal payments. In addition, it has been demonstrated that redundancy pay will raise the aggregate payoff if there is no firing-cost mark-up but a positive tax rate on labor, while the dismissal probabilities b and h are constant. However, if dismissals become more costly, the probability of a job loss will fall for a given level of aggregate employment. In such a situation, severance payments may no longer have adverse employment consequences in the absence of wage adjustments. Subsection 5.2 investigates how the results are affected by the assumption of given dismissal probabilities.

5.1   Excludability of Shirkers from Dismissal Pay Entitlements

Suppose that firms do not have to make dismissal payments to shirkers with probability one, but can avoid payments with the probability $1 - \alpha > 0$. Alternatively, the parameter α can be interpreted as the fraction of dismissal pay for an individually dismissed non-shirker which a shirker obtains. If a worker takes into account that a job loss owing to shirking yields an expected dismissal pay αD when deciding whether to provide the required effort level $\bar{e}$, firms can adjust the efficiency wage. In the limiting case of $\alpha = 0$, dismissal and redundancy pay become equivalent (compare equations (4) and (5)) since shirkers can be excluded from both types of transfers. Furthermore, it can be noted from equation (4) and the steady-state condition for the labor market, that wages continue to rise with dismissal pay for a value of

$$\alpha > \alpha^{\text{crit}} \equiv b(1 - N)/(b + h) + b/r.$$

Accordingly, as long as the fraction of shirkers which can be excluded from the receipt of dismissal pay is less than $1 - \alpha^{\text{crit}}$, the prediction derived in subsection 4.1 continues to apply, namely that such transfers reduce the aggregate payoff.

If the fraction of shirkers which obtains dismissal pay falls below the critical value α^{crit}, the efficiency wage will decline with dismissal payments. In such a case, the aggregate payoff of workers, firms, and the government may increase. However, unless the exclusion of shirkers is perfect ($\alpha = 0$), the increase in the overall payoff will be smaller than that which is obtained from redundancy pay for $\tau > \xi$. To illustrate this finding, suppose that shirkers can be completely barred from the receipt of dismissal pay. In this case, dismissal pay, being equivalent to redundancy pay, represents an incentive not to shirk since only non-shirkers can obtain such payments. For intermediate cases $(0 < \alpha \leq 1)$, however, redundancy pay provides stronger incentives to reduce shirking than dismissal payments because shirkers obtain the latter with a greater probability than the former. Moreover, the direct cost effect of dismissal pay will be the same as that of redundancy pay. Accordingly, an increase in the combined payoff of workers, firms and the government is more likely to occur for redundancy pay in the event of collective redundancies than for dismissal pay for individual dismissals. The basic prediction of section 4 will not be affected, namely that redundancy pay is better suited than dismissal pay to mitigate the shirking problem and, thus, more likely to be found in economies in which wages are a means to restrict or prevent shirking.

5.2 Variable Dismissal Probabilities

Firing costs, irrespective of their nature, tend to reduce the number of employees because expected labor costs rise. Conversely, such cost might also have positive employment consequences to the extent that firms become more hesitant to dismiss workers.[22] In terms of the above model, the potentially positive employment effects of severance payments have been ignored since the probabilities b and h of dismissing workers have been treated as constants. However, if higher severance payments lower dismissal probabilities, the overall effects of changes in such transfers will also depend on the impact of these probabilities on profits, tax receipts and the utility streams of workers. From equation (4) it can be seen for $\alpha = 1$ that the efficiency wage rises with the probability of a shock.[23] Applying the same argument as in section 4, it can be shown that the wage and tax effects will cancel out for a given level of employment if firms, workers, and the government are considered in aggregate. Moreover, lower dismissal probabilities entail fewer instances of severance payments. However, fewer transfers do not change the aggregate payoff since the gain of one economic actor is the loss of another. Therefore, the additional effects of lower dismissal probabilities on the aggregate payoff result from the increase in employment and the reduction in firing costs other than severance payments. Given an additional positive effect on the aggregate payoff, the incentives for introducing or raising redundancy payments for collective redundancies are strengthened. By the same token, the reduction in the aggregate payoff due to dismissal pay for individual job losses will be mitigated if dismissal probabilities fall. If a given variation in dismissal and redundancy pay affects dismissal probabilities in the same way, the payoffs will be altered in the same manner and the relative superiority of redundancy payments remains.

Summary

The starting point of this analysis has been the question of how the more extensive entitlements to payments in the event of a collective redundancy relative to those for an individual job loss in many OECD countries can be explained. Using a shirking model of efficiency wages it has been shown that redundancy payments for collective redundancies can reduce the incentives to shirk and, thereby, mitigate the adverse welfare consequences of asymmetric information about the employees' behavior. The increase in the combined payoff of firms, workers, and the government will materialize if

• the entire tax rate on labor exceeds the firing-cost mark-up on redundancy payments,

• workers who have been caught shirking do not obtain redundancy pay,

and

• the budgetary effects of more people obtaining wage payments instead of unemployment benefits are greater than the impact of the firing-cost mark-up on firms' profits.

Endogenizing dismissal probabilities does not change the qualitative result. Moreover, it has been demonstrated that dismissal payments for individual dismissals will reduce the aggregate payoff of firms, workers, and the government if

• shirkers cannot be excluded from the receipt of severance payments with a sufficiently high probability

and

• dismissal probabilities are fixed.

Relaxing either of these assumptions can entail an increase in the aggregate payoff. However, unless workers who have been caught shirking can be excluded from dismissal payments for individual job losses with a greater probability than from an entitlement to redundancy pay for collective redundancies, redundancy pay will be more beneficial for society than dismissal pay.

Appendix

Efficiency Wage

Solving equations (1) and (2) for $V(\bar{e})$ and $V(0)$, respectively, yields

$$V(\bar{e}) = \frac{w - \bar{e} + bU(\bar{e}, i) + hU(\bar{e}, m)}{r + b + h} \tag{A.1}$$

and

$$V(0) = \frac{w + (b + q\alpha)U(0, i) + q(1 - \alpha)U(0, s) + hU(0, m)}{r + b + q + h}. \tag{A.2}$$

The instantaneous expected utility streams $rU(e, x)$ of a worker who becomes unemployed, where e denotes the effort level ($e = 0$ or $e = \bar{e} > 0$) and x whether the worker has lost the job individually (i), in the wake of a mass redundancy (m), or due to shirking (s), are given by the following equations:

$$rU(e, i) = \bar{w} + D + a[V(e) - U(e, i)], \tag{A.3}$$

$$rU(e, m) = \bar{w} + R + a[V(e) - U(e, m)], \tag{A.4}$$

$$rU(0, s) = \bar{w} + a[V(0) - U(0, s)]. \tag{A.5}$$

Equations (A.3)–(A.5) can be simplified to yield

$$U(\bar{e}, i) = \frac{\bar{w} + D + aV(\bar{e})}{r + a} = U(\bar{e}, m) - \frac{R - D}{r + a} \tag{A.6}$$

and

$$U(0, i) = \frac{\bar{w} + D + aV(0)}{r + a} = U(0, m) - \frac{R - D}{r + a} = U(0, s) + \frac{D}{r + a}. \tag{A.7}$$

Substituting in (A.1) and (A.2), we can calculate the utility streams of employed workers:

$$V(\bar{e}) = \frac{(w - \bar{e})(r + a) + (b + h)\bar{w} + bD + hR}{r(r + b + h + a)}, \tag{A.8}$$

$$V(0) = \frac{w(r+a) + (b+q+h)\bar{w} + hR + (b+q\alpha)D}{r(r+b+q+h+a)}. \quad\text{(A.9)}$$

A worker will not shirk if $V(\bar{e}) \geq V(0)$. Solving this condition as equality yields equation (4) in the main text. Substituting w^e into (A.8) then gives expression (5). Note that all derivations are based on the constraint $V(\bar{e}) > U(\bar{e}, m)$, which holds for a value of $R < \bar{e}(r+a)/q + \alpha D$ (for similar restrictions, see Saint-Paul 1995, Fella 2000, or Goerke 2002b).

Profit Maximization

A firm will employ $Tn > n$ people if there is a positive shock and Cn (Pn), $0 < P < C < 1$ people if a small (large) adverse shock occurs, where T, C, and P are assumed to be fixed. The probability that a firm experiences a positive shock because the output price rises from unity to $\bar{T} > 1$, and the company employs $Tn > n$ workers, is β, where $0 < \beta < 1$. In case of a small shock, the output price will fall to $\bar{C} < 1$ and employment will be Cn. This state occurs with probability c and implies that dismissal pay D is obtained by $(1 - C)n$ workers. A mass redundancy due to an output price $\bar{P} < 1$ takes place with probability p, leaves employment at Pn, and entitles $(1 - P)n$ workers to redundancy pay R. If firms experience either a positive or a negative shock, the probability of a positive shock will be $\beta = 1 - c - p$. Given the firing-cost mark-up $\xi \geq 0$, total cost per worker in the case of an individual dismissal amount to $D(1 + \xi)/(r + a)$. Thus, expected profits are

$$E(\Pi) = (1 - c - p)[\bar{T}f(Tn\bar{e}) - w^e nT(1 + \tau)]$$

$$+ c\bar{C}f(Cn\bar{e}) + p\bar{P}f(Pn\bar{e}) - (cC + pP)w^e n(1 + \tau).$$

$$- \frac{[c(1 - C)D + p(1 - P)R]}{r + a}n(1 + \xi). \quad\text{(A.10)}$$

A steady state implies $(b + h)N = a(1 - N)$. Inflows due to individual dismissals $\mu nc(1 - C)$ have to match aggregate inflows bN, i.e., $b = c(1 - C)$. The respective equalities for mass redundancies and employment expansions entail

$$h = p(1 - P),$$

$$a(1 - N) = (1 - c - p)(T - 1)\mu n,$$

and

$$(1 - c - p)T + cC + pP = 1.$$

An according substitution and maximization of (A.10) yields

$$\frac{d(\mathrm{E}(\Pi))}{dn} \equiv \pi_n = 0$$

(cf. equation (6)), where the marginal expected output $\hat{f}'\bar{e}$ is defined as

$$\hat{f}'\bar{e} \equiv \bar{e}\{\beta \bar{T} f'(Tn\bar{e})T + (1 - \beta)[(1 - c - p)f'(n\bar{e})$$

$$+ c\bar{C}(f'(Cn\bar{e})C + p\bar{P}(f'(Pn\bar{e})P]\} > 0. \tag{A.11}$$

The second-order condition $\pi_{nn} < 0$ will be warranted if f is strictly concave, as was assumed above.

Employment and Payoff Effects
The variation in employment per firm n due to severance payments for $\alpha = 1$ can be derived as follows:

$$\left.\frac{dn}{dD}\right|_{\alpha=1} = \frac{\dfrac{\partial w^{\mathrm{e}}}{\partial D}(1 + \tau) + \dfrac{b}{r + a}(1 + \xi)}{\pi_{nn}} = \frac{(1 + \tau)(r + h + a) + (1 + \xi)b}{(r + a)\pi_{nn}} < 0,$$
$$\tag{A.12}$$

$$\frac{dn}{dR} = \frac{\dfrac{\partial w^{\mathrm{e}}}{\partial R}(1 + \tau) + \dfrac{h}{r + a}(1 + \xi)}{\pi_{nn}} = \frac{h(\xi - \tau)}{(r + a)\pi_{nn}} > 0 \quad \text{for } \tau > \xi. \tag{A.13}$$

Aggregate employment effects are found using the steady-state condition $a = (b + h)N/(1 - N)$. Substituting in the definition of the efficiency wage (4) implies, for $\alpha = 1$,

$$Z = w^{\mathrm{e}} - \frac{\bar{e}}{q}(r + b + q + h + a(N)) - \bar{w} + \frac{hR}{r + a(N)} - \frac{D(r + h + a(N))}{r + a(N)} = 0. \tag{A.14}$$

Aggregating labor demand over all μ ex-ante identical firms, one obtains from (6)

$$Y = \hat{f}'(N)\bar{e} - w^{\mathrm{e}}(1 + \tau) - \frac{hR + bD}{r + a(N)}(1 + \xi) = 0. \tag{A.15}$$

The derivatives of Z and Y are given by

$$Z_w = 1,$$

$$Y_w = -(1 + \tau) < 0,$$

$$Z_R = h/(r + a) > 0,$$

$$Y_R = -(1 + \xi)h/(r + a) < 0,$$

$$Y_D = -(1 + \xi)b/(r + a) < 0, \tag{A.16}$$

$$Z_D = -1 - h/(r + a) < 0,$$

$$Y_N = \hat{f}''(N)\bar{e}^2 + \frac{hR + bD}{(r + a)^2}(1 + \xi)a_N,$$

and

$$Z_N = a_N \left[-\frac{\bar{e}}{q} - \frac{h(R - D)}{(r + a)^2} \right] < 0 \quad \text{for } R \geq D. \tag{A.17}$$

The subsequent analysis is based on the assumption of a negatively sloped labor demand curve $(dN/dw < 0)$ and $R \geq D$ in accordance with fact 2. This entails $Y_N < 0$ as $dN/dw = -Y_w/Y_N < 0$, while $Y_w < 0$ holds and guarantees $Y_N Z_w - Z_N Y_w < 0$. Thus, the changes in employment N due to higher severance payments are found to be as follows:

$$\frac{dN}{dR} = \frac{h(\xi - \tau)}{(r + a)(Y_N Z_w - Z_N Y_w)} > 0 \quad \text{for } \tau > \xi, \tag{A.18}$$

$$\frac{dN}{dD} = \frac{b(1 + \xi) + (1 + \tau)[r + a + h]}{(r + a)(Y_N Z_w - Z_N Y_w)} < 0. \tag{A.19}$$

The changes in expected profits $E(\Pi)$ due to severance payments, taking into account the variation in wages (equations (4) and (6)), are as follows:

$$\left. \frac{dE(\Pi)}{dD} \right|_{\alpha=1} = -\frac{n}{r + a}[(r + h + a)(1 + \tau) + b(1 + \xi)] < 0, \tag{A.20}$$

$$\frac{dE(\Pi)}{dR} = \frac{nh}{r + a}[\tau - \xi] > 0 \quad \text{for } \tau > \xi. \tag{A.21}$$

Acknowledgments

I am grateful for comments by Thomas Moutos, Susan Vroman, Jim Albrecht, Mick Keen, Alfons Weichenrieder, Jonas Agell, two anonymous referees, and participants in the CESifo/ISPE conferences on Labour Market Institutions and Public Regulation, and for financial support by the Deutsche Forschungsgemeinschaft.

Notes

1. Bentolila and Bertola (1990) and Siebert (1997) provide theoretical arguments. The OECD (1999, pp. 119–125) and Addison and Teixeira (2003) survey the empirical evidence.

2. See Garibaldi and Violante 2002, Bertola 2004, or Goerke 2002a for the first response, Blanchard and Wolfers 2000 or Belot and van Ours 2001 for the second, and Bertola et al. 1999, 2000 for the third reaction.

3. Payments in the event of a job loss are usually labeled severance pay. This is also the term chosen by the OECD (1999). The terms "redundancy" and "dismissal pay" can be found as well. However, a terminology which allows to distinguish between payments in the case of individual dismissals and collective redundancies has not yet been established. In this paper, *severance* pay encompasses all types of payments, as reflected by the title, while *dismissal* pay refers to transfers to workers who are individually dismissed and *redundancy* pay denotes transfers in the case of collective redundancies.

4. For details see, inter alia, OECD 1999, pp. 98–100; European Commission 1999, pp. 86–89.

5. OECD 1999, pp. 101–103; EIRR 1999; Mosley and Kruppe 1993, p. 148; Schömann et al. 1998, pp. 24–71.

6. See Emerson 1988, EIRR 1999, or Bertola et al. 1999 for according information. Schömann et al. (1998, pp. 35, 38, 49, 57, 60) report that summary dismissals—which generally imply that workers forfeit all entitlements to dismissal pay—require gross misconduct in France, Germany, Italy, Portugal, and Spain. In Germany gross misconduct implies persistent disobedience, fighting, or theft; in Portugal the respective list of behavioral criteria includes disobedience of orders, aggravation of other workers, intentional acts of damage, fighting, and false declarations. In the Netherlands a summary dismissal is feasible for "the persistent refusal to obey orders" (Delsen and Jacobs 1999, p. 159).

7. Bureau of National Affairs, Employee Discipline and Discharge, PPF Survey No. 1309, January 1985, p. 1, cited in Krueger 1991 (p. 646, n. 3).

8. See, for example, Mortensen 1978; Burda 1992; Booth 1997; Alvarez and Veracierto 2000; Goerke 2002b; Garibaldi and Violante 2002; Bertola 2004.

9. For these results see Levine 1989; Sjostrom 1993; Carter and De Lancey 1997; Alvi 1998; Lin 2002.

10. In the European Union, for example, directive 98/129/EC classifies a mass redundancy as a dismissal of a minimum number of employees relative to the size of an establishment. More specifically, the directive states: "... 'collective redundancies' means dismissals effected by an employer for one or more reasons not related to the individual workers concerned where, according to the choice of the Member States, the number of redundancies is: (i) either, over a period of 30 days: at least 10 in establishments normally employing more than 20 and less than 100 workers, at least 10% of the number of workers in establishments normally employing at least 100 but less than 300 workers,

at least 30 in establishments normally employing 300 workers or more ... (ii) or, over a period of 90 days, at least 20, whatever the number of workers normally employed in the establishments in question...." See *Official Journal of the European Communities* no. 225 (12.8.1998) and no. 48 (22.2.1975).

11. See, for example, Atkinson 1999, pp. 86–89; Grubb 2000; Tzannatos and Roddis 1998, pp. 30–33.

12. Bull (1985), Atkinson (1999, pp. 83–105), and Goerke (2000) investigate unemployment benefits in efficiency-wage models from which shirkers can be fully or partially excluded.

13. The presumption that workers cannot save requires the definition of severance pay as a transfer per unit of time. Moreover, the assumption that workers receive severance pay only during an unemployment spell ensures that their utility stream does not change over time and, moreover, warrants the existence of a stationary equilibrium.

14. This presumption is the same as in the original analysis by Shapiro and Stiglitz (1984), but contrasts, for example, with the approach of Gibbons and Katz (1991).

15. For a corresponding approach see, for example, Acemoglu and Angrist 2001.

16. Garibaldi and Violante (1999) calculate that the transfer component of total firing costs in the UK (Italy) amounts to more than 90% (88%), translating into a firing cost mark-up ξ between 11% and 14% ($D(1 + \xi) = 1$ for $D = 0.9$ or 0.88). In a later study, the authors calculate that dismissal cases which go to trial in Italy and, thus, involve an above average fraction of firing costs, still entail a "transfer component of the total firing costs (which) varies from 66 to 74 percent" (Garibaldi and Violante 2002, p. 22).

17. See Picard and Toulemonde 2001.

18. See, inter alia, Mendoza et al. 1994; Leibfritz et al. 1997; Mongay-Martinez and Fernandez-Bayon 2001.

19. The finding illustrates the assertion by Summers (1989, pp. 180–181) that "in terms of their allocational effects on employment, mandated benefits represent a tax at a rate equal to the difference between the employer's cost of providing the benefit and the employee's valuation of it, not at a rate equal to the cost to the employer of providing the benefit."

20. In Goerke 2002b it is, furthermore, shown that in the absence of a firing cost mark-up the increase in profits exceeds a possible decline in tax receipts such that the combined payoff of government and firms rises.

21. A detailed computation can be found in Goerke 2002a.

22. Bentolila and Bertola 1990; Bertola 1990, 1999, 2002.

23. Actually, the positive relation between the efficiency wage and the probability of a large shock h only applies for a level of redundancy payments $R < \bar{e}(r + a)/q + D$. This restriction, it can be demonstrated, implies that the utility stream of an employed non-shirker exceeds that of someone who loses the job due to a collective redundancy and, therefore, applies in a world in which workers benefit from re-employment, relative to remaining unemployed subsequent to a mass redundancy. Moreover, given $\alpha > 0$, it could be argued that dismissal pay reduces the probability of firing a shirker who is detected. Since a shirker does not contribute to output ($e = 0$), firing a detected shirker with probability 1, however, continues to be optimal.

References

Acemoglu, Daron, and Joshua D. Angrist. 2001. Consequences of Employment Protection? The Case of the Americans with Disabilities Act. *Journal of Political Economy* 109: 915–957.

Addison, John T., and Paulino Teixeira. 2003. The Economics of Employment Protection. *Journal of Labor Research* 24: 85–129.

Alvarez, Fernando, and Marcelo Veracierto. 2000. Labor-Market Policies in an Equilibrium Search Model. In *NBER Macroeconomics Annual 1999*, ed. B. Bernanke and J. Rotemberg. MIT Press.

Alvi, Eskander. 1998. Job Security and Unemployment in an Efficiency-Wage Model. *Journal of Labor Research* 19: 387–396.

Atkinson, Anthony B. 1999. *The Economic Consequences of Rolling Back the Welfare State*. MIT Press.

Belot, Michèle, and Jan C. van Ours. 2001. Unemployment and Labor Market Institutions: An Empirical Analysis. *Journal of Japanese and International Economies* 15: 403–418.

Bentolila, Samuel, and Giuseppe Bertola. 1990. Firing Costs and Labor Demand: How Bad is Eurosclerosis? *Review of Economic Studies* 57: 381–402.

Bertola, Guiseppe. 1990. Job Security, Employment, and Wages. *European Economic Review* 34: 851–886.

Bertola, Guiseppe. 1999. Microeconomic Perspectives on Aggregate Labor Markets. In *Handbook of Labor Economics*, volume 3c, ed. O. Ashenfelter and D. Card. North-Holland.

Bertola, Guiseppe. 2004. A Pure Theory of Job Security and Labour Income Risk. *Review of Economic Studies* 71: 43–61.

Bertola, Guiseppe, Tito Boeri, and Sandrine Cazes. 1999. Employment Protection and Labour Market Adjustment in OECD Countries: Evolving Institutions and Variable Enforcement. Employment and Training paper 48, International Labour Office.

Bertola, Guiseppe, Tito Boeri, and Sandrine Cazes. 2000. Employment Protection in Industrialised Countries: The Case for New Indicators. *International Labour Review* 139: 57–87.

Blanchard, Olivier, and Justin Wolfers. 2000. The Role of Shocks and Institutions in the Rise of European Unemployment: The Aggregate Evidence. *Economic Journal* 110: C1–C33.

Booth, Alison L. 1997. An Analysis of Firing Costs and Their Implications for Unemployment Policy. In *Unemployment Policy: Government Options for the Labour Market*, ed. D. Snower and G. de la Dehesa. Cambridge University Press.

Bull, Clive. 1985. Equilibrium Unemployment as a Worker Discipline Device: Comment. *American Economic Review* 75: 890–891.

Burda, Michael C. 1992. A Note on Firing Costs and Severance Benefits in Equilibrium Unemployment. *Scandinavian Journal of Economics* 94: 479–489.

By the Numbers. 1996. Severance Pay and Downsizing. *Journal of Accountancy* 181(6), 23.

Carter, Thomas J., and Paul R. De Lancey. 1997. Just, Unjust, and Just-Cause Dismissals. *Journal of Macroeconomics* 19: 619–628.

Deakin, Simon, and Frank Wilkinson. 1999. The Management of Redundancies in Europe: The Case of Great Britain. *Labour* 13: 41–89.

Delsen, Lei, and Antoine Jacobs. 1999. The Management of Redundancies in Europe: The Case of the Netherlands. *Labour* 13: 123–182.

EIRR (*European Industrial Relations Review*). 1999. Individual Dismissals in Europe, Parts 1–3, 306: 30–36, 308: 20–23, 311: 31–35.

Emerson, Michael. 1988. Regulation or Deregulation of the Labour Market: Policy Regimes for the Recruitment and Dismissal of Employees in Industrialised Countries. *European Economic Review* 32: 775–817.

European Commission. 1999. Die Regelung der Arbeitsbedingungen in den Mitgliedstaaten der Europäischen Union, volume 1: Vergleichendes Arbeitsrecht der Mitgliedstaaten.

Fella, Guilio. 2000. Efficiency Wages and Efficient Redundancy Pay. *European Economic Review* 44: 1473–1490.

Franz, Wolfgang, and Bernd Rüthers. 1999. Arbeitsrecht und Ökonomie. *Recht der Arbeit* 52: 32–38.

Galdón-Sánchez, José E., and Maia Güell. 2003. Dismissal Conflicts and Unemployment. *European Economic Review* 47: 127–139.

Garibaldi, Pietro, and Giovanni L. Violante. 1999. Severance Payments in Search Economies with Limited Bonding. Mimeo, University College London.

Garibaldi, Pietro, and Giovanni L. Violante. 2002. Firing Tax and Severance Payment in Search Economies: A Comparison. Discussion paper 3636, Center for Economic Policy Research.

Gibbons, Robert, and Lawrence F. Katz. 1991. Layoffs and Lemons. *Journal of Labor Economics* 9: 351–380.

Goerke, Laszlo. 2000. On the Structure of Unemployment Benefits in Shirking Models. *Labour Economics* 7: 283–295.

Goerke, Laszlo. 2002a. On Dismissal Pay. *Labour Economics* 9: 497–512.

Goerke, Laszlo. 2002b. Redundancy Pay and Collective Dismissals. *Finanzarchiv* 59: 68–90.

Grubb, David. 2000. Eligibility Criteria for Unemployment Benefits. *OECD Economic Studies* 31: 147–184.

Krueger, Alan B. 1991. The Evolution of Unjust-Dismissal Legislation in the United States. *Industrial and Labor Relations Review* 44: 644–660.

Lazear, Edward P. 1988. Employment at Will, Job Security, and Work Incentives. In *Employment, Unemployment and Labor Utilization*, ed. R. Hart. Unwin Hyman.

Lazear, Edward P. 1990. Job Security Provisions and Employment. *Quarterly Journal of Economics* 105: 699–726.

Leibfritz, Willi, John Thornton, and Alexandra Bibbee. 1997. Taxation and Economic Performance. Working paper 176, OECD Economics Department.

Levine, David I. 1989. Just-Cause Employment Policies When Unemployment Is a Worker Discipline Device. *American Economic Review* 79: 902–905.

Lin, Chung-cheng. 2002. Effects of Job Security Laws in a Shirking Model with Heterogeneous Workers. *Southern Economic Journal* 69: 479–486.

Mendoza, Enrique G., Assaf Razin, and Linda L. Tesar. 1994. Effective Tax Rates in Macroeconomics: Cross-Country Estimates of Tax Rates on Factor Incomes and Consumption. *Journal of Monetary Economics* 34: 297–323.

Mongay-Martinez, C., and R. Fernandez-Bayon. 2001. Effective Taxation, Spending and Employment Performance. In *Taxation, Welfare and the Crisis of Unemployment in Europe*, ed. M. Buti et al. Elgar.

Mortensen, Dale T. 1978. Specific Capital and Labor Turnover. *Bell Journal of Economics* 9: 572–586.

Mosley, Hugh, and Thomas Kruppe. 1993. Employment Protection and Labor Force Adjustment—A Comparative Evaluation. Discussion paper FS I 92-9, Wissenschaftszentrum Berlin.

OECD. 1999. Employment Protection and Labour Market Performance. *Employment Outlook* 47–132.

Pencavel, John H. 1991. *Labor Markets under Trade Unionism*. Oxford University Press.

Picard, Pierre M., and Eric Toulemonde. 2001. On the Equivalence of Taxes Paid by Employers and Employees. *Scottish Journal of Political Economy* 48: 461–470.

Saint-Paul, Gilles. 1995. Efficiency Wage, Commitment and Hysteresis. *Annales d'Economie et de Statistique* 37/8: 39–53.

Schömann, Klaus, Ralf Rogowski, and Thomas Kruppe. 1998. *Labour Market Efficiency in the European Union*. Routledge.

Shapiro, Carl, and Joseph E. Stiglitz. 1984. Equilibrium Unemployment as a Worker Discipline Device. *American Economic Review* 74: 433–444.

Siebert, Horst. 1997. Labor Market Rigidities: At the Root of Unemployment in Europe. *Journal of Economic Perspectives* 11: 37–54.

Sjostrom, William. 1993. Job Security in an Efficiency Wage Model. *Journal of Macroeconomics* 15: 183–187.

Staffolani, Stefano. 2002. Firing Costs, Efficiency Wages and Unemployment. *Labour* 16: 803–830.

Summers, Larry H. 1989. Some Simple Economics of Mandated Benefits. *American Economic Review* 79 (Papers and Proceedings), 177–183.

Toharia, Luis, and Antonio Ojeda. 1999. The Management of Redundancies in Europe: the Case of Spain. *Labour* 13: 237–267.

Tzannatos, Zafiris and Suzanne Roddis. 1998. Unemployment Benefits. Social Protection discussion paper 9813, World Bank.

Willemsen, Heinz Josef. 2000. Kündigungsschutz—vom Ritual zur Rationalität. *Neue Juristische Wochenschrift* 38: 2779–2786.

6

Some Macroeconomic Consequences of Basic Income and Employment Subsidies

Thomas Moutos and William Scarth

Recent years have witnessed both growing income inequality and persistently high unemployment. In the United States and in the United Kingdom, the worsening prospects have taken the form of decreases in the real earnings of lower-skilled workers—in the United States the real hourly wages of young males with 12 or fewer years of schooling have dropped by more than 20 percent in the last two decades (Freeman 1995). In continental Europe, real wages at the bottom of the skill distribution have risen, but at the cost of significant increases in unemployment—especially for this group (Machin and Van Reenen 1998). Although there have been competing explanations concerning the primary reasons behind these phenomena, for some authors the increased pace of global economic integration (popularly referred to as globalization) has had a major role to play (Wood 1995; Rodrik 1997).[1] Moreover, in conjunction with the need for more social insurance programs—which the increased exposure to globalization generates— many authors fear that globalization (of capital markets in particular) erodes the ability of the nation state to satisfy these needs. According to this view, governments will find it increasingly difficult to raise revenue from the taxation of mobile factors of production. As a result, redistribution and employment creation are viewed as initiatives that may be increasingly difficult to pursue.

These developments have stimulated renewed interest in policies that may redistribute income in ways that minimize undesirable indirect effects. This is particularly so since one of the usual charges made against the social welfare system is that in many countries it nourishes a collectively sub-optimal incentive structure, ranging from excessive early retirement to "poverty traps" for unemployed workers (especially single mothers) who return to low-wage employment. In many countries, the implicit tax rate at the low end of the earnings distribution is often very large because of the phasing out of transfer programs as income rises. For example, Atkinson and Sutherland (1990) report that in Britain in 1989 almost half a million families faced marginal tax rates of 70 percent or higher, as a result of means-tested social assistance benefits. Blundell and MaCurdy (1999) also provide an extensive analysis of marginal tax rates faced by low-income households in the United States and in the United Kingdom, and show that the implicit tax rate may sometimes exceed 100 percent when two or more transfer programs are phased-out simultaneously. Despite these costs, the welfare state can still have a net positive (efficiency enlarging) effect in modern industrialized economies. Indeed, as Sinn (1995) and Atkinson (1999) have persuasively argued, the welfare state should not be viewed as something that only disturbs the market process. Especially in a second-best setting, it is something that can encourage risk taking, foster efficiency, and facilitate growth.

In this paper, we argue that the fears regarding globalization may be exaggerated. We show that, in a second-best setting, even when taxing perfectly mobile factors, governments can acquire the necessary revenue to facilitate policies that can both reduce unemployment and increase the incomes of those already working. As a base for comparison, we first examine a closed economy in which the source of the second best lies in the labor market. The payment of efficiency wages by firms intent on maximizing profits results in involuntary unemployment. Then, we focus our attention on small open economies.

Three policies are considered.

The first involves the unconditional payment of a guaranteed income to all citizens. The features that distinguish the Basic Income (BI) proposal—variously called "guaranteed annual income," "universal basic income," or "demogrant" (Meade 1948, 1972; Tobin et al. 1967; Atkinson 1995; Van Parijs 1995, 2000)—from other social security proposals, are that it is paid irrespective of any other income, it does not require any present or past work performance, it is not conditional on the willingness to accept a job, and it is paid to individuals rather than households (Van Parijs 1992). Some proponents argue that a BI system should be accompanied by widespread social security reform, including deregulation of the labor market. For Atkinson (1995), the BI proposal, in its pure form, would replace all social security benefits and it would be accompanied by a flat comprehensive income-tax rate that would replace the existing income taxes and social security contributions.[2] In this way, proponents of BI hope to provide a solution to the "impossible trinity" of welfare reform objectives: to raise the living standards of low-income families, to encourage employment, and to keep budget costs low.

The second policy proposal involves the government paying employment subsidies to firms, as advocated by Phelps (1997) and Solow (1998). The direct aim of this policy is not so much to increase worker's income but to reduce the unemployment rate. It could, nevertheless, indirectly help those remaining unemployed after the enactment of the policy if it results in higher wages and unemployment benefits (if the replacement ratio stays constant).

The third policy we examine is more straightforward, in the sense that it does not involve the government setting up an entirely new program. Instead, it involves simply the lowering of the tax rate applied to labor income.

Throughout our analysis, we assume that all initiatives—basic income, employment subsidies and household wage-income-tax cuts—are financed by raising the tax on capital—which is a perfectly mobile factor in the open-economy case. We make this financing assumption, despite the fact that some proponents of BI expect this initiative to be financed by cuts in existing social programs. We do so for two reasons.

First, we want to examine the possibility of redistribution—especially in an open economy. All previous analyses of the effects of introducing BI have assumed that it will be "financed" by cutting down on existing social security programs in a closed economy (Bowles 1992; Atkinson 1995; Groot and Peters 1997; Van der Linden 1999, 2000).

Second, we are concerned about political feasibility. In this respect we note that even within the European Union, there are significant differences across countries in the relative importance attached to redistributive social policy goals, in the instruments used, and in the extent to which social policy achieves its intended effects.[3] The evolution of the social welfare system in each country has created constituencies that strongly resist any reductions in the benefits to which they have become "entitled." Even more importantly, for many supporters of advanced European welfare states, the fully developed welfare state deserves priority over BI because it is considered to accomplish what BI cannot: it guarantees that certain specific human needs will be met. It is argued that although both the current advanced welfare states and BI can reduce inequality of "condition," the welfare state does so with greater efficiency because it takes better account of inequalities due to differences in needs. For example, if person A needs expensive medical treatment and person B does not, giving both of them a BI grant will not go far to make their situations more equal; only the public provision of health services has the chance of accomplishing that (Bergmann 2001). Thus, both to respect this political feasibility constraint, and to address some of the concerns raised about globalization, we consider financing all initiatives by taxing the "rich."

In section 1, we introduce the macro model that underlies the paper's conclusions. It is quite standard and highly simplified. There are two factors of production: labor (which we think of as unskilled, since the government wishes to raise workers' incomes), and "capital" (which we think of as standing for both physical capital and skilled labor—the source of the human capital that is also to be taxed). It is assumed that the owners of capital are the "rich." To the extent that "capital" involves skilled workers, we make the assumption that these individuals find their employment so rewarding that the possibility of reduced efficiency and effort on the job does not arise. But with the less skilled who do not have "good" jobs, it is assumed that these individuals are dissatisfied with their work. It is, therefore, in firms' interest to pay efficiency wages to generate the profit-maximizing level of labor productivity. We use Summers's (1988) compact exposition of efficiency wages to specify this set up for the "labor" input in our model. All initiatives that are designed to help labor are financed by taxing the owners of capital. In the closed economy, these "rich" individuals cannot migrate to escape this taxation; in the small open economy they can.

In sections 2 and 3, the results for the closed-economy version and the small-open-economy version of the model are explained. In section 4, we consider a sensitivity test (allowing unemployment to follow from unions instead of efficiency wages) and discuss several possible extensions of the analysis.

1   The Model

There are two factors of production: labor (L) and capital (K). Since we think of "labor" as unskilled and deserving of some government attention, and since it is more difficult for such individuals to move great distances, we assume that labor is immobile internationally. (We set $L = 1$.) In contrast, in the open economy, we assume that capital can move in and out of the country without cost.

Firms (correctly) believe that wages exert an influence on the productivity (effort) of their workforce. Firms have an incentive to manipulate the wage offered to the unskilled so that costs per efficiency unit of unskilled labor are minimized. As a result, while still equaling the marginal product of labor, the wage rate exceeds the level that would clear the market, and this determines the equilibrium unemployment rate for labor. Firms have no incentive to pay a similar premium for capital. Thus, capital is paid its marginal product, and in the open-economy case, capital mobility insures that the after-tax return is determined exogenously in the rest of the world.

We view the unemployment that emerges in an efficiency-wage setting as "involuntary." This is why it is appropriate for the government to consider intervening with a policy initiative. Efficiency-wage theories are based on market failure—the premise that employers cannot acquire full information about the productivity of their workers (Akerlof and Yellen 1986). This proposition is reflected in most employment contracts, since they do not involve precise specifications of productivity. A higher wage offer by the firm may increase the average productivity of its workforce for several reasons. First, a high-wage firm may (on average) attract workers of higher quality. Second, a higher wage increases the magnitude of punishment incurred by a worker who is fired after being found offering a sub-standard amount of effort. Third, high wages may lead workers to believe that they are treated "fairly," and they may reciprocate to this "gift" by offering higher effort. The implication of this dependence of worker productivity on wages is that the firm will want to choose a wage rate such that the marginal benefit from a wage increase is equated with the associated increase in costs. Thus, the profit-maximizing wage rate chosen by firms is compatible with involuntary unemployment. The unemployed may be willing to work at lower wages, yet if firms employ them, marginal revenue would decline more than marginal cost.

The firms' production function is

$$Y = K^{1-\gamma}(bL)^{\gamma}, \tag{1}$$

where γ is a positive fraction and b is the index of work effort. We rely on a particularly compact version of efficiency wages, due to Summers (1988) and highlighted by Romer (2001), that is compatible with any of the motivations mentioned above. (It is also more readily calibrated than the Shapiro-Stiglitz (1984) specification—see Pissarides 1998.) Following Summers, we specify

$$b = [(w(1 - t) + pw) - x]^\alpha. \tag{2}$$

The term in parentheses defines what individuals receive if they are working; x denotes their alternative option that is available should they leave their current job. t is the income-tax rate applied to labor earnings, and p is a parameter that defines BI. This parameter measures the generosity of an unconditional (and tax-free) transfer of income from the government to all (unskilled) individuals—independent of employment status. We assume that this BI (which is the same for all individuals) is proportional to the wage rate. α is a positive fraction; as a result, a higher wage in the current job raises each worker's return relative to her alternative, and thereby induces higher productivity. The worker's alternative option is defined as

$$x = (1 - u)(1 - t)w + ufw + pw, \tag{3}$$

where f is a parameter measuring the generosity of the unemployment-insurance system. That is, benefits paid to the unemployed are a proportion (f) of the wage, and these benefits are untaxed. The worker's alternative option is a weighted average of the wage offered at other firms (which equals w in full equilibrium) and what is received if the individual cannot find work. The weights are the employment rate, $(1 - u)$, and the unemployment rate, u, respectively. When firms optimize, they regard x as independent of their individual wage and employment decisions.

Each firm's profit function is

$$\pi = Y - (w - Q)L - rK,$$

where r is the interest rate (the wage or rent paid to each unit of capital); as above, w is the wage rate; and Q is a per-employee subsidy paid to the firm. We assume that Q is proportional to the economy-wide wage rate, that is, $Q = qw$. Nevertheless, when individual firms optimize, they do not think of this equation holding at the individual level. That is, when choosing w, firms do not think that the subsidy rate that they will receive depends on their individual wage policy.

Setting the derivatives of the profit function with respect to w, L and K equal to zero, manipulating the first-order conditions, and using the definition of x, we derive the following relationships:

$$u = \alpha(1 - q)(1 - t)/(1 - t - f), \tag{4}$$

$$(1 - \gamma)Y/K = r, \tag{5}$$

$$\gamma Y/L = (1-q)w. \tag{6}$$

Equation (4) states that the unemployment rate depends positively on the generosity of unemployment insurance and the wage-income-tax rate paid by workers, and negatively on the subsidy rate paid to firms for employing individuals. Equation (5) states that the marginal product of capital should be set equal to the rental cost of capital. In similar fashion, equation (6) states that the marginal product of labor should be equal to its (net of subsidy) rental rate (the pre-tax wage).

In the open economy, the assumption that capital is perfectly mobile internationally implies that its after-tax reward is equal to what prevails in the rest of the world. This implies that

$$r(1-\tau) = \bar{r}, \tag{7}$$

where τ is the tax rate applied to capital rents and $\bar{r}$ is the after-tax reward that can be had by the owners of capital in the rest of the world. Equation (7) constrains the government's ability to redistribute income, since it implies that the "rich" stand ready to withdraw their services to whichever degree is required to insulate their net returns from any taxes imposed.

There is one additional limitation on the government's use of fiscal incentives and transfers—the fact that it must respect its budget constraint. A balanced budget is stipulated as follows:

$$G + fwu + pw + qw(1-u) = tw(1-u) + \tau rK. \tag{8}$$

It states that spending on goods (G), unemployment insurance, unconditional income transfers (the BI), and employment subsidies must equal the sum of the two forms of income-tax revenue. Equation (8) involves the definition that individuals must be either employed or unemployed:

$$L = 1 - u. \tag{9}$$

The open-economy version of the model involves equations (1)–(9) solving for Y, L, K, u, w, r, b, x and one government policy variable (which is p in the case of BI, q in the case of employment subsidies, and t with the wage-income-tax cut). In each case, we impose an increase in the tax rate on capital, τ. In the closed-economy case, equation (7) is dropped, and K becomes an exogenous variable. Proceeding with the solution of the model, we first divide both sides of equation (8) by Y, define $g = G/Y$, $k = K/Y$ and use equation (6) to substitute out w/Y. Equation (8) becomes

$$\gamma = [fu + p - (t - q)(1 - u)] = (1 - u)(1 - q)[\tau(1 - \gamma) - g].$$

To derive policy effects, we take the total differential of the system, and then simplify the coefficients of the resulting system (that relates the changes in all variables) in two ways. First, we evaluate the coefficients subject to the restrictions implied by the initial full equilibrium. Second, we set the initial values of BI (p) and the employment subsidy (q) equal to zero, and the initial value of Y to unity. We focus on four effects that follow from each policy initiative—the effects on: the unemployment rate (u), the level of productivity (b), the expected income of each individual (who undergoes periods of employment and unemployment, x), and (in the closed economy only) the income of capitalists (v). The percentage change in expected labor income is given by

$$\frac{dx}{x} = \frac{dw}{w} - [(1 - u)/\psi] \, dt - [(1 - t - f)/\psi] \, du + (u/\psi) \, df + (1/\psi) \, dp,$$

where $\psi = (1 - t)(1 - u) + uf + p$ and the percentage change of the income of capitalists (in a closed economy) is given by

$$\frac{dv}{v} = \frac{dY}{Y} - \frac{1}{1 - \tau} d\tau.$$

Recall that the incomes of the owners of capital are unaffected in the small open economy (given equation (7)).

The formal results are summarized in the appendix. The discussion in the following sections of the text is limited to verbal and graphic analyses.

2   A Closed Economy

The most convenient way of appreciating the results in the closed-economy case is by considering figure 6.1. This diagram shows the perfectly inelastic supply curve for capital, and the downward sloping marginal product of (demand for) capital curve. The position of the demand curve is affected by the quantity of effective labor, bL. For example, an increase in bL increases the marginal product schedule for capital (as shown by the dashed demand curve in figure 6.1). Initially,

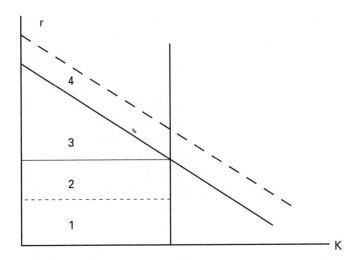

Figure 6.1

before any such shift, the economy's outcome is given by the intersection of the solid demand and supply curves. Total output (Y) is given by the sum of three areas (numbered 1–3). Capital owners receive a total income equal to the area of regions 1 and 2, while labor receives a pre-tax-and-transfer level of income equal to region 3.

Now consider the introduction of BI. Since this policy is independent of each individual's employment status, there are no incentive effects, and hence no income effects. As a result, labor productivity, the unemployment rate, and the wage rate are all unaffected. There is a zero-sum outcome since capital owners are captive. They pay more taxes, and exactly this total is transferred to workers and the unemployed. All that happens in figure 6.1 is that an amount of income equal to region 2 is transferred to the workers/unemployed. This policy cannot be recommended on the basis of the hypothetical compensation principle, since—if the winners compensated the losers—there would be precisely nothing left over.

A more discouraging result emerges with employment subsidies. This policy does involve incentive effects, so—at first glance—it would seem to be recommended. Firms respond by increasing employment and paying higher wages, and—together—these developments raise the expected income of each individual (variable x). But there are competing effects on the level of labor productivity. Worker effort is increased by the higher wage rate, but it is decreased by the increased probability that the unemployed can find a job. As proved in the appendix, the latter effect *must* dominate, so productivity falls. There are competing effects on the overall level of GDP as well, and the value of the formal model is that it allows us to evaluate which effect is stronger. Total output is pushed up by the fact more people are working, but total output is pulled down by the reduction in productivity. Again, as proved in the appendix, the lower productivity effect must dominate. In terms of figure 6.1, this means that the marginal product of capital curve shifts down, so that total output (represented by the area under that marginal product schedule) falls. In other words, this initiative generates a negative-sum outcome. The winners (labor) cannot compensate the losers (capital) even if they transfer their entire winnings. By the hypothetical compensation criterion, then, this policy is not recommended.

Finally, consider a cut in the wage-income-tax rate financed by a higher tax on capital. Since this policy raises the relative return individuals receive from employment, its direct effect is to push up productivity. This makes it sensible for firms to cut the wage premium they had been offering to stimulate productivity, and with lower wages, the unemployment rate falls. It is proved in the appendix that productivity *must* increase—despite the fact that lower pre-tax wages and lower unemployment both push productivity in the opposite direction. The dominant influence is the fact that the lower tax rate makes the *after-tax* wage *higher*. In terms of figure 6.1, the marginal product curve for capital shifts up since both b and L are higher. Total output is now the sum of areas 1, 2, 3, and 4. With this increase in overall product, the winners can compensate the losers and still have something left over. So, according to the hypothetical compensation principle, this policy is recommended. However, this criterion is unappealing since there is no way for the government to perform this transfer back to capitalists without simply reversing the original initiative.

We conclude that none of the policies represent a Paretian improvement. Thus, according to this model, we should expect resistance to all these policies on the part of the owners of capital. One might expect that the support for these initiatives could be even more limited in the open-economy case, since—in this case—capitalists can protect themselves by migrating away from the higher tax, leaving workers to operate with a lower quantity of capital. We see in the next section, however, that the analysis does not support this conjecture concerning decreased support.

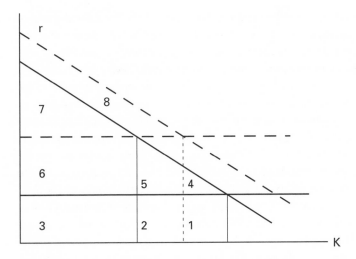

Figure 6.2

3   The Open Economy

The open-economy results are illustrated in figure 6.2. In this case, the supply curve for capital is perfectly elastic. There is no change on the demand side of the model, so the downward sloping marginal product relationship appears as in figure 6.1, and (as before) its position is affected by bL. Before any of the policy initiatives, the economy's outcome is given by the intersection of the solid demand and supply curves, and total output (Y) is given by the sum of seven areas (numbered 1–7). Capital owners get regions 1, 2 and 3, while labor gets regions 4–7.

Before focusing on the model's results, let us use figure 6.2 to review the standard analysis of why taxing elastically supplied capital is not recommended. That standard setting involves a competitive labor market (so the parameter b is unity), and a fixed labor supply (so L is unity). As a result, there is no mechanism that permits a shift in the position of the capital demand function. When the government raises the tax on capital, the higher (dashed) supply curve becomes relevant. Domestically produced output falls by the sum of regions 1, 2, 4, and 5. Capital owners do not lose regions 1 and 2, since they now earn this income in the rest of the world. Labor loses regions 4, 5, and 6, but if the revenue is used to make a transfer to labor, their net loss is just the sum of regions 4 and 5. But this is a loss, so capital is a bad thing to tax.

But if there is a pre-existing distortion, capital *can* be a good thing to tax. Before illustrating this proposition in figure 6.2, we review the original article on the second best (Lipsey and Lancaster 1956). One example discussed in that seminal paper concerned sales taxes in a two-good world. With perfect competition, a tax on just good 2 is not recommended, since this levy makes that price exceed marginal cost, and there is no similar wedge in the other market. But if there is market failure in the first place (say in the form of a monopolist producing good 1), the tax on good 2 can make sense. Now a sales tax on the competitive sector can raise that good's price-to-marginal-cost ratio to what prevails in the monopoly sector, and a selective excise tax is optimal after all. The tax in the second sector fixes the initial problem—that the output of good 1 is too small. Figure 6.2 illustrates a similar situation involving two factors, instead of two goods.

With asymmetric information, the employment of factor 1 (labor) is too small in the second best starting point. A tax on capital induces firms to shift more toward employing labor and that helps lessen the initial distortion. But can this desirable effect of the tax outweigh the traditional excess-burden cost (the loss of income represented by region 3 in figure 6.2)? It appears that this is possible. For instance, if the government uses the tax revenue in a way that induces higher labor productivity and/or lower unemployment, the higher b and L values would shift up the marginal product of capital curve in figure 6.2. The new outcome is given by the intersection of the dashed demand and supply curves. Total income available to labor is affected in two ways. It is reduced by region 4 (as usual) and it is increased by region 8. The two questions of interest are: Can we identify a use of the tax revenue that leads to the marginal product curve shifting up, not down? and Can we identify a circumstance in which region 8 can be bigger than region 4?

With this intuitive background in place, let us now consider each policy in turn. We begin with BI. As is evident from figure 6.2, the financing of BI raises the cost of capital to firms, and it induces them to set a lower wage rate. In this efficiency-wage setting, lower wages lead to lower productivity, so this policy lowers b, and the demand for capital curve shifts down, not up. As a result, the total income available for labor shrinks, and this is why average labor income (x) falls. So, with capitalists unaffected and labor losing, BI is not supported by this analysis.

The analysis is a little more complicated with employment subsidies, since there are two reasons for the marginal product of capital schedule to shift—both b and L adjust. The reduction in unemployment has both favorable and unfavorable effects. The direct (favorable) outcome is that it increases the marginal product of capital, but the indirect (unfavorable) outcome is that (other things equal) increased job prospects and lower wages (as explained above) lead to lower labor productivity (a lower value for b). It is proved in the appendix that this downward pressure on b must be the dominant consideration, so that both wages (w) and the average labor income (x) must fall. As with BI, then, the demand for capital curve (in figure 6.2) shifts down, and the total income available for labor falls. Employment subsidies are not supported by the analysis.

Finally, we consider the balanced budget tax substitution—increasing the tax on capital to finance a tax cut for labor. As with the employment subsidy, unemployment falls, but in this case there are competing effects on labor productivity. As before, increased job prospects lead to decreased work effort, but in this case, the lower tax on employment earnings stimulates increased work effort. It is proved in the appendix that this favorable effect must dominate, so that the work effort index, the parameter b, rises. With both b and L rising, we finally have an initiative that shifts the marginal product of capital schedule up, as shown in figure 6.2.

As was noted above, for it to be possible for this tax substitution to represent a Paretian improvement, we must establish that region 8 in figure 6.2 can be larger than region 4. As explained in the appendix, an appeal to illustrative parameter values is required to make this case. Up to this point, there have been some ambiguities in some of the formal multipliers that are reported in the appendix, but in all cases these uncertainties are resolved by appealing to three simple conditions. A sufficient—though not necessary—set of conditions for all results reported thus far is that the initial unemployment rate be smaller than the replacement rate parameter in the unemployment insurance system, and that this, in turn, be smaller than 1 minus the initial tax rates:

$$u < f < (1 - t) = (1 - \tau).$$

Since these restrictions are not remotely controversial, we are confident of all results that have been reported. However, to establish the effect on average labor income in this open-economy tax-substitution case, we need to consult illustrative parameter values in a more detailed fashion.

We have considered many sets of representative parameter values, and the results are unaffected by this sensitivity testing. Our baseline parameter assumptions are $u = 0.12$ and $f = t = \tau = \gamma = 0.33$. These values are based on the assumption that broadly defined capital (which we think of as including skilled labor) receives an income share of $\frac{2}{3}$ (Mankiw, Romer, and Weil 1992). Since the model involves the assumption that skilled individuals are fully employed, the $u = 0.12$ assumption implies that the nation's overall unemployment rate is 6 percent if (initially) there are equal numbers of skilled and unskilled individuals. Readers can readily verify that this is one set of parameter values that involves both average labor income, x, and work effort, b, rising with this balanced budget tax substitution (despite the fact that wages, w, fall). Since capitalists are unaffected by this initiative, and since labor is helped—both in terms of lower unemployment and in terms of higher average income—we conclude that the analysis supports this policy. It delivers support for low-income individuals in a globalized setting.

Further intuitive understanding of some of our results can be achieved by focusing on the fact that an employment subsidy increases the gross wage, while an income-tax cut lowers the gross wage. As a result, the employment subsidy makes unemployment benefits more generous, and since unemployment benefits are not taxed in our model, the income-tax cut makes benefits less generous. Since, within this framework, more generous benefits raise unemployment, it is much more difficult for the employment subsidy to receive a positive verdict (than it is for the general tax cut to find support in this analysis).

To allow readers to have some feel for the possible magnitudes involved with all policies, we note the following implications of the baseline parameter values. If the tax on capital rises by 10 percent (by 0.033), x falls by 1.3 percent with BI; x falls by 1.2 percent with employment subsidies; and x rises by 0.9 percent with the tax cut for labor. The unemployment rate is unaffected by BI; it falls from 12.0 percent to 10.8 percent with the employment subsidy; and it falls to 10.7 percent with the tax cut for labor.

Finally, it is useful to summarize the differences between the closed and open-economy analyses. There is some support for those concerned about the proposition that globalization may make low-income support more difficult. As we move to the global case, both BI and employment subsidies shift from being policies that help labor to ones that hurt labor. Also, in the case of BI, the effect of the policy on overall output shifts from one that involves no change to one that reduces the size of the overall economic "pie." But the outcome is different for the wage-income-tax cut. Labor wins in both settings, and the overall economic "pie" grows in both cases. But, since there is no political economy problem (no compensation required) in the open-economy case, this policy receives *stronger* support in the global setting. We conclude that the analysis provides at least a partial response to anti-globalization protesters, since it shows that the scope for at least one low income support policy can be increased by globalization.

As was noted in the introduction, we have been heavily influenced by the challenge posed by globalization—does a small open economy have sufficient degrees of freedom to perform meaningful income redistribution? We are drawn to this focus because, over time, the assumption of perfect mobility for both capital and skilled labor may become ever more relevant. Since no studies of BI and employment subsidies have focused on the small-open-economy constraint, we felt that it was important to start filling at least part of this gap. We conclude that globalization does pose a threat to the efficacy of these policies, but that there is a substitute initiative that appears to be less limited by these constraints.

We close this section by reiterating the intuition that lies behind the support we have found for the tax substitution policy. With an asymmetric information problem and market failure in the labor market (and only one other factor: capital), the optimal tax on capital is no longer zero. Even though capital is supplied elastically, and (therefore) this tax distorts, it permits a lower tax to be paid by labor. This decreases the difference between the net wages of the employed and the income received by those out of work, and this reduces unemployment and increases overall consumption possibilities. This conclusion—that it may make sense to tax internationally mobile capital—is similar to the one derived by Koskela and Schöb (2000) in the context of optimal factor income taxation. They note that, in the presence of involuntary unemployment, labor supply is locally infinitely elastic. Thus, the inverse elasticity rule suggests that labor should not be taxed at a higher rate than capital (whose supply is also infinitely elastic at the world rate of interest). Moreover, the presence of unemployment due to the wage rate being higher than the competitive one implies that the private marginal cost of labor is higher than its social marginal cost. Thus, welfare can be increased by taxing the labor input less heavily relative to the capital input (whose social marginal cost equals the world interest rate).[4]

It must be admitted that our model does not address the concern that fiscal competition among countries in a world of mobile capital might eliminate the tax on capital as an option (see, for example, Edwards and Keen 1996; Sinn 1994). A similar point—applied to mobile skilled labor—is made by Wildasin (1991). But Kessler, Lülfesmann, and Myers (2000) have considered mobile capital and labor together. In this setting, fiscal competition is lessened. When redistribution is pursued in one country, the immigration of labor raises the tax base and decreases the incentive to attract capital. Kessler, Lülfesmann and Myers identify circumstances in which increased redistribution in one country makes the majority of the population in both countries (in their two-county model) strictly better off. We conclude that fiscal competition may not undermine the applicability of analyses such as ours after all.

4 Specification Issues

In this section, we address two questions: an alternative rationale for unemployment, and issues surrounding the specification for labor supply.

Since there is controversy concerning how best to model unemployment, we consider an alternative to efficiency-wage theory. In particular, in Europe, the role of unions in pushing the wage above market clearing levels is often stressed. Pissarides (1998, p. 162) outlines a compact specification of the interaction between unions and firms. It involves firms choosing employment after the wage is set as a result of a Nash bargaining process. If individuals are risk neutral, and the production process is Cobb-Douglas, Pissarides shows that the closed-form solution for the unemployment rate is precisely our equation (4) above. In this case, the parameter α is defined differently:

$$\alpha = \frac{\varepsilon(1 - \gamma)}{\gamma(1 - \varepsilon)},$$

where, as above, γ is labor's exponent in the production function and ε is labor's bargaining-power parameter in the Nash product involved in the theory of wage setting. (This parameter determines the share of the surplus resulting from the employment relationship that goes to workers.) The only other changes in the model are that, with unions instead of efficiency wages, the parameter b is unity and the exponent for capital in the Cobb-Douglas production function is specified as β, where $\gamma + \beta < 1$, since there must be a surplus to be bargained over.

With the structure of the model almost identical, it is not surprising that many of the results (and the intuition provided by figures 6.1 and 6.2) are the same as what have been explained above. The major difference is that there is an implicit third factor—which we can think of as the entrepreneurs—receiving income equal to $(1 - \gamma - \beta)/Y$. For the surplus that is bargained over to remain in full equilibrium, we have to assume that the entrepreneurs are not mobile internationally. Thus, we are forced to treat the entrepreneurs in a group along with the (unskilled) workers. This is unappealing since there is not the same public concern about entrepreneurs. Thus, while our results are very similar with unions replacing the efficiency-wage specification (and our analysis therefore passes this sensitivity test), we prefer the efficiency-wage model on motivation grounds.

We now discuss our specification of labor supply. In effect, we assume that labor force participation is independent of the policy changes that are examined. This may seem especially controversial in the case of basic income, since some proponents stress possible differences between BI and other forms of income support on this front. As a result, we provide a brief review of the empirical literature concerning the impact of income taxation on work incentives.

The empirical literature on labor supply has identified two margins in which labor supply can respond.

First, there is the response along the intensive margin. That is, individuals can vary their hours or effort intensity on the job. If leisure is a normal good, the income and substitution effects of tax changes work in opposite directions. The empirical literature has been at pains to establish the size of the net effect. Killingsworth (1983), Burtless (1986), and Blundell (1992) conclude that the evidence suggests a labor supply elasticity far closer to 0 than to 1.

Second, individuals may respond along the extensive margin; that is, they decide whether or not to enter the labor force. With respect to the extensive margin, the Negative Income Tax (NIT) experiments and Earned Income Tax Credit (EITC) policies in the United States have provided most of the evidence. It is well established that, relative to a NIT program, incentives to work are enhanced with an EITC because the implicit tax rate inherent in the latter program is smaller. Nevertheless, some authors (for example, Browning (1995) and Eissa and Hoynes (1998)) have still pointed to some problems regarding the incentive structure of the EITC. A major concern in this respect is that the EITC is effectively subsidizing married mothers to stay at home (while it has only a small positive effect on married men's labor supply). Eissa and Hoynes (1998) suggest that a possible reform of the EITC (that it be based on individual earnings as opposed to family earnings) would offset the incentives for secondary earners to leave the labor force. Since the BI proposal provides support to working age individuals (rather than families), it should be less prone to causing reductions in participation rates. This consideration, when taken together with the small effects identified by Eissa and Hoynes, lead us to regard the assumption of no effect of BI on aggregate labor force participation as a reasonable approximation of reality.

Conclusions

Our analysis of basic income and employment subsidies has drawn attention to some of the complications that follow from the financing of these initiatives. Even in a closed economy setting, the analysis identifies political economy questions concerning how such policies can achieve support when segments of the population suffer income losses. The analysis indicates that these concerns are increased in the open-economy setting, where those who are taxed have an increased ability to avoid any loss in income. Nevertheless, we have stressed that in a second-best initial situation, Paretian improvements are possible. Further, a balanced budget tax substitution was identified as one initiative that could thereby avoid any political economy support problem —even in a global setting. We think that the identification of this possibility should allay some of the fears of those who think that globalization may weaken our ability to effect low-income support policy in a small economy. The analysis suggests that more research on tax substitutions of this sort may bring at least as big a return as will further analysis of basic income and employment subsidies.

In related work, we have begun some of this additional investigation. We are considering a specification of technology that allows for an explicit difference between skilled labor and physical capital (the former being essential in the production process). Also, we allow the skilled individuals to save (so that their consumption and income are not identical, and so that the analysis allows for the effects of each policy initiative on long-run wealth accumulation). Preliminary results suggest that some of these changes in model specification can increase the support for basic income and/or employment subsidies. We hope that the present paper stimulates others to work on extensions such as this one.

Of course, even with extensions, it may not be possible to incorporate within the analysis all aspects of the debate concerning basic income and employment subsidies. For example, proponents of BI stress issues such as its beneficial effects on the level of real freedom for disadvantaged groups, while some opponents stress self-sufficiency and the value people derive from making a contribution through employment. These wider philosophical issues are well summarized in a debate in the *Boston Review* between Phelps (2000) and Van Parijs (2000). Some of these wider issues can be included in an extended version of our analysis. One relates to the encouragement of work sharing, and a second to reductions in administrative costs. (BI would do away with complicated means-tested benefits.) Another issue stressed by proponents of the BI is that—when it replaces unemployment insurance—it offers incentives for skill acquisition. It remains to be explored how BI may affect behavior if it also replaces a public pension system. Nevertheless, our work in progress involving a formal skilled-unskilled distinction and long-run wealth accumulation are designed to allow theses issues to be explored. In the meantime, it is hoped that the present paper has clarified some of the basic macroeconomic trade-offs involved with the provision of basic income and employment subsidies.

Appendix

For the closed economy, the policy results are as follows. With BI,

$$\frac{du}{d\tau} = \frac{dw/w}{d\tau} = \frac{db/b}{d\tau} = \frac{dY/Y}{d\tau} = 0.$$

Also,

$$\frac{dv/v}{d\tau} = -1/(1-\tau) < 0$$

and

$$\frac{dx/x}{d\tau} = \frac{(1-u)(1-\gamma)}{\gamma\psi} > 0.$$

With the employment subsidy,

$$\frac{du}{d\tau} = \frac{-u(1-\gamma)(1-u)}{\gamma\lambda} < 0,$$

$$\frac{dw/w}{d\tau} = \frac{(1-u)(1-\gamma)(1-\alpha\gamma - (u(1-\gamma)/(1-u)))}{\gamma\lambda(1-\alpha\gamma)} > 0,$$

where

$$\lambda = \psi - uf/(1-u) > 0;$$

$$\frac{db/b}{d\tau} = \frac{-\alpha u(1-\gamma)(1+\gamma)}{\gamma(1-\alpha\gamma)\lambda} < 0;$$

$$\frac{dY/Y}{d\tau} = \frac{-\alpha\gamma u(1-u)(1-\gamma)}{\gamma\lambda(1-\alpha\gamma)} < 0.$$

With the wage-income-tax cut,

$$\frac{du}{d\tau} = \frac{-(1-\gamma)(1-u)(u-\alpha)}{\gamma\Omega\phi} < 0,$$

where

$$\Omega = 1 - t - f > 0$$

and

$$\phi = 1 - u - \frac{f(u-\alpha)}{\Omega(1-u)} > 0;$$

$$\frac{dx/x}{d\tau} = \frac{(1-u)(1-\gamma)\theta}{\gamma\phi(1-\alpha\gamma)} > 0,$$

where

$$\theta = [(u-\alpha)(1-\alpha\gamma)[(\Omega/\psi) - (1/\Omega(1-u))]] + [(1-u)(1-\alpha\gamma)/\psi]$$
$$+ [\alpha\gamma^2/u\Omega] > 0;$$

$$\frac{dY/Y}{d\tau} = (1-u)(1-\gamma)\frac{(\alpha^2/u) + ((1-\alpha)(u-\alpha)/(1-u))}{\Omega\phi(1-\alpha\gamma)} > 0;$$

and

$$\frac{dv/v}{d\tau} < 0.$$

Not all the signs reported are certain *a priori*. Nevertheless, as noted in the text, sufficient—though not necessary—conditions for all but the very last result are

$$u < f < (1 - t) = (1 - \tau).$$

Since these restrictions are not at all controversial, we can be confident of the signs that are reported.

For the small open economy, the policy results are as follows. With BI,

$$\frac{du}{d\tau} = 0,$$

$$\frac{\hat{w}}{d\tau} = \frac{-(1 - \gamma)}{\gamma((1 - \tau)(1 - \alpha)} < 0$$

$$\frac{\hat{b}}{d\tau} = \frac{-\alpha(1 - \gamma)}{(1 - \tau)(1 - \alpha)\gamma} < 0,$$

$$\frac{\hat{x}}{d\tau} = \frac{(1 - \gamma)\delta}{\gamma} < 0,$$

where

$$\delta = \frac{1}{(1 - t) + (uf/(1 - u))} - \frac{1}{(1 - \tau)(1 - \alpha)} < 0.$$

With the employment subsidy,

$$\frac{du}{d\tau} = \frac{-u(1 - \gamma)(1 - u)}{\gamma\lambda} < 0$$

and

$$\frac{\hat{w}}{d\tau} = \frac{(1 - \gamma)[(1 - u)(1 - \alpha) - (\lambda/(1 - \tau))]}{\gamma(1 - \alpha)\lambda} < 0.$$

The x response is calculated from these component multipliers (as in earlier cases). The result is unsigned. Nevertheless, we have experimented with many parameter values, and the results are unaffected.

Readers may wish to use our baseline parameter assumptions (noted in the text) to verify that, for representative parameter assumptions, x falls with the introduction of employment subsidies.

With the wage-income-tax cut,

$$\frac{du}{d\tau} = \frac{-(1-\gamma)(1-u)(u-\alpha)}{\gamma\Omega\phi} < 0,$$

$$\frac{\hat{w}}{d\tau} = \frac{-(1-\gamma)[(\phi/(1-\tau)) - (\alpha^2(1-u)/u\Omega)}{\gamma\phi(1-\alpha)} < 0,$$

and

$$\frac{\hat{b}}{d\tau} = \frac{-\alpha(1-\gamma)}{\gamma(1-\alpha)\phi}[(\phi/(1-\tau)) - (\alpha(1-u)/\Omega u)] > 0.$$

Acknowledgments

The work was first presented at the CESifo-ISPE conferences on Labor Market Institutions and Public Regulation at Munich, October 26 and 27, 2001 and Cadenabbia, June 2–4, 2002. We wish to thank our discussants, Martin Werding and Marcel Thum, the organizers (Jonas Agell, Michael Keen, and Alfons Weichenrieder), two anonymous referees, and the conference participants for many helpful comments and suggestions. Finally, we are grateful to Manos Matsaganis, Apostolis Philippopoulos, Krishna SenGupta, and those attending the seminar at the University of Canterbury (July 19, 2002) for very helpful input.

Notes

1. Some economists have pointed to alternative explanations, such as a shift in relative demand in favor of skilled labor. Gordon (1996) has argued that the weakening of labor-market institutions and the erosion of the real value of the minimum wage are responsible for the increased inequality in the United States.

2. The BI proposal, although it can be traced as far back as Augustin Cournot and John Stuart Mill, must be seen in tandem with the current policy trend in many OECD countries to "make work pay." By conferring tax credits and benefits to employees, policy makers in many countries attempt to increase employment and net incomes of low-wage earners without imposing too large a burden on the state's budget (e.g. the Earned Income Tax Credit (EITC) in the United States, the Child Tax Benefit in Canada and the Working Families' Tax Credit in the United Kingdom). Nevertheless, the measures implemented do not aim at guaranteeing a subsistence level. All these programs are conditional on employment, and the level of the implied subsidy is inversely related to the income (or hours of work) of the recipients. To the proponents of BI, this is the Achilles'

heel of these programs, since the implied marginal tax rate for households in the phase-out range of these programs can be as high as 80 percent (Brewer and Gregg 2001).

3. Following Esping-Andersen (1990), we can identify four "models of welfare capitalism" in the EU: the Scandinavian model of universal social protection as a right of citizenship; the "Bismarckian" employment-based model of Germany, Austria, France and the Benelux countries; the Anglo-Saxon model of the United Kingdom and Ireland; and the fragmented and highly idiosyncratic arrangements of the remaining southern EU members. Also, Heady, Mitrakos and Tsakloglou (2001) document the very large variance of social transfers in the EU. Social transfers as a percentage of GDP vary between 16.9% (Portugal) to 37.6% (Sweden). Wide differences also exist in the allocation of such transfers by type of benefit (for example, family related benefits account for 0.7% of total social transfers in Spain and for 15.2% in Ireland), by their impact on inequality (the proportional decline in the Gini index of inequality due to social transfers in cash varies between 46% for Denmark and 22.7% for Portugal), and in poverty (the existence of unemployment benefits reduces poverty by 66.4% in Denmark and by 1.7% in Greece).

4. For related analyses (stressing the median voter's choice of the size of an employment subsidy, financed by a tax on mobile capital) see Leite-Monteiro, Marchand, and Pestieau (2003) and some of the references cited there. Manning (1995) and Rebitzer and Taylor (1995) have shown that—in a second-best setting—other non-standard results can emerge. For example, in their efficiency-wage models, minimum wage laws can raise employment. We have verified that this is not possible in Summers' version of efficiency-wage theory that we rely on in this paper.

References

Akerlof, G., and J. Yellen, eds. 1986. *Efficiency Wage Models of the Labor Market*. Cambridge University Press.

Atkinson, A. 1995. *Public Economics in Action: The Basic Income/Flat Tax Proposal*. Oxford University Press.

Atkinson, A. 1999. *The Economic Consequences of Rolling Back the Welfare State*. MIT Press.

Atkinson, A., and H. Sutherland. 1990. "Scaling the 'Poverty Mountain': Methods to Extend Incentives to All Workers." In *Improving Incentives for the Low Paid*, ed. A. Bowen and K. Mayhew. Macmillan.

Bergmann, B. R. 2001. A Swedish-Style Welfare State or Basic Income: Which Should Have Priority? Discussion paper 10, United States Basic Income Group.

Blundell, R. W. 1992. "Labour Supply and Taxation: A Survey." *Fiscal Studies* 13: 15–40.

Blundell, R. W., and T. MaCurdy. 1999. "Labour Supply: A Review of Alternative Approaches." In *Handbook of Labour Economics*, volume 3A, ed. O. Ashenfelter and D. Card. North-Holland.

Bowles, S. 1992. "Is Income Security Possible in a Capitalist Economy? An Agency-Theoretic Analysis of an Unconditional Income Grant." *European Journal of Political Economy* 8: 557–578.

Brewer, M., and P. Gregg. 2001. Eradicating Child Poverty in Britain: Welfare Reform and Children since 1997. Discussion paper 01/18, Institute of Fiscal Studies.

Browning, E. 1995. "Effects of the Earned Income Tax Credit on Income and Welfare." *National Tax Journal* 48: 23–43.

Burtless, G. 1986. "The Work Response to a Guaranteed Income: A Survey of Experimental Evidence." In Lessons from the Income Maintenance Experiments, ed. A. Munnell. Conference Series No. 30, Federal Reserve Bank of Boston.

Edwards, J., and M. Keen. 1996. "Tax Competition and Leviathan." *European Economic Review* 40: 113–134.

Eissa, N., and H. W. Hoynes. 1998. The Earned Income Tax Credit and the Labour Supply of Married Couples. Working paper 6856, National Bureau of Economic Research.

Esping-Andersen, G. 1990. *The Three Worlds of Welfare Capitalism*. Polity Press.

Freeman, R. 1995. "Are your Wages Set in Beijing?" *Journal of Economic Perspectives* 9: 15–32.

Gordon, D. N. 1996. *Fat and Mean: The Corporate Squeeze of Working Americans and the Myth of Managerial "Downsizing."* Free Press.

Groot, L., and H. Peters. 1997. "A Model of Conditional and Unconditional Social Security in an Efficiency Wage Economy." *Journal of Post-Keynesian Economics* 19: 573–597.

Heady, C., T. Mitrakos, and P. Tsakloglou. 2001. "The Distributional Impact of Social Transfers in the European Union: Evidence from the ECHP." *Fiscal Studies* 68: 547–565.

Kessler, A., C. Lülfesmann, and G. Myers. 2000. "Redistribution, Fiscal Competition and the Politics of Economic Integration." Discussion paper 00-11, Department of Economics, Simon Fraser University.

Killingsworth, M. R. 1983. *Labour Supply*. Cambridge University Press.

Koskela, E., and R. Schöb. 2000. Optimal Factor Income Taxation in the Presence of Unemployment. Working paper 279, CESifo.

Leite-Monteiro, M., M. Marchand, and P. Pestieau. 2003. "Employment Subsidy with Capital Mobility." *Journal of Public Economic Theory* 5: 327–344.

Lipsey, R. G., and K. Lancaster. 1956. "The General Theory of the Second Best." *Review of Economic Studies* 24: 11–32.

Machin, S., and J. Van Reenen. 1998. "Technology and Changes in Skill Structure: Evidence from Seven OECD Countries." *Quarterly Journal of Economics* 113: 1215–1244.

Mankiw, N. G., D. Romer, and D. Weil. 1992. "A Contribution to the Empirics of Economic Growth." *Quarterly Journal of Economics* 107: 407–437.

Manning, A. 1995. "How Do We Know that Real Wages are Too High?" *Quarterly Journal of Economics* 110: 1111–1126.

Meade, J. 1948. *Planning and the Price Mechanism*. Allen and Unwin.

Meade, J. 1972. "Poverty in the Welfare State." *Oxford Economic Papers* 24: 289–326.

Phelps, E. 1997. *Rewarding Work*. Harvard University Press.

Phelps, E. 2000. "Subsidize Wages." *Boston Review* 25: 5.

Pissarides, C. 1998. "The Impact of Employment Tax Cuts on Unemployment and Wages: The Role of Unemployment Benefits and Tax Structure." *European Economic Review* 42: 155–183.

Rebitzer, J., and L. Taylor. 1995. "The Consequences of Minimum Wage Laws: Some New Theoretical Ideas." *Journal of Public Economics* 56: 245–256.

Rodrik, D. 1997. *Has Globalization Gone Too Far?* Institute of International Economics.

Shapiro, C., and J. Stiglitz. 1984. "Equilibrium Unemployment as a Worker Discipline Device." *American Economic Review* 74: 433–444.

Sinn, H.-W. 1994. "How Much Europe? Subsidiarity, Centralization, and Fiscal Competition." *Scottish Journal of Political Economy* 41: 85–107.

Sinn, H.-W. 1995. "A Theory of the Welfare State." *Scandinavian Journal of Economics* 97: 495–526.

Solow, R. 1998. *Work and Welfare*. Princeton University Press.

Summers, L. 1988. "Relative Wages, Efficiency Wages and Keynesian Unemployment." *American Economic Review, Papers and Proceedings* 78: 383–388.

Tobin, J., J. Pechman, and P. Mieszkowski. 1967. "Is a Negative Income Tax Practical?" *Yale Law Journal* 77: 1–27.

Van der Linden, B. 1999. Is Basic Income a Cure for Unemployment in Unionized Economies? A General Equilibrium Analysis. Document de Travail No. 49, Chaire Hoover d' Ethique Economique et Sociale, Universite Catholique de Louvain.

Van der Linden, B. 2000. "Fighting Unemployment without Worsening Poverty: Basic Income versus Reductions of Social Security Contributions." In *Policy Measures for Low-Wage Employment in Europe*, ed. W. Salverda et al. Elgar.

Van Parijs, P. 1992. *Arguing for Basic Income: Ethical Foundations for a Radical Reform*. Verso.

Van Parijs, P. 1995. *Real Freedom for All: What (If Anything) Can Justify Capitalism?* Oxford University Press.

Van Parijs, P. 2000. "A Basic Income for All." *Boston Review* 25: 5.

Wildasin, D. 1991. "Income Redistribution in a Common Labor Market." *American Economic Review* 81: 757–774.

Wood, A. 1994. *North-South Trade, Employment and Inequality*. Clarendon.

Contributors

Jonas Agell Stockholm University

Lars Calmfors Stockholm University

Robert Dur Erasmus University, Rotterdam

Anders Forslund Swedish Office of Labour Market Policy Evaluation

Laszlo Goerke Johannes Gutenberg University, Mainz

Maria Hemström Swedish Office of Labour Market Policy Evaluation

Michael Keen International Monetary Fund

Thomas Moutos Athens University

Rafael Lalive University of Zurich

Gilles Saint-Paul University of Social Sciences, Toulouse

William Scarth McMaster University, Hamilton

Coen Teulings Erasmus University, Rotterdam

Alfons Weichenrieder Johann Wolfgang Goethe University, Frankfurt

Josef Zweimüller University of Zurich

Index